Back to the Miracle Factory is a book about music from the point of view of a listener. It is a collection of recent critical essays by a writer who has spent almost thirty years attempting to close the gap between people who listen to and observe art professionally (academics, reviewers, the musicians/artists themselves) and those who listen solely because they want to, because they get something from the experience. The link between me and my readers is that we both want to know, or at least get into words, what that "something" is.

—Paul Williams

Praise for *Back to the Miracle Factory*

"Williams may have published the first rock 'n' roll magazine—*Crawdaddy!*—in the 1960s and may be regarded as the father of rock criticism, but he has never rested on his laurels or turned his ear from the latest music."

—*Library Journal*

"A significant writer . . . His essays are very close to thought . . . [to] the thinking process itself. Williams obviously loves music, people, words, playing with thoughts, shifting gears, exclaiming, emoting, shouting, contemplating, jiving, joking, thinking, writing."

—*Los Angeles Free Press*

"I can't remember a time when I—and everyone I knew—wasn't interested in what Paul Williams had to say about pretty much anything."

—Samuel R. Delany

"The pioneer of modern rock journalism."

—*Twilight Zone*

"Paul Williams uses no props, has no disguises. The pure joy of his writing is that it comes from a heart that speaks the truth, from a pen of deep talent."

—Bill Graham

"A perceptive eye, a sensitive ear. Williams was one of the first in this country to see rock music as a core of the lives of his generation, as a common jumping-off place for exploring shared experience and awareness."

—*San Francisco Examiner*

FORGE BOOKS BY PAUL WILLIAMS

The 20th Century's Greatest Hits
Back to the Miracle Factory

BACK
TO THE
MIRACLE
FACTORY

ROCK
ETC. 1990s

Paul Williams

A TOM DOHERTY ASSOCIATES BOOK
NEW YORK

Book design by Heidi Eriksen

A Forge Book
Published by Tom Doherty Associates, LLC
175 Fifth Avenue
New York, NY 10010

www.tor.com

Forge® is a registered trademark of Tom Doherty Associates, LLC.

Library of Congress Cataloging-in-Publication Data

Williams, Paul.
    Back to the miracle factory : rock etc. 1990s / by Paul Williams.
        p. cm.
    ISBN 0-765-30352-3 (hc)
    ISBN 0-765-30353-1 (pbk)
    1. Rock music—1991–2000—History and criticism. I. Title.

ML3534 .W58 2002
781.66'09049—dc21   2001054539

First Hardcover Edition: February 2002
First Trade Paperback Edition: January 2003

Printed in the United States of America

0 9 8 7 6 5 4 3 2 1

For Cindy Lee Berryhill
and
Alexander Berryhill-Williams

CONTENTS

Back to the Miracle Factory is a book about music from the point of view of a listener. It is a series of critical essays by a writer who has spent his life attempting to close the gap between people who listen to and observe art professionally (academics, reviewers, the musicians/ artists themselves) and those who listen solely because they want to, because they *get something* from the experience. The link between me and my readers is that we both want to know, or at least get into words, what that "something" is.

Our relationship with music, as individuals, is for most of us a mysterious and fascinating subject. And a very personal subject. Like our relationship to nature, it is of great importance in the shaping and sustaining (and, often, reawakening) of our basic values, those vital intangibles that affect both our everyday actions and our major life decisions. People who listen to music tend to *love* the music they listen to. It is an intense relationship: source of pleasure, source of identity, source of self-awareness.

As a writer I want to talk about what's going on in our lives and our world. I founded *Crawdaddy!*, the first U.S. rock magazine, in January 1966 specifically for that purpose. The magazine played its pioneering role in the rock explosion of the late 1960s, and provided me with front-row seats and/or a place on stage for many of the dramatic moments of that half-decade. It was fun. And reviving *Crawdaddy!*—which I did in January 1993 largely so I could write and publish the essays that make up *Back to the Miracle Factory*—has also been a lot of fun. There is as much or more good music being released today as there was in the 1960s. What is missing (if anything) is a sense of context: What is rock? Who are we? The purpose of this book is to aid and abet the sometimes revolutionary process of discovering (or restoring) the contexts in which we listen together. Yes, we listen as individuals. But in the case of all musics— popular, folk, and others—we listen with an awareness of, or a conjecture about, a community of listeners who are sharing this experience with us. Miracles create communities. And vice versa.

—Paul Williams

January 1993. Bill Clinton. Somalia. Bosnia. *Automatic for the People*. We know already: This is what we'll remember, one of those moments that sticks in the memory, and an album that may always, for many of us, be the soundtrack of that moment. Everyone's listening to it. Sure seems that way. And not just once, but over and over. A hit? No, something much more meaningful than that. A touchstone. A common reference point. Something private and collective, both at once. Shared intimacy on a universal scale. Why? What do we like about this record? I'm not claiming to be able to answer this question. But I think it's worth asking.

Why?

The album *Automatic for the People* reminds me of is *Rubber Soul*. The texture or mood of it, most of all, and a modest yet very striking fresh creativity (inventiveness!), and then the way the record hangs together as a whole. I like every track. That's very unusual. And there's no single song I want to hear over and over at the expense of the others. Want to hear 'em all over and over, a few favorites at any given moment and different ones every day. Keep playing the record. Like *Rubber Soul*: more than the sum of its parts. Album as unitary, total experience, hanging together as slick and mysterious as a song. Like *Murmur*, like (my personal favorite still) *Fables of the Reconstruction*. Welcome back. To me, as well as you. This is what music is s'posed to do for us.

So this is an essay about hearing voices. Familiar voices, for the most part. R.E.M., Neil Young, Bob Dylan, Bruce Cockburn, Television, and Sonya Hunter are the authors of the new albums in and beside my CD player this week, and of these Sonya's is the only voice I haven't communed with on many a past occasion.

But what's exciting is this feeling that I'm hearing new messages.

What messages? Big game with *Automatic for the People*: What's he saying? Sometimes it's better not to know for sure. Leaves doors open. Allows the mind to go wandering. The mind needs to go wandering. That's one of the gifts words and music can give us.

The quantity and quality of new music being released nowadays is overwhelming. One of my difficulties in writing this essay is I actually feel guilty about the exciting new albums I'm not choosing to talk about here—a few that I've heard and liked, and *many* others I'm simply unaware of. Then there are whole categories of music unrepresented here—my self-image wants to present me as someone who's aware of all the best new bands, alternative, metal-edged, hip-hop, techno, grunge, whether underground/indie or worthy megaplatinum or bubbling on the edge of famiosity. But I'm not, not even a little bit. I'm a guy in a record store, dazzled and confused and eager to get out without spending too much money but with at least one CD under my arm that will speak my language and make me feel special for a few weeks or years. I'm forty-four, but I think I could be just as confused and self-conscious if I were fifteen or twenty-one. Too many choices. What speaks for me?

I know it may very well be *Copper Blue* by Sugar, but I haven't got around to buying that one yet. Let me tell you about the ones that have ended up on my turntable.

AUTOMATIC FOR THE PEOPLE.

R.E.M. First track: "Drive." Just what the doctor ordered: It pulls me in and in and in and excites me so I shout and sing along, and never reveals anything. A very good beginning. The last couple of R.E.M. album-openers left me cold—why, I ask myself, does this one, another conscious effort to make a radio-friendly single, work so well for me? I like the way it goes round and round; I like the tension that builds and builds and breaks open in unexpected places (strings and "ollie ollie ollie" climax erupting somewhere just past the halfway point). I like the impenetrable but still satisfying lyrics ("nobody tells you where to go"), whereas I hated the words to "Radio Song"—did the singer's attitude shift, or mine, or maybe we met in the middle somewhere? This is not perhaps too early to mention R.E.M.'s songwriting process: The three instrumentalists work out stuff together (each bringing ideas in) and then give working tapes to the singer who chooses some of these not-yet-songs to put words to. Process goes on from there, but anyway we can understand that first there was a hypnotic little thing going through (in this case) Peter Buck's mind, then the thing was wrestled into something approaching form (odd form, lovably unorthodox form) by Berry, Mills, and Buck, and then Michael Stipe put these words on top of it and into it, magnifying riff and mood and augmenting structure and feeding the whole concept back into itself until with a few further twists it became a performance, a recording, a statement. "Hey! Kids! Rock and roll!" It's the tone of voice that matters, that speaks of something neither straightforward nor ironic. And tone of guitars. The quality and particular texture of the echoes. R.E.M. is a riff-oriented band, but not at all like the Rolling Stones. It's like these riffs are exo- rather than endoskeleton. Anyway, the damn thing works. Not as apocalyptic as "Gimme Shelter," certainly (these are different times), but a no-release-of-tension album-opener worthy of being mentioned in the same breath. Speaking of which—

Second track: "Try Not to Breathe." Good thought. Good sound. Sometimes R.E.M. seem to achieve the *sound* of thought. Good vocals deserve a lot of credit. And good production. Some mysterious evenness of sound (amidst and made up of all sorts of eccentricities). Good harmonies in new places. I like it when arrangement and vocals and melody and sound and words are all moving in the same direction, and it's a firm and unfamiliar direction. I like being carried along like this. And the music does not betray the words' seriousness—nor vice versa. For a song about dying, I find it oddly heartening, full of encouragement towards life. Thanks for the good advices.

Third track: "The Sidewinder Sleeps Tonite." If there's a contest on to see who can borrow and bend and update a riff most tastefully and effectively, these guys win hands-down. The Beatles used to be masters of this sort of assimilation, but R.E.M. in a good year (1985, 1992) have a quirky intelligence that actually helps me hang in for those desirable multiple listenings (Beatles used to and still do wear thin on me faster; *de gustibus*, of course). The *Cat in the Hat* and insufficiently-substantial-soup sections of this song are magnificent, in lyric and particularly in performance of lyric. Pay attention: top-level rock-and-roll singing happening here. The riff (performance of riff; band action) makes it possible, creates singer's and listener's mood, pushes and supports that freeness and subtlety and humor, one form of delight feeding another, which obligingly feeds back. Did someone ask how it's done? Creativity breeds more of the same, we spark off each other, somehow also helping each to stick to the project at hand.

"Phoning to wake her up"—the pictures come through loud and clear, even if the words don't always. Music is simple but steady as Gibraltar or Creedence. And melody! And those surprisingly perfect string parts, crafted by John Paul Jones. (Led Zeppelin meets Atlanta Symphony Orchestra and the Tokens at an R.E.M. session. Hey, only in the never-never land of rock and roll are such things possible.) "You've got a boogie-woogie groove on this one!" indeed. Pluck a track from this album to stand beside anything R.E.M. has created and I think this'd be my candidate. The message? Love of life again. Why do they say this is a downer record?

Maybe it has to do with the "feel" of the next bunch of performances, and especially "Everybody Hurts" (fourth track). Sounds so sad. But it isn't. At first I thought this was the track that would grate on me after a few listenings, the one I'd want to skip over. But it isn't. It pushes it, that's for sure—that lugubrious pace, right on the edge of schmaltzy classical or the worst of new age; hell, I think R.E.M. may actually be doing their own cocktail version of Pachelbel's "Canon" here, but . . . I am surprised. Again. It works. Get closer and it doesn't get uglier, nor tedious; it gets prettier and lighter and pleasantly underspoken. The words—what they are and what they are not—help tremendously, but still I wouldn't want to hear this song done by anyone else. It's that group-mind performance, coming from a good space this time out, playful, sincere, inquisitive, respectful of each-other-self, specifically including the listener. Song sounds sad to catch the ear of our sadness. And because of the respectfulness, it works (some) even for proud ones like me who think we're not gonna slut our self-pity around, or be seduced by would-be (platitudinous) comforters. But in fact what the song title says is true. And the song touches me. Even ends up seeming bold and risky. And caring. Oh well. Thanks. I'm not admitting anything here but (maybe) I needed that. Hmm. A song sung like a self-absorbed cry of pain that turns out, as we listen more, to be rather the antidote ("No no no, you're not alone"—great moment). I probably wouldn'ta listened to it on any other album.

Fifth track: "New Orleans Instrumental No. 1." Good programming. We needed a break. CDs are too long. This sweet interlude relaxes and refreshes and helps the whole thing hang together somehow.

Sixth track: "Sweetness Follows." Peter Buck, quoted in Q, says he doesn't play lead guitar (i.e., his job is rhythm and riff and sound sculpture, not soloing)—"but I love guitar feedback. 'Sweetness Follows' doesn't need a solo, a melodic restatement, so instead you get a wash of sound that fills the space and pushes the song to a different level." Yes. Sound of pain again (especially since the only words you're sure to catch are about burying your father and mother) (and this is not a teenage hate song), but instead of walking the schmaltz line this one is elegant, feedback keening like a Celtic rite, furious and gentle. Another insight into R.E.M.'s technique (Buck again, quoted in *Pulse*): "Michael likes to conflict what the lyrics are saying with the music or the way he's singing it sometimes." The thing with riddles is they have to be timed properly: solve 'em too fast and you lose the magic. I loved "Roxanne" (first Police hit) until I realized the crazy intense "You don't have to put on the red light" refrain was actually a literal bit of narrative in a song about falling in love with a hooker. Blah. Stipe is very good at riddles, and he varies 'em nicely: "Sidewinder Sleeps" reveals parts of itself as you listen closely (and parts of itself on first listening too; feelings and sonic pleasures that aren't betrayed as you get to know the lyrics better) and other parts of it delight but never resolve as segments of a larger narrative, leaving the mind free to, um, do whatever. "Sweetness Follows" is very hard to catch (don't know how long it would take to hear the chorus phrase if it hadn't been chosen to be the title), but the funny thing is if you sit down with pencil and paper and write the words, you can get ninety percent of 'em with no trouble. And the song unfolds as an excellent essay on just what it feels to be about, only simpler, more straightforward. The singer has learned the power of indirection: "Readying to bury your father and your mother"—but he sings just that first word in such a way that you can't be sure what you're hearing, and that leaves the meaning of the whole verse up in the air. Also an intentional touch of openmouthed Southern accent on "why" ("why did you bother") turns it into "what" when it runs up against the "*d*" sound of the next word, and again we are so effectively and gently thrown off the chase. Not a game, but (this time out) a kind of artfulness. It works. (My mantra for this record.) The speaker has something to say. If he's too direct about it, it will sound condescending. He doesn't want that. He finds a way. And he is guided, in his finding, by the music he's listening to, the nonverbal form of that message, ever pointing a subtle and specific direction. Collaboration. They in turn respond to him. Something comes together, comes forth. Something really beautiful this time, and yet again it's a song I thought would get old quickly; instead gets younger and fresher slowly and steadily, pulling me into this mood where I don't want anything but *Automatic for the People* on my phonograph. Wow. Those two words (the title) are a superb marriage—it's all about sounds, isn't it—and the connotations of sounds. "Flows" and "swallows" are conjured up without ever being brought in directly. And melody. The history of these R.E.M. creations is all about the moment(s) of the arrival of melody. Music then words; words implied by music; melody implied by words and born in singing and brought forward by more musicking. Process. Mystery. Finally I have to acknowledge the way he balances specific sister and brother image with addressing you and me as "my sister and my brother"—perfect, he dodges the disadvantages of either interpretation while reaping the full benefits both ways. Ambiguity rules and flourishes. Swell ending to side one of the record, and how come that comes through so clearly even though I have a CD?

Seventh track: "Monty Got a Raw Deal." Ambiguity is not enough. Michael Stipe and R.E.M.'s DNT (Disjointed Narrative Technique) works because (and when) they truly do have a story to tell. Substance lurks behind, and peeks through, the disjunctions. My wife Donna, after a few dozen listenings, hadn't read the song title but loves the song, and couldn't quite catch that first word ("Monty," as in the first line and natural title of the song: "Monty, this seems strange to me"). I wondered, then, what it seemed to her to be about. She suggested "forgiveness," as in the phrase that jumps out at (and lingers with) her: "You don't owe me anything." More generally, she feels it as a song of lost love, which also (my personal favorite attribute in a rock-and-roll song) is about "what seems to be going on on the planet now." Planet news. Planet waves. Late world roundup. Okay. This is important information about how we hear songs, particularly "rock" songs: strong impressions left by snatches of phrase, rather than by the narrative as a whole. "I can't get no sat-is-fac-tion" or "How does it *feel?*" are the messages that sink in; the verses often are more of a blur, an experience, a *sound*. Felt by the body. Whereas those phrases that jump out are simultaneously felt by the body and heard by the mind. Powerful effect. Donna notes the attractive quality of an album that urges us (track four), "Hold on, hang on" and (track seven), "Just let go; just let go." Good! It works! Contradictory feelings are normal; we recognize them; we like having them acknowledged and celebrated. We know, without having to think about it, that "try not to breathe" as a sung phrase, with this music and this timing, evokes the value of breathing. It is like saying, "appreciate breath"—but it's a cooler way of saying it.

So. Disjointed narrative. Behind the phrases and images that jump out at you, a story is being told. Sometimes it's implicit: "Everybody Hurts" is exhortatory, but when you hear it as a guy—assumed persona—speaking to a girl, it can become a fictional fragment, a story. "Sweetness Follows," by offering more specifics, more overtly conjures up story context, while still speaking in a monologue addressed to an intimate "you." (Lots of self-reflective stuff, too, as though he's speaking to himself, but still standing in front of "you.") "Monty Got a Raw Deal" is in the form of explicit (third person, past tense, "this happened and then that happened") narrative: "I saw you buried in the sand." "I saw you strung up in a tree." These could be dream images or visions (à la "Hard Rain"), except that they are preceded by establishing circumstances ("I went walking through the street") and followed by little conversations in which the person (stranger) with you tells me not to look at what's going on, not to speak of it. (Donna wonders if the woman saying "hold your tongue" is also saying the next words, "You don't owe me anything / Don't you waste your breath.")

These scenes, added to the repeated word "mischief" in the second and last verses, suggest that this is a story about someone who is being messed with in a playful but sinister fashion. The word "movie" in the second line fits in with the cinematic effect of the narrative: song starts in second person, narrator addressing "Monty," and continues in that form (except for that nice elusiveness in the bridge regarding who's saying "you don't owe me anything," and to whom) until the last verse, which is still second person but seems directed towards listener/record producer/journalist or police secretary writing this down . . . "Monty" here is in the third person, and he's lying low (so low, the singer clearly implies, he may in fact be six feet under). But I'm cheating.

I'm cheating, or I've been cheated, because I have a more specific idea about this narrative, communicated not through the song itself but (in a trick used particularly by U2 and R.E.M. over the years) through an interview in the press with a band member, which interview may also be recommunicated through a disc jockey's comments on radio or MTV or through regurgitation in a review like this one. Monty (I "know" from reading R.E.M. talking in *Pulse* and *Q*) is Montgomery Clift; during the recording sessions, Michael Stipe heard some stories from a guy who took photos of Clift during the shooting of *The Misfits*, and this song resulted. It takes place on a movie set. The narrator is (partly) the photographer: a stranger who notes that something peculiar is going on. The song gets this across extremely well—even when one doesn't have this "clue" dropped into the media. I say I may have been cheated because I can't hear the song now without thinking about what might have been going on during that movie shoot; I may in fact receive less of its magic now that its context has been made (irreversibly?) more specific for me. And I've just passed the contagion on to you. Sorry.

But all this talk of words, which are the most familiar elements of narrative, certainly, mustn't distract us from the pleasures and misdirections of the musical part of the story. That wonderful bit of Orientalia—clichéd Japanese/Okinawan scales, that recurs at key moments—what's that? How does it fit with any of this? And yet it fits so deliciously! Disjunction à la Stipe and Company is achieved as much through tone of voice or tempo of music at odds with apparent emotional content of lyrics, as through juxtaposition/mystification/omission in the lyric-writing. But always what is vital (and somehow this is true even in the music that apparently existed before there were words and a title and a conscious subject) is that there is a real story in each performer's mind (not always the same story), and it's something he wants and needs to share. (Why the obfuscation, then? Hey, we all do this, a lot of the time. We cry for help while concealing and denying our feelings. We want to tell our secrets almost as much as we want to protect them, or is that vice versa? R.E.M. just picks up the common usage and runs in some funny directions . . .)

Eighth track, "Ignoreland," is angry and *fun.* Hmm. Definitely the best "political" song R.E.M. has yet recorded. By way of disjunction/obfuscation I particularly appreciate the "1979" motif in the semi-audible narrative, which somehow saves the song from being an overobvious blast at the Reagan-Bush gang. (It is, but what is this story he's telling about 1979? If it were 1980—election year—or '81, first year of their administration, it'd all fall neatly in place, but thankfully it doesn't, and is an infinitely better song, in my opinion, as a result.) I like picking up words a few at a time, after one, ten, a hundred listenings ("CBS-TV tells a million lies"). Great beat, great sound. Again, it's all a matter of personal taste, but (although there are days when I'd rather not hear it) I find myself listening to this track with pleasure, enthusiasm, satisfaction, long after the point at which "It's the End of the World as We Know It" had passed saturation for me. This one goes beyond cute. It's righteously and rightly angry, and funny, and intelligent, and it builds and builds and breaks at the right places and builds again. "I know that this is vitriol . . . but I feel better having screamed it!" Me too. A very necessary and timely release. Especially since the title/chorus points past all the obvious villains of the tale, through to those of us who are in fact responsible. Yeah. Yeah. Yeah. "Someone's got to take the blame . . ." All right. Rock and roll.

"Fuck Me Kitten" (track nine) is announced as "Star Me Kitten" on the album packaging, in the tradition of the Rolling Stones' "Starfucker" (aka "Star Star"). Funny though, how, if it were called (and sung) "Star Me Kitten," it could be the one unsuccessful song on the record—that one word, and the charge it still comes with (especially when used as a transitive verb), give this odd excursion shape and personality and the drama it needs to be effective. Among other things, the title phrase offers a neat mélange of the appealing (to me; but then Brigitte Bardot always did more for me than Marilyn) and the repugnant (there's something demeaning about the phrase "Fuck Me Kitten," isn't there?, ok or great in a moment of passion maybe but out of place in anything as public as a recorded love song). So we get, on the surface, another example of the patented Stipe love song as anti–love song (pop song as anti–pop song), a genre I'm tired of in general but hey this particular one in the context of these other performances twists my tail appropriately, comes through finally as another riddle (to which only the listener has the answer). Singer's really gargling this time. So we hear a monologue that's deliberately unintelligible until climaxing in the final stuff about "You are wild, and I am your possession . . ." This is the key. I first heard it (and I imagine I ain't alone) as "You are mine, and I am your possession," which is ordinary and somehow depressing: Hey, let's objectify each other, and then have sex. But "You are wild" puts things in a totally different light, because now he never claims ownership of her; quite the opposite. A song of surrender, and courtship. Rekindling old fires. (I think I hear him say ". . . from our driveway"; domestic touch, eh?) And these singsong chords, that could easily be repugnant, they're appealing, too; that one word (not "fuck" but "wild") transforms the speaker's intention for me, and I sympathize, identify, am caught up in the possibility of these people's rediscovery of each other. Molasses tempo on this one. Does it work? Mmmmm . . .

(Mike Mills on the creation of those ghostly background vocals on "Kitten": "I sang seven or eight different notes and put them on faders on the board. You play the board like an instrument, fading the notes in and out." God, you get the impression these guys actually *enjoy* making records.)

Tenth track: "Man on the Moon." Okay, a great chance to talk about melody. How am I going to do this? Maybe it's not possible. I want to say melody is like beauty, like color, but these comments are neither helpful nor true. What I do know about melody is that it's attractive, and it puts hooks in us, won't let go, "lingers on," as the old song has it. This song can be seen as a sort of acknowledgment and celebration of the power of melody: This tune is so pleasing, so catchy, the lyricist seems to be thinking, so beguiling and articulate in and of itself, that I can juxtapose a handful of half filled-in word-pictures here with no discernible link between 'em except the momentum of the music, and get away with it. Indeed, the result may be more charming, more full of delight, more appropriate to the tune, than if a comprehensible narrative thread had been offered. When melody takes charge, it puts feelings first; it asserts the meaningfulness of these feelings regardless of the mind's ability or inability to make sense of them. "If you believe they put a man the moon . . ." Where's the declarative clause that's supposed to follow a conditional one? Implied. Like a missing subject implied by a verb, here's a statement that sums up and ties together everything, missing, known only through the implications of the dependent clause that tries to introduce it, and through the music that dances and shouts its message.

Jaunty rhythm. Good melody has something to do with that, too: it helps inspire a groove. In music, melody and rhythm come together (within a structure; could be a sonata, a jazz improvisation, a pop song) and create something magical, and the purpose of words if any is to direct our minds towards the intended feelings while simultaneously distracting them and keeping them out of the way.

"Here's a little legend for the never-believer" ("yeah yeah yeah yeah"—those "yeahs" so similar to and so different from the ones in the chorus of "Ignoreland," subtle symphonic touches on this album, links between different movements), "here's a little ghost for the offering." Yes. Song about song, about the power of belief, if you will, about the intimacy we can feel with a character on our TV set (even if or especially if he's been dead for years), or a singer calling to us from a CD. With historical characters, even. And the desire to be children together, playing games. "Andy did you hear about—?" Gotta like this one. It's funny (that echo, "man on the moooooon"). It's bouncy. It's the melody, and the way the performance delights in it. Got me spellbound. Got me mindless. Got me feeling something.

I appreciate it. (Don't always appreciate having it still on my brain when I wake up the next morning, though . . .)

Eleventh track: "Nightswimming" ". . . deserves a quiet night." Now we come to the heart of the matter. Is this the only track on the album where virtually all of the words can be heard easily, and where those words, on close attention, resolve into a single train of thought? (I realize in this essay I've used the word "narrative" to mean the train of thought that moves through a song or poem or essay, as well as in its more literal sense of the act of telling a story—because each train of thought in an aesthetic context is in fact a story, a deep, sequential story about who the person is who's speaking, with at least hints of everything that's brought him or her to this moment, these feelings.) (And R.E.M. use multiple and/or broken narratives—both qualify as "disjointed"—to represent accurately the complexity of who we are. I mean our shapes are fractal, not geometric. We are the intersections of waves, of many waves.) Maybe. Certainly it stands out in many ways, while remaining very much a part of the fabric of the album-as-a-whole. We are also told, through the interviews, that it is a lyric written back before the previous album was completed, a lyric that arrived before the music in this case, and that the band failed, in a number of tries, to fit music to it to their own satisfaction. Until now.

Until now. My friend Jonathan, suddenly raving to me about this song while we sat waiting for Television to come onstage at the Great American Music Hall in San Francisco, pointed out its connection to one of R.E.M.'s defining moments, the exquisite "Gardening at Night" on their early EP *Chronic Town*—he believes/feels both these songs to be metaphoric references to that which the group's name also refers to, our night life, that huge mysterious fearful and vital realm of sex and dreams. Nightswimming. "And what if there were two side by side in orbit, around the fairest sun?" A song also about swimming through the ocean of stars, our metaphysical and astrophysical existence (*In the Night Kitchen*).

Ahem. But not a pretentious song (for me, even "Losing My Religion" is somewhat contrived or pretentious, though I dearly love it). "Nightswimming" is primarily and simply about seeing a photograph reflected in a car's windshield while driving at night, a photo presumably of a night swimming party at a neighbor's waterhole in Athens, back when BBM&S and the community around them were more innocent and youthful ("fear of getting caught" because the neighbor didn't appreciate these naked kids on his property), a song full of respect for a past moment and the implications, not of its passing, but of its memory and continued existence inside us. A song not of sentiment but of sentience, remembering, awakeness. "I'm not sure all these people understand. It's not like years ago." A simple evocation of a specific scene and moment, framed within a second scene (friends standing by the water; individual driving around town) and so perfectly realized, so astonishingly beautiful, it's surprising how quietly its beauty sneaks up on you, and how gently it holds you (heart to heart) once it has your attention.

Mike Mills (surely the secret genius of this album, as Stipe is the obvious one, and the group as a gestalt—four plus more—the ultimate and necessary one) is responsible for the magnificent piano-playing on this; the only other musical accompaniment is John Paul Jones's string section. And it works so well, heartfelt vocal actually a foil for the shattering eloquence of the words and the piano, strings filling in the musical spaces and tying this track in tight with the sound of the album as a whole. "These things they go away / Replaced by everyday." Easy couplet. And, in this song, on this record, at this moment in our individual and collective lives (age fifteen or twenty-one or forty-four or seventy-three), as brilliant and successful an expression of "how it feels" as any poet might pray for. "The recklessness of water. They cannot see me naked." Go boys go. An amazing performance.

Twelfth track: "Find the River." Back to disjointed narrative. Washing over us. Great words (and melodic fragments) jumping out at us here and here and there. Reminds me of "Maps and Legends." I love it. New sounds from beginning to end of this record. Mills (in Q): "I asked everybody to sing a background part for the chorus without hearing any of the other guys. Mine was really emotional, and Bill's was totally the opposite, cool and low-key. They really worked together. That's the kind of thing that keeps it from being too processed; that lets you know that it's not being machined to death, that there are human beings doing it." Amen. A demo, but it sounded so good they just kept it. "This life will pass before my eyes." A very good ending. Was that really forty-nine minutes? Let's hear it again . . .

Then there's these other records (CDs, actually; and I've also copied them onto tapes for the car and the Walkman) I've been listening to. Where do they fit in? This is complicated. *Automatic for the People* isn't perfect, but it is extraordinary, larger than life, (almost) endlessly nourishing: that which we look for in a musical album and very seldom find. And yet it's not enough for me.

The geography of my current listening would be simpler to describe if it were limited to a single disc. But that's not what's happening. My attention spills over, spills out, and just this once I want to write about this larger, messier experience. I'm not sure how to do it. I'm not going to go track by track through five more records. Instead, I guess I'll just start talking—

HARVEST MOON

[Neil Young] is strange. It's the nearest thing to a failure among the records discussed here. There isn't a single great song on it, the lyrics throughout are unsuccessful at best, banal and embarrassing at worst, and some of the melodies and arrangements go over the line into real sappiness. And yet there's something about it . . .

It sounds like I'm trying to find something nice to say about a mediocre record because I like the artist. No. Neil Young is a great songwriter/performer/creative force, but he's famously uneven, and if this were another forgettable record like *This Note's for You* or *Long May You Run* I'd say so. But it's not. It's certainly not a great great great record like *Ragged Glory*, but it doesn't try to be. It's another concept album (no one else has come close to making as many albums, each with its own goofy and/or brilliant [subtle and/or obvious] unifying "concept," as Neil Young, undisputed king of the concept album, yessir)—and what an intriguing idea. *Harvest*, Neil's fourth solo album, released in 1972, was his most commercially successful record (if others have sold more units it's because the market as a whole has expanded; but no Neil Young album since *Harvest* has been close to as popular in absolute terms). Ever since then record companies have been pressuring Neil to "make another *Harvest*" . . . and now he's done it, self-consciously, twentieth-anniversary edition, same all-star band and backup singers, and with a title meant to ensure that you don't miss the point. But how to go about making "another" version of an existing album? Neil's answer hinges, as does the R.E.M. album, on the question of melody. It's a less successful, far less satisfying use of melody than R.E.M.'s triumph, but it is innovative in an odd way, and definitely rewarding if you can scale your expectations down far enough. Why bother? Because it might give you a new perspective on how music communicates. And because you might (I've been taking a survey of Neil fans whose musical tastes

I respect, and the odds seem to be about fifty-fifty, much higher than I expected) like it.

I'm not certain if I like it.

I know what most gets in the way of my liking it: the lyrics. Many of Neil's most endearing lyrics have been dumb and/or absurd ("Sugar Mountain," "Cowgirl in the Sand"), but they've *worked*, hit the bell, they still do, they're evocative, attractive, affecting, compelling. That doesn't mean, however, that any sort of nonsense can be okay just because it's dumb (or just because it's Neil). My friend Jonathan said he thinks "Natural Beauty" (the album-closer) may turn out to be a great song on repeated listenings; my response was and is that the central lyrical statement, "Natural beauty should be preserved like a monument," is such bad poetry, such an unapt and inappropriate image, that it serves as an insurmountable obstacle to the song's achieving what it reaches for. Let's be literal, okay? Natural beauty should *not* be preserved like a monument. That's really the opposite of what Neil presumably wants to say. A monument is, to most of us (language is what we hear, images are what we see when the word is spoken, get away from that dictionary), a dead stone thing, solid unmoving and made by human hand. Natural beauty should be "preserved" (already a bad word) in the wild, as a living thing, unemasculated, full of its native power. Like a hurricane. Natural beauty is an expression of God, of life, not (as the song's refrain seems to suggest) an abstract concept to be legislated. Truthfully, "should be," "preserved," and "like a monument" are all three inappropriate, clunky, contrary word-phrases to attach to the feeling of "natural beauty" that this song's melody and performance clearly strive to evoke. Is there some value, maybe, in the contradiction? No, not this time. It's too unconscious.

There's no grace, not even goofy awkward wacked-out grace (Neil's specialty). It's a simple case of fucking up.

There are redeeming aspects. "Don't judge yourself too harsh, my love" is a good line, could be a very moving line if the song weren't built on such a wimpy verbal foundation. I don't care for the "video screen" image but it's the sort of thing that Neil can force on me and make it work (stretch me, surprise me) when he's inspired. Some of the dumb words and images in *Ragged Glory* achieve transcendence (others, including entire songs, remain dumb, but I still flat-out love the album). But "Natural Beauty" is crippled by infelicitous word choices and perhaps by something deeper: a shallowness or laziness that's in direct contrast to the commitment required by the subject matter. I grant you I like it better than "Mother Earth (Natural Anthem)" on *Ragged Glory*. Oh well. It would be easy to say Neil should stick to love songs (and angry/passionate/sensitive/confused observations on the rock-and-roll life). But in fact it's probably more true that he's reaching for something here he really cares about, and he should go back and work it even harder, till he captures in sound-story what's biting him, till he untangles this truth and makes it bite back with all the ferocity and beauty of "Over and Over" or "Love to Burn" or (soft sentimental melody-sound okay, just as long as it *works*) "After the Gold Rush."

David Geffen sued his former friend Neil to try to force him to deliver an album like this (rather than a computer music album followed by a fifties retro album followed by a mainstream country album) when he was under contract to Geffen Records. Neil resisted. Now he takes up the challenge as though it's an aural experiment, like 1991's *Arc* (a thirty-five-minute CD composition made up entirely of feedback segments from the Neil/Crazy Horse tour earlier that year; a surprisingly likeable piece of music).

Taken purely as sound, *Harvest Moon* works. The weird thing is, it works best at arm's length, CD playing in the background while you go about the everyday business of your life. To call an album "background music" is an insult where I come from, though Brian Eno's Ambient series may have removed some of that stigma; the thing about Neil Young, however, is that he's made so many albums he has a right to narrowcast them, and this one may just retain its dignity by virtue of the fact that it's self-consciously "adult contemporary" (aging ex-rockers seek mellow sounds, identify Neil Young with memories of "Heart of Gold" and his sensitive singer-songwriter days) and that Neil *knows* that them AC fans aren't listening too, er, *closely*. So he gathers up the *Harvest* musicians and backup vocalists (big-name talent used modestly: James Taylor, Linda Ronstadt), goes for similar instrumentation, mix, overall *sound*, and then consciously recasts the memorable melodies and rhythms of the earlier record into slightly new combinations, a little like Holland-Dozier-Holland rewriting the last Motown hit to make the next one, but lovingly, and with a wink (like the wink HDH gave us when they put out a Four Tops hit called "Same Old Song"). A sonic patchwork meant to be heard peripherally. Okay, but . . .

But where's the meat? *Ragged Glory* re-created and updated the sound of "Down by the River" and "Like a Hurricane" so successfully that it actually becomes a new reference point, quite possibly Neil's best album. *Harvest Moon* re-creates but doesn't update the sound of *Harvest*, and the identity of its own that it takes on is a very modest one. "Come a little bit closer, hear what I have to say," he sings to his wife on the title track, and if we take him at his word we find that there's very little to hear, neither lyrically ("From Hank to Hendrix" is promising, but the payoff line—"Can we make it last, like a musical ride?"—is almost as bad as the dreadful "American Dream" stuff Neil wrote for the last CSN&Y album) nor melodically ("Unknown Legend" promises good old musical delights in its intro and then bops us with every possible steel guitar and backup vocal cliché before the first verse is over).

"I'm still in love with you" is a perfectly valid message, but we've heard much more convincing expressions of it on the last two studio albums, *Freedom* and *Ragged Glory*. Ironically, what's lacking on this journey into sensitive-songwriter land is vulnerability. The original *Harvest* was in fact a very uneven record ("There's a World" is Neil at his emptiest and most overblown, "Alabama" is musically clichéd and horribly condescending lyrically, and "Words [Between the Lines of Age]" is just boring), but the vulnerability of the best songs was totally authentic and I still get my guts twisted listening to both the sound and the words of "Out on the Weekend" or "A Man Needs a Maid." *Harvest Moon* is an experiment to see what happens when you sample yourself, when you bring your famous old sounds and melodies back together for a twenty-year reunion to see what's become of them and us, without compromising your self-honesty. And what it proves, I think, is that though melody may be at the heart of the magic, sound and melody alone are not enough. The R.E.M. album achieves what it achieves because each band member struggles mightily and at considerable personal risk to pursue the uncharted paths that a good melody can point us towards, over and over, song after song. And as a result the ambiguities and obfuscations in both lyrics and performance can take on profound meaningfulness, moment to moment, for both performer and listener. Neil's ambiguities and obfuscations have done the same for us at many's the past moment, and will again, but not on *Harvest Moon*. And yet . . .

"I wanna see you dance again." He knows what we want. And maybe we love him because we identify with his conflicted desire to satisfy us and to withhold himself at the same time. Maybe—in fact I'm sure of it—this album that comes down strongly on the side of withholding is more palatable and reassuring to our everyday selves than albums that scream "You'd better take a chance!!" to cacophonous Crazy Horse accompaniment. And wasn't *Harvest* all about self-conflict in the first place? Yes. But I don't just want to see you dance. I want you to win my heart. Every time. *Harvest Moon* doesn't deliver. But it does add an important new footnote to the saga of how it feels to try to be (both in public and private) "Neil Young."

NOTHING BUT A BURNING LIGHT.

Bruce Cockburn. A great album. I bought a copy when it came out last June, and didn't connect with it at first; I guess I got the impression it was slow, dark, not fun. Wrong! Fortunately it crept back onto my stereo sometime this fall, and this time grabbed ahold and wouldn't let go. An amazing set of songs and performances by one of the finer troubadours (traveling song-poets) of our era. Terrific production by T-Bone Burnett. Terrific guitar-playing (as my musician pal Cindy points out, Cockburn is an underrated master, and he outdoes himself here).

It's an unusually long record (sixty minutes; bye-bye, vinyl), and I'm not always in the mood for the leisurely pace of the second half. But when I am in the mood, it delights me, even or especially the oddball stuff: the two instrumentals—the first cooks deliciously, worthy of an album that features Booker T. on organ on nine out of twelve tracks; the second strikes me as a deeply moving nonverbal coda to the previous song, "Indian Wars"—and Cockburn's charming but plodding retelling of the Christmas story, "Cry of a Tiny Babe."

But if you ask me "Why great?" I have to point to the first seven songs (every CD has an EP inside it, consisting of the first batch of songs in the sequence, which is heard two or three times more often than the album as a whole), and to three performances in particular: "Mighty Trucks of Midnight," "Soul of a Man," and "One of the Best Ones." These seem immediate candidates to stand with Cockburn's finest work, alongside the likes of "Hills of Morning" and "If I Had a Rocket Launcher" and "Tibetan Side of Town." Worthy also to stand beside *Automatic for the People* as music that speaks to and for the heart of our personal, political, spiritual moment. We need songs like these. They make a difference.

They make a difference, first of all, by being different. "Mighty Trucks of Midnight" would be a huge hit single in the aesthetically appropriate alternate universe of my imagination, blaring at us over this seven-week period from storefronts and boom boxes and every radio we happen to turn on. It has that clean fluid soulful electric blues sound reached for by most every rocker and captured on record by very few, and then only at rare and magical, unforgettable, moments. And the lyrics fill that sound and amplify it, sending it out as a personal message of pain and reaffirmation and awakening to all those parts of our bodies that feel most deeply. Cockburn's version of Disjointed Narrative Technique involves, in this case, seeming to change the subject with every new verse—and then commanding us, by the sound of his voice on the unchanging chorus, to understand viscerally that these separate and even contradictory stories are in fact facets of a single, chilling, liberating truth. "Mighty trucks of midnight, moving on . . . moving on." I see the night highways of North America, full of sinister power, rearranging our financial and physical realities in ways we can neither affect nor comprehend. This vision arises naturally from the lyric of the first verse, a novel compressed into a song stanza, perfect poetic summation of 1993:

> "Used to have a town but the factory moved away
> Down to Mexico where they work for hardly any pay
> Used to have a country but they sold it down the river
> Like a repossessed farm auctioned off to the highest bidder."

Hair-raising. The next verse starts appropriately with a comic portrait of the aggressive manipulators of Ignoreland, efficiently conveyed in the form of a declaration of independence therefrom ("Wave a flag, wave the Bible, wave your sex or your business degree / Whatever you want but don't wave that thing at me"), but then takes the sort of quick turn for which seatbelts were invented: "The tide of love can leave your prizes scattered / But when you get to the bottom love's the only thing that matters."

This is true. And once again, like the first verse, it is a novel or epic poem condensed into a couple of lines. (I apologize to Mr. Cockburn for quoting his entire song here, but it's the only way I can effectively share my awe and appreciation for what he has crafted. Besides, exquisite as the lyrics are, they have nil resale value separated from their music. Buy the record, folks.)

But what shall we do with this non sequitur between job flight and the destruction of communities—and the pathos of those who articulate the "moral" rationale for all such godless, self-serving activities—and the sudden appearance of love in the song, passionate, painful love, the kind that may break hearts, families, self-images, but that, when you get to the bottom, cannot be gainsayed, cannot be dismissed on behalf of something more "important"?

And (chorus chimes in) what do those mighty trucks have to do with love, anyway?

Third verse is last, and must resolve (Stipe songs don't always, I know, but Cockburn songs come at you from a different angle of incidence). Now we get personal (starting with the word "I") and philosophical (for Cockburn "philosophical" and "spiritual" are practically the same word, and my own sympathies lie very close) in a big way:

> "I believe it's a sin to try and make things last forever
> Everything that exists in time runs out of time someday
> Got to let go of the things that keep you tethered
> Take your place with grace and then be on your way."

What is he saying? Well you'll listen and feel for yourself, of course, but what I hear is a direct contradiction to the implicit or expected political argument of the first verse, which is that there are evil forces tearing apart everything of value, forces that must be identified, fought, and stopped. This last verse says, in effect, not, "Don't stand in the way of progress," but rather, "Don't try to stand in the way of death." This, like so much else on the album (and for better or worse, I guess), is a mature perspective. And for Cockburn it's a hopeful, defiant, and even loving perspective. Don't stand in the way of death, because death and change are inevitable, are freedom, are finally the only sources of new life. Meanwhile we must shine as best we can during the brief moment of our presence.

"Mighty trucks of midnight," after this extraordinary stanza, are still sinister and powerful, but the image they convey has become bigger and more intimate both at once—out between these cities, through all the hours of darkness, Time and Fate are doing their work, rolling down the road, silent and relentless but not perhaps merciless if we open ourselves to the mystery of Time's mercy, Death's mercy, God's inexplicable mercy which makes it possible for us to be here, to love, to lose, and finally makes it possible for us to leave here again, free at last. And now I/we can find the sequitur in the split middle verse: the subject is values. These are indeed separate novels that have been compressed here, but novels that belong together— the story of the (seemingly purposeless) loss of what's valued, and the story of the discovery (rediscovery, probably) of love as the only reliable value, the only one worth fighting for, except you fight for it by loving, by having the courage to love even in the shadow of the inevitability of loss. (Who was it in *Pogo* who said that the reassuring thing about life is that "it ain't nohow permanent"?)

Which is not to say, "Don't resist the forces of decay." It is simply to acknowledge that the political life and the spiritual life, both exemplified in the work of Bruce Cockburn over the last twenty-three years, raise questions and feelings (anger hope despair acceptance) that totally engage us but that cannot be answered or resolved except perhaps in our knowledge of God, and insofar as love itself can be an answer. We fight the forces of decay by loving, and this song/performance is an example of that activity at its best.

One person's opinion. This is (part of) what I experience and feel, as I listen.

"Soul of a Man" is almost equally profound, and it fits the album so well and sounds so much like Cockburn's lyrical and musical voice, it is a shock to discover it's a Blind Willie Johnson song from circa 1930. What a great sound Cockburn and Burnett (and the players; on this track, Michael Been on bass and veteran Jim Keltner on drums and washboard) have created here! As marvelous as the guitar-playing is, it is always contained within the glorious rhythmic framework built by bass and percussion; and Cockburn's intense but restrained vocal rounds out the effect—a piece of music that drips power at every moment yet never distracts from the lyrical narrative that is the proper focus of the listener's attention.

"Won't somebody tell me," song and singer ask, "tell me what is the soul of a man?" What makes Cockburn relatively rare among popular artists of this or any era is that he lives with his eyes, ears, and heart open, looking, listening, and feeling, so when he does write and record a song he (more often than not) speaks with the voice of someone who genuinely has something to say. This is achieved in the performance as much as in the writing: anyone might sing these words, but very few could succeed in making them so immediate, so personal, so heartfelt.

I don't mean to suggest that this is primarily a matter of vocal (or guitar) technique. It has to do with something both simpler and more mysterious, something that's approached by words like vulnerability, humility, honesty, aliveness. Maybe I just like this song because the answer Cockburn and Johnson come up with is the same one I arrived at (in part through twenty years of studying the I Ching) and wrote about in a book called *Remember Your Essence*; they report:

"*I read the Bible often*
I try to read it right
As far I can understand
It's nothing but a burning light."

Gooseflesh. But maybe you had to be there. Which is, I think, the opportunity this record offers.

There are a lot of fine songs on this album. "Kit Carson" is spooky, a history lesson in a handful of words, reminding us that evil is not always impersonal, that in fact it usually comes down to the acts of individuals, based on the decisions each of us must make, over and over, as to what is right, and how we express those decisions in our actions. "A Dream Like Mine" is a good album-opener, a likable rocker with an inspiring message having to do with where courage and conviction can be found. "Indian Wars" is a well-written finger-pointer, calling attention to the fact that genocide is not just something our forefathers perpetrated. "Great Big Love," "Somebody Touched Me," and "Child of the Wind" are familiar, effective, rhythmic/melodic Cockburn love songs that express the joy of being alive in the world of nature (a world that includes both "the pounding of hooves" and "engines that roar") and in the presence of both divine and earthly (man-woman) love.

Attractive songs, performed with affection, fire, grace. My favorite, alongside "Mighty Trucks of Midnight" and "Soul of a Man," is "One of the Best Ones," a gentle (almost mournful) love song to the singer's spouse or life companion. This is the song Neil Young tried to write, over and over, on *Harvest Moon*, without success. It's not an easy song to write. The lyrics, and the way the melody wraps itself in and around the lyrics, like a shy toddler in his mother's skirts, speak of love and passion from the perspective of one who has "paid a lot of dues to get here," looking into the eyes of another such. They (words and melody both) ring like haiku, mysteriously simple and touching. How long does it take to learn (or even care about) the meaning of the word "sincerity"? This quiet song has an immediately recognizable depth of life experience within it and behind it. The verses drop like petals onto a pond, the shimmering water of the performance, beautiful and silent and full of personal meanings for each listener. "Guess I'd get along without you / If I had no choice" (reminding us almost unavoidably of how we'd have said and felt the opposite at twenty, and how, paradoxically, these words show a shift towards more, not less, commitment). "Done a lot of getting ready for this / Some things we learn so slow." "There are eight million mysteries / In the naked body." This music invokes for each listener what we value most in our love relationships: the affection, the sharing, the respect. And the wonder. Cockburn really is our poet laureate of wonder. Long may he ride.

TELEVISION.

Television. I went to see these guys when they came to town last month—for me it was a historic event, my favorite band of the late 1970s reunited after fourteen years, and I expected the club would sell out quickly. Naw. Television was a critics' favorite during their brief era (two albums, in 1977 and '78), and has been acknowledged as a primary influence and inspiration by the members of U2 and R.E.M., but most folks have never heard of them, and the band's astonishing comeback passed without much notice even in musically hip San Francisco.

Too bad. The shows were thrilling. Certain rock guitarists—Neil Young, Jerry Garcia, Pete Townshend—can get a sound from their instruments that is uniquely their own, and Tom Verlaine and Richard Lloyd, playing together, belong to this pantheon and have not lost the magic. With the other two original members, Fred Smith on bass and Billy Ficca on drums, they filled the Great American Music Hall with what can only be called Television music. I'm sitting here at a loss as to how to describe what it is about that sound that makes my heart beat fast and the hairs stand up on the back of my neck, but anyway the important news about those shows and this new album is that they are in fact the real thing; the passage of years and the rise and fall of rock empires have meant nothing to this band who sounded from the beginning like they existed outside of normal time.

How to describe it? This album, which would be easier to talk about if it had a title, is not quite the equal of the two from the seventies, *Adventure* and *Marquee Moon*, but it is very much a continuation of the same eccentric vision, sonically and musically as well as lyrically. Tom Verlaine, who sings and writes the words as well as playing lead guitar much of the time, is a professional weirdo—when he sings "that cat's from Mars!" we know he's only echoing what people say about him. The songs he creates with Television have a sound that may be partly a matter of playing at a certain pitch, choosing chords and keys that resonate with the textures of the songs, music pictures (and rhythm pictures) to go with the word pictures. Whatever it is, it's addictive; even when the songs as songs don't seem memorable, their sound is—you want to hear it again, be transported like that again, and you won't find it anywhere but here. That weird voice. Those metallic guitars.

What do we listen for? Different reasons at different times. *Television* can never be the sort of intimate friend that *Automatic for the People* is for me, but it offers another kind of friendship. Like Neil Young, Tom Verlaine projects the archetype or persona of "the loner"; and there are times when the loner in me needs nothing so much as sitting quietly nearby another loner (not too close), staring together at something unseeable in the middle distance.

I say "sitting quietly"—the quietness is in the music, even though it is strong rhythmic rock and roll throughout. The lead track of the album, "1880 or So," is a good example (the song could have been called "Rose of My Heart," but then we might actually be able to remember it by name—Verlaine works hard at erasing such conveniences). It has a lovely metronomic (nonelectronic) drum figure running through it, creating (with bass and rhythm guitar) an exquisite feeling of regularity, universal pulse, solid, steady, full of the quietness of waves eternally and reliably breaking on a sandy shore. There is quietness also in the tone of Verlaine's voice, along with tremendous color and character. The voice doesn't try to ride the rhythms of the music, exactly, but it draws its power from its relationship with them.

The next song, "Shane, She Wrote This," is louder and more emphatic but still has that feeling of regularity and calm running through it, forming a beautiful contrast with the excitement and intensity in the song's melodic and rhythmic structure. What am I saying—that there are two sorts of rhythm here, both conveyed by bass and drums, one soft and steady and the other fierce and explosive? Yes, but they coincide in a manner I can't quite explain. This music bounces—not cutely but in some way that speaks directly to certain pulses in my own nervous system. I twitch along to the music, feeling mysterious happiness.

In these songs, guitar solos generally speak more clearly than words. And sound of voice communicates where words alone would mystify. Feeling and emphasis are primary. Words, like instrumental sounds, lack specific firm conceptual meanings but carry emotional weight. Occasionally a phrase emerges: "In my world, come and go / What I want, I just don't know" (from "In World," the third song on the album). Mostly the words are cryptic. We suppose the first track is a love song because of the repeated "rose of my heart" phrase. A close listen makes it possible to identify almost every word but the narrative remains elusive. "I don't belong to misery." Well, I can certainly make that mean something. "In the fragrant sweep of the evening air / I could leave this world quite without a care." But is he talking about love, or detachment? It's a lovely phrase anyway, evoking feelings even if I can't give a name to what it is I feel. Something. Something rather precious. And that tasteful lead guitar commentary that follows, movement one and movement two, and the way it interacts with the drumming. The closer I listen, the more seems to be going on here. "The time is brief, now the shadows swim." The words will never yield up their mystery. The guitar lines too stay ambiguous in their eloquence. But my tapping foot knows something.

I like the first three tracks particularly well. While each track on the R.E.M. album strives (successfully) to find some way to stand out for us, to establish its special identity, the songs on *Television* strive for anonymity. It's an album that grows on you, sounds much better after six or seven listens, and takes another huge leap forward after maybe fifty spins. No reason to think you'll be moved to make such a commitment to it, but if you are, you'll be rewarded. Some kind of endorphin feedback effect kicks in, and the pleasures of the music suddenly multiply themselves. Pleasures of guitars, of rhythm instruments, vocal performance, song structure, and of bits of lyric and melody sticking to the mind and helping it feel its unity with the body and soul and all that.

What do we listen for? Pleasure? Insight? Companionship? An opportunity to release emotions (anger, anguish, confusion, joy)? All of the above? No doubt. And then when we say we do or don't like a particular record, what are we reporting? That it doesn't do anything (none of the above) for us? That it doesn't meet the expectations we had? That it gives us everything we ever wanted from a record album and more, across the spectrum of possibilities? That it makes us feel good in certain ways that are fulfilling and that right now we're not finding anywhere else?

Sometimes I listen to the *Television* album and it's opaque to me, I just don't get it. Other times, however, it pleases me so much more than I expect it to, and then I wish I had words to explain, even to myself, what it is I'm so delighted by, what I'm responding to. "Shane, She Wrote This" is a wonderful song. Why do I like it? I like the rhythm. I like the chorus, the chord that starts it and the funny guitar figure that follows: chord / "She gives me" / guitar fig-

ure / "all her love" / guitar figure again / "Maybe I don't understand" / follow-up figure . . . Hey, I can't even describe it, but that
follow-up thing, transitioning back to the word "Shane" and the
next verse, is so great, the sound of it, the rhythm (bass/drums/gui-
tar), the way it comments on and incorporates the music that's
gone before, the unique *tone* of it, and then the extraordinary instrumental break halfway through the song, blossoming out from the
chorus, all sorts of stuff going on in here that tickles me, that illu-
minates, suffuses me, without my being able to begin to say what it
is I feel or see.

The words don't help me explain. They're good words, like the
sounds are good sounds, but this is not the kind of song (not like
Bruce Cockburn's, say) that speaks in words to my conscious mind
even as it speaks with music and the sound of words to some larger
part of me. There's no verbal anchor here. I mean, the song is about
the singer's feelings for a woman, or it purports to be, or it partly is.
It's also about a kind of religious experience. ("Rapture is mine now
as I behold / All turning holy and bright"—or is that "altar," and are
there words I'm missing?) It's certainly about that repeated phrase
that builds to the song's climax, "I want to know," but at the same
time I could turn to you after you've listened to this record fifty times
and ask you which song he sings "I want to know" on and you could
look at me like, Yeah, that rings a bell, but I'm not sure, I mean I'm
drawing a complete blank. These songs hide within themselves. They
are perfect puzzles that, unlike the songs on R.E.M.'s album, don't
require or request solving. We experience them without thought.
They wash over us. They touch our bodies in magical ways and then
disappear into the night.

They are brilliantly realized creations, built to exacting specifications that no one but Tom Verlaine would ever have come up with
and that no one but Television (not even Tom alone) could possibly
meet. The discipline involved is remarkable, and the results are—
peculiar. But inspiring. I said this album is not quite the equal of
Marquee Moon and *Adventure* but I'm not sure about that. It doesn't
have a single song that I love as much as "Carried Away" or "Friction"—
but ask me again in six months or a year and I may tell a different story.
This stuff fits no mold. It just grows on you. At first you try to brush it
off. But it won't go away.

Like a ringing in the ears. I don't know what Tom Verlaine's
intention was in writing and recording this album, but I can tell
somehow that it's exactly as he wanted it to be. Weird person. And

then what about me—why do I enjoy listening to it so much? It's those sounds. You can hear them particularly in the instrumental passages ("No Glamour for Willi," say), although I suspect the sound of the voice is what sets us up to really hear the instrumental stuff. New colors, or rather ancient colors newly rediscovered, brought to light. Textures dimly remembered by brain cells, revived and set to dancing, and it stirs my DNA, stirs something long-forgotten and deeply significant. Not significant like the Archduke's assassination, significant like the smell of a particular childhood neighborhood on a rainy day. And those rhythms. They unlock things—

I don't like this record at all sometimes. Sometimes I love a handful of songs and am uncomfortable with the others. Sometimes it all sounds amazing to me, perfect in its eccentricity, its musical freshness and clarity. If I had to say what it is, I'd call it a collection of love songs, to girls with different names who may nevertheless be the same person, that are also love songs to music and deeply personal expressions of that most valuable of our possessions: a sense of wonder. Verlaine is in awe of this world he finds himself in. He shares his awe, points to some of what is most striking to him, rhythms and colors and chords and sounds, representations of the immeasurable. Synapse music, some kind of synesthesia. It crosses my wires. "When I see the glory . . ." That's a line from the second album, but they haven't stopped seeing it. Haven't forgotten how to turn it into music, either.

I delight in this album. It may or may not tickle you, but if you think it might, give it five or six spins before deciding. If it is for you, you'll be glad you made the effort. No one else speaks this musical language. And no other language can capture the people and places and spaces enclosed in these songs. This is what we listen for: new messages. We don't have to be able to say what they mean. We just like the way it feels when we receive them.

FAVORITE SHORT STORIES.

Sonya Hunter. I didn't precisely choose the records included in this essay; this one in particular chose me, catching my attention (I met a guy who runs a small record company and he sent me some things; this CD jumped out from the group and demanded to be heard again and again) at a moment when I was in a mood both to listen, and to write about this experience of listening. The point is, I guess, that I am defined not only by my favorite album of the moment, but by the cross-section of stuff I'm currently into. I have an almost-eighteen-year-old son who is currently enthusiastic about Arrested Development, Pearl Jam, and Garth Brooks. This is normal, though you won't find a radio station that plays all three of these talented and popular artists. We have to be our own radio stations now, punching buttons in the car and stacking CDs on the home player, maybe making compilation tapes for the Walkman if we're so inclined. We mix and match, painting subtle or blatant self-portraits as we do so. I am not trying to paint a self-portrait here. I am trying to paint a portrait of the universe, at this instant in time, based on what I see when I look out the window. Window of music. This 1991 album that just showed up in my life is part of what I see hear feel this month. It pleases me. I'm not writing about it because I want to introduce you to a new artist. I'm writing about it because it makes me happy.

I like the songs (some more than others). I like Sonya Hunter's singing—the sound of her voice and the way she makes use of it, her performance. I like the arrangements. I like the way the album hangs together as a whole, the "feel" of listening to it.

A good voice is something new under the sun. Once you meet it, your world is bigger. In a certain sense a voice and a personality are the same thing. Or voice and individuality. An artist's voice (paint on canvas, words on paper) is, at best, the soul of that person, shared with someone else at this moment of contact. Monet's voice—unmistakable. Shakespeare's voice. Billie's voice. Chaplin's voice (the voice of silence, the voice of face). It surprises me that this modest album has grown on me to the point where I'm not ashamed to speak of it in terms of what art is all about for me. It's about meeting real people. Voices that touch me. Voices I listen for, look for, wait for. Voices I remember.

Thank God for new voices. Thank God for old voices, too.

On this album, I am starting to realize, Sonya Hunter stakes her claim to possibly be an old voice, old musical friend, someday. Hello. A future Neil Young, perhaps, and people will say, "How come she doesn't do another album like *Favorite Short Stories?*" Oh well. I'm not saying this is a great record. But it's a wonderful record. There's a subtle distinction.

Three things that help it to be wonderful, help it to be an effective introduction: its length, its ensemble, and its thematic unity.

Its length: It's short. You can get the full experience in half an hour (thirty-one minutes), which especially when you're first meeting someone is a real advantage over hourlong albums like Cockburn's, Young's, and Dylan's. There are eleven songs here, and they all feel whole and complete (except "View from a Sidewalk," which isn't supposed to), though most of them are less than three minutes long. Refreshing.

The ensemble: Musicians are used with some of the sparkle and intelligence that occurred on Bob Dylan's early ensemble recordings. These are people with voices of their own, and they are encouraged to use them full heart while at the same time they have the advantage that here there is a strong guiding musical vision for them to be themselves within. Because of this strong vision, different sets of musicians and different combinations of instruments can exist side by side very effectively. "Once I Had a Sweetheart" features a brilliant Chuck Prophet rave-up on electric guitar; "Foggy Moon" showcases Steven Strauss on upright bass, Ben Demorath on oboe, and Chris Cacavas on accordion—along with Sonya on acoustic guitar, a fantastic combo. "The Frost Will Melt" is piano-based, with bass and percussion; "Feathers" is just acoustic guitar and upright bass; "Not Yet," guitar and cello; five other songs feature electric guitar/bass/percussion combinations with various excellent musicians; and the last song, "New Year," is the only solo performance (acoustic guitar). Good arrangements and well-chosen instrumentation and songs and sequencing can turn an album into a tapestry, some kind of rich remarkable texture, unity in diversity. It happens here.

The thematic unity is partial and understated and it works very well. It is announced with marvelous flourish in the opening track, the only "cover" on the album (song not written by the songwriter/performer, in this case a traditional, probably Irish, folk lament): "Once I Had a Sweetheart (But Now I Have None)," done with gloriously intense rock and roll (or electric blues) keening and hypnotic marching-band rhythms, all supporting Sonya's cool, devastatingly believable vocal. She seems to move effortlessly between detachment and desperation, perhaps because (for the character she's portraying) each is a mask for the other. Whatever. The point is that she plays this character (note the album title; these songs, true or not, are presented as narratives, as fictions), the jilted woman, with irresistible conviction. The character shows up again on the other three standout tracks, nicely spaced through the album (1, 4, 8, 11): "Wedding," "Not Yet," "New Year." The closing song, "New Year," is subtle in its expression of the theme (balancing the opener's flamboyance)—only her voice makes it clear that she's singing about loss of love. Great lyrics: "No resolution / My plans have all gone / A good vacation / Who doesn't need one?" Great singing. The singing on all four of these jilted woman songs is exceptional, and anyway, the effect is that the album grabs hold of the listener—on first listen (and second and third) it is clearly *about* something—and it communicates that something uniquely and indelibly. We are happy to give the other songs a chance to grow on us while we wait breathlessly to hear these performances again.

The other seven songs all have their charms, particularly the vocal and instrumental performances. The "jilted" songs showcase the bluesy side of Hunter's voice and personality; there is also a lyrical, playful side displayed on songs like "Feathers" ("Get your free feathers here!"—my teenage daughter immediately responded to this one), "Paint," and "Foggy Moon." The elasticity and expressiveness of her voice as she subtly changes mood and attitude, between and within songs, is striking. "Foggy Moon," a personal perspective on crime in the city, is my favorite after the big four already mentioned. "Break the lock, come right in / Browse around, steal something," she sings cheerily and sadly. Catchy tune. The hook in the chorus—"Trust is dangerous . . ."—is memorable, even haunting. I like the light, sure way she sings against the pulse of the upright bass. The phrasing and timing of her performance illuminate these songs, making her seem at times a better songwriter than she really is. "The Frost Will Melt" is a useful example of the risks of disjointed Narrative Technique; the intriguing pieces of implied story that don't quite fit together have to not fit together in just the right way (Stipe a master of the technique; Neil Young more of an intuitive primitive, a hit-or-miss genius). Many aspects of this song are terrific but I find it hard to love because I can't quite juggle together the title phrase and the "obedient dog" images and the Jezebel reference and end up with any kind of satisfying sense of what she's trying to tell me. Is she flirting, or being humiliated? Is she the Jezebel (I do get that it's a song about talking to oneself), and if so, why? I'm left hanging. Some fine vocal moments, though. Check out "View from a Sidewalk" for an example of Sonya as songwriter dancing just out of reach of my comprehension and making it work for me; good DNT, I like the words even though I'm not sure what they are.

Straightforward narrative techniques still have their place, of course, and the standout short story on the album, "Wedding," uses ironic understatement and unusual dramatic perspective (song sung by a woman involved in a prenuptial affair with the groom) to splendid effect. Funny, deadly performance. This and "Sweetheart" are the performances that hooked me on first listen to this album and brought me back for more. But the tracks that have weathered the best for me are the plaintive (definitely haunting) "Not Yet" and the equally sad, equally delicious "New Year." Melody plays a big part here. Good melodies are pleasing to the soul. Good melody combined with good story (conveyed by good performance) keeps me coming back real well. Sing it for me again please.

The album is highly recommended, not for promise but for what it powerfully and richly delivers. As for promise, I recently heard Sonya sing live (opening for Television at the Great American Music Hall). She was killer the first night, way off the second (opening act is a tough gig, and anyway, in my experience real performing artists blow hot and cold while "entertainers" stay tepidly consistent). But what I want to tell you, apart from seeing her sing if you get a chance to, is that I heard more than enough outstanding new songs at her shows to know she's got a next album in her that should be better than the first, and probably many more after that if she can hang in there. Not an easy thing to do, of course, as one tries to pay the rent and keep the faith and catch the ear of those music biz investment banker guys (still guys, mostly). But I wish her Godspeed and perseverance. This first album (co-produced by Sonya Hunter and Patrick Thomas) is a textbook example of how it's possible to make a great-sounding record on a tiny budget. Also a textbook example of how hard it is to sell any records on a tiny budget, no matter how wonderful the album is. Oh well. If voice is personality, it is also spirit, and we can hope that this woman's strong, distinctive voice is indicative of an equivalent strength of spirit that will allow her, somehow, to keep singing and making records.

I want to hear more.

Speaking of endurance, **Good as I Been to You** is **Bob Dylan**'s fortieth album (including the two with the Traveling Wilburys). It's also, remarkably, the first solo acoustic album he's made in twenty-eight years. Why so long? Probably (ask Neil Young) because he just didn't want to do what people wanted him to do.

And he hasn't. He's found a new way instead. New old way. He's playing acoustic guitar and harmonica and he's singing songs he never wrote. An album of covers, not goofy and detached like *Self Portrait* or quirky and wildly uneven like *Down in the Groove*, but affectionate, modest, intimate, and committed. My friend Jonathan nailed it: "There are no grand gestures on this album." That's right. I love the grand gestures Dylan performed in his solo cover spots on tour in 1988—showstoppers all, the climax of each evening—"Barbara Allen," "Trail of the Buffalo," "Eileen Aroon," "The Lakes of Ponchartrain." But this isn't that. This is something new, again. A new way of being with a song, of speaking through performance.

In a different way from *Blood on the Tracks*, in a different way from *The Basement Tapes*, it is an intimate album. I think indeed it may be the most intimate album Bob Dylan has ever recorded.

Secrets of the heart.

Singers love songs. It's a simple truth, but not always remembered in this day and age. They love 'em, they love to mess with them, they love to hang out with them, they love to sing them. Bob Dylan successfully uses his voice and his guitar-playing to express and explore his great affection and respect for every one of the thirteen songs on this record.

This is an astonishing accomplishment, and I know I'm not the only listener who finds his thoughts turning to something Dylan said to Nat Hentoff in 1962, quoted on the back cover of *Freewheelin'*: "I don't carry myself yet the way Big Joe Williams, Woody Guthrie, Leadbelly and Lightnin' Hopkins have carried themselves. I hope to be able to someday, but they're older people."

We know a friend is sharing a secret of the heart, a privacy, when he tells us straight-out about his pain and longing, as Dylan does on "You're a Big Girl Now" or the less obviously confessional "Most of the Time." But we also feel our friends' hearts' truths when they speak of them indirectly, speak of them through tone of voice, through posture while sitting or walking, through movements of hands and shoulders and facial muscles, through a fleeting look in the eyes. Often this is inadvertent, but there are also moments when we know a friend is consciously, purposefully communicating with us in this fashion, asking us to receive something that cannot be put in words. This album's like that, I think. You can come real close on this one.

At the risk of repeating myself: Intimacy is not the same as confession. Our confusion on this point is a reflection of our *People* magazine culture. Intimacy is closeness, mutual sharing. Dylan's embarrassing and/or incomprehensible performances on national television in recent years are expressions of his inability to pretend to be communing with another person (his listener) in a context which in fact he experiences as extremely uncomfortable, dishonest, and humiliating. "One should never be where one does not belong." The converse of this statement is that when one is where he belongs—as determined by the heart, not the intellect—then one enjoys a certain freedom from prosecution, from the pressures of outward censure or inner guilt. It is in this personal oasis that intimacy exists. Time out from the universe. You and me in this room.

Stories have drifted down through the years, of Dylan playing songs for the other musicians before or during a recording session, or sitting around with friends in a hotel room, folk songs, rockabilly, country, blues, pop standards, even "White Christmas"—amazing snatches of performance that are often incomplete, that come and go in a moment, but that are remembered with awe by the people who happened to be there. This album, recorded rather spontaneously (Dylan had done a lot of recording for a completely different record, involving various other musicians, when he suddenly went into the studio for a day or two and did this one instead), seems to me to be the official opportunity for a public peek at the backstage Dylan, not what he says or does, but what songs he sings, and how he sings and plays them, when he's by himself or with one or two other people.

All of the songs on "Good as I Been to You" are traditional, with the exception of "Hard Times" by Stephen Foster, "Tomorrow Night" by Coslow and Grosz (a huge hit record for Lonnie Johnson in 1948), "Sittin' on Top of the World," which was written and recorded by Jacobs and Chatman of the Mississippi Sheiks in 1930, and "You're Gonna Quit Me," recorded and probably written by Blind Blake in 1927.

The range of source material is fascinating, and reveals a side of Dylan few people are aware of: He is, in his own way, a song scholar, and throughout his career has learned many more songs than he has ever performed publicly. He likes oddball sources, though he's not a showoff about it; he doesn't hesitate to include very familiar songs— "Frankie and Albert," "Blackjack Davey," "Froggie Went A Courtin' "—alongside more unusual choices. He has not gone out of his way to rework these songs—rather, each is to some extent a tribute to the source he learned it from, and it comes out sounding similar to or different from that source, depending on Dylan's mood as he sings it, what feels good to his fingers or his voice, what key he's comfortable playing it in, and so forth. Dylan apparently learned "Arthur McBride," an Irish song from the eighteenth century, from Paul Brady's 1976 recording; and his appreciation of Brady is there in the performance even though Dylan's assumption of the personality of the narrator is so complete you'd swear the cousin in question just told you the story himself.

It's a virtuoso performance. Dylan's ability to identify with victims of injustice and members of the underclass fills this story— about a couple of punks who verbally and then physically resist the predations of His Majesty's recruiters—with an immediacy that is riveting. The subtlety of the singing and the guitar-playing is characteristic of this album, and very much the work of a mature artist. His voice is amazing—it reminds me of what a peculiar and brilliant creation Dylan's original assumed vocal persona was, that hybrid Okie accent, not measurable against any standard because it was sui generis, a "Bob Dylan accent," his private vehicle. This Irish accent of Dylan's is not Irish nor American but is born rather of the song itself, its key and chords and musical texture, its ironies and understatements and emphases. It is an accent created spontaneously by an inspired, hardworking artist who is looking for the right vehicle to transverse the space between this singer and this song at this moment of performance, a place where the feelings he gets from the song can become sounds, a place where the sounds of the words can become music and the colors and textures in the melody can become narrative. A voice. Every song on this album has its own voice, each a unique creation and not for show but for the specific purpose of honoring and getting across the song. Each performance full of respect for history, and for the human feeling and experience that is back of that history. "Christmas morning." When he sings the words he is not Bob Dylan. He is Arthur McBride's cousin. We've met him, and unlike the sergeant in the story, our lives have been enriched by the experience. New messages. As great artists mature, their work often becomes simpler and more deeply felt. Dylan—Dylan the performer, not Dylan the songwriter, who's semiretired despite the genius displayed at the *Oh Mercy* sessions—is no exception.

This is not an album for all moods and moments. It's a thrilling musical and emotional expedition better suited to regular rediscovery than to saturation repeat listenings. Not a pop record, in other words, though it is certainly capable of speaking directly to many different sorts of listeners.

"Jim Jones," an early-nineteenth-century song about a prisoner's boat trip to the penal colony in Australia, is an exquisite example of the beauty Dylan's ravaged voice is capable of when it finds a melody that delights it. This is a song about the dignity of the human spirit; Dylan's portrait of Jim Jones is compassionate, unsentimental, uncompromising, and extraordinarily lucid—his voice is a paintbrush, wielded by a free and confident hand, subtle, supple, exulting in the finest detailwork while never losing the sweep and character of the performance as a whole. The guitar's support is invaluable, full of imagination, intelligence, consciousness. Listen to him sing this couplet: "With the storms raging round us and the winds of blowing gales / I'd rather have drowned in misery than gone to New South Wales." Maybe you're still looking for some other Bob Dylan, voice of some great remembered collective moment. That's okay. But are you missing, through the singleness of your search, the ongoing work of a great artist alive and actively working among us now?

Every song a painting. Every painting filled with light, and full of details that become visible at different moments, on different listenings. The first four songs on the album are classic narratives, their purpose is to tell a linear story; this is also true of "Arthur McBride" and "Froggie Went A Courtin' " (though in the latter we're not so much interested in the story as in the chain of images the storyteller conjures up, lightly, of course, almost a parody of narrative, but still your basic "series of pictures" song in a tradition that Dylan reinvented for much of his most distinctive work, from "Hard Rain" to "Chimes of Freedom" to "Series of Dreams"). Other songs here are what I might call "implied narratives," where there's clearly a story behind the song but we aren't told it directly or in sequence—"Little Maggie," "You're Gonna Quit Me," "Diamond Joe." We know the singer of "You're Gonna Quit Me" is going to jail, but we don't know why, and the song's not intended to tell that story. Rather, it speaks of the situation, a man speaking to his woman whom he believes is abandoning him (presumably because he's no good to her in prison). A song like "Tomorrow Night" is pure situation; no story except, Tonight you're here with me but I wonder how you'll feel tomorrow. And yet it is still Dylan's character as a performer to imbue the song with an astonishing narrative moment. He sings, "Your lips are so tender / Your heart is beating fast / And you willingly surrender / [long pause] To me, but darling will it last?" That pause is so rich in sexuality (I imagine Dylan heard the song as a young teenager and thought it very daring, which it is), and more than that: the dominance of the male, he who is surrendered to, is immediately transformed into vulnerability; the singer feels helpless in the face of his desire for this moment to be repeated, and his knowledge that his fate is now entirely in her hands. The narrative quality I refer to is the feeling we get, largely because of that pause, that he has just described their actual lovemaking, that we are there as it's happening. We also feel the shift take place as confident lover becomes uncertain supplicant. It's a sweet song. Dylan's voice, to my tastes, is gorgeous here; his harmonica playing full of compassion, appreciation of beauty, and resignation. And other things. No simple answers. Rich complexities of the human heart.

I also love the texture of his voice on "Hard Times." This is purely a matter of taste (no accounting for it), I think, the way one is drawn to a particular color in a painting or finds beauty in a particular body and face. I hear the sound of his voice here and I get chills, I get all sorts of feelings, there's a quality to it that pulls me, ear candy, someone else might hear it as nails on a blackboard and how could I argue or explain? I can praise, however, the uniqueness of the sound here created, another new message, new creature. I am intrigued by Dylan's ability to convey to me both the guilt and compassion of the narrator, who is part of a more privileged class ("While we seek mirth and beauty . . ."), and also the feelings of the sufferers themselves—when he sings the chorus he is not the narrator quoting the miserable ones, he is himself one of them, feeling and living the pain, hope, hunger, and despair of the situation and again deeply communicating the dignity of the human spirit at the same time. (This dual role of the singer can be expressed also in the question, is it the hard times that are lingering "all around my cabin door," or is it the poor themselves, or the song they sing that plucks at the conscience? I suppose it is probably all three.) Obviously a timely and well-chosen song, and far from simple in its implications and reverberations. But it is a vehicle for feelings first; thoughts and politics are strictly secondary, or more accurately, the singer believes they appropriately arise from feelings.

The album is full of moments. When Dylan sings, in "Blackjack Davey," "She answered him with a loving smile," I can see and feel that smile. It's the inflection in his voice, the way he's inside the song, the charm and conviction of the storyteller. Lust in his voice— the girl's lust, not the gypsy's. How does he do that? And how about that guitar-playing? My god. I don't think he practiced for months in preparation for making this album, but the difference between what he does here and on the other songs and what he's been doing onstage (as a guitar player) for the last many years, is staggering. It seems clear that the gift is in him, as great as ever or more so, needing only an occasion it's willing and inspired to rise to. The seducer, the charmer, the gypsy poet guitarist comedian rock-and-roll star, has resources he'll always be able to call on if so moved. It's the sweetness of the lady that's the variable, from his point of view—is there an audience I care to charm, after all these years, can you somehow make me want to strut my stuff? Evidently someone was able to.

Maybe Bob just woke up in love with his audience one week, and moved quickly to execute this project before the feeling passed.

(Actually, this happens all the time at his live shows—I mean affection for and openness to his listeners, expressed in the performance of a song. But it's not such a consistent occurrence in the studio. And I can think of only a few occasions—certain concerts or segments of concerts over the years—when he has shared himself so openly and unself-consciously.)

"Step It Up and Go" is in some ways a key to the album: it reminds us that the guitar is a rhythmic instrument as much as a melodic one, and that there is a strong rhythmic element in the performance of all these songs, even if this is the only real rock-and-roller in the bunch. It's an old jug-band song, often called "Bottle Up and Go," and among other things it tells us that Bob Dylan understands the history of American music in the twentieth century, knows where rock and roll came from and maybe where it's going to. Certain feeling, makes you want to get up and dance. Listen to that voice! His fingers are a complete band. "Everybody's gonna have a wonderful time tonight." He doesn't sing that but we can hear it. I can also hear, for example, "Silvio," but this is a much better song (or is transformed into one by a much better performance). Twenty-eight years ago I used to listen to "Snaker" Dave Ray sing "Go My Bail" accompanied by himself on 12-string and wonder why I loved it so much and what was the difference between that and rock and roll? I'm still trying to work it out.

Rhythms. How come he plays the same "Sittin' on Top of the World" he helped Big Joe Williams record thirty-one years ago, and yet it sounds like Reverend Gary Davis (and the Stones) doing "You Got to Move"? Just something his fingers got into, I guess. Rhythms. They float freely between songs and performers and eras and styles of music just like melodies do, recurring over and over in new forms and permutations. With melodies it's called "the folk process" (steal everything) (it ain't theft if it never was private property to begin with). Anyway. I appreciate that none of these songs are primarily nostalgic in content or effect. The point is just the opposite, really: They are alive now, have as much or more to say about our present condition as any new stuff that's being written.

And I like the album title, too. Very funny. Certainly Bob Dylan has been good to us. But certainly he hasn't done it because we wanted him to. No chance. He just happened to notice that we were walking in the same direction, and thought he might offer to entertain us while we walk along. "Hey, I know a love song, and a dance tune, and a story about a girl who disguised herself as a tar and shipped out on a Navy boat. You wanta hear them?" And he tapes a list of songs to his guitar strap. And starts singing them to us.

And we can't get him to stop.

I've been listening to Bob Dylan for more than thirty years. I've been listening to R.E.M. since 1985. A friend gave me Television's first single in 1975, but like a fool I didn't go see them live while I lived in New York, and didn't really get into them till *Marquee Moon* came out in 1977. I've been fascinated with Neil Young since I first saw Buffalo Springfield, in 1966. There've been a few albums of his I didn't buy over the years, because he'd disappointed me the last few times, I guess, but I've always come back and so has he. I got turned on to Bruce Cockburn and *Dancing in the Dragon's Jaw* in 1983, three years after the album came out. Sonya Hunter, as you know, is a 1992 addition to the ever-changing list of voices I'm interested in. What does it mean to have all these voices in my life?

It is a blessing. I don't listen to music all the time. I like to be able to give it my attention, which is one reason I like to write about it: it gives me an excuse to spend hours and hours and hours with *Automatic for the People*, intimate time, quality time, diving deep into each song, each performance, and the feelings it draws forth from me. I recommend this process to you, as much or more than I recommend any given record I've talked about here. Music offers education, self-healing, communication and connection with "the world," that amorphous, huge, ill-defined community of common consciousness that we try to make real by apportioning it into smaller communities that we feel some link with, Americans, Democrats, Christians, Jews, men, women, rock-and-roll fans, R.E.M. listeners. Artists create their own audiences; popular artists create communities of listeners. Less popular artists create smaller (often more intense) communities of listeners. We benefit from our participation in these communities. They expand and deepen our awareness of "the world."

"Maybe I ride, maybe you walk, maybe I try to get off, baby . . ." "Hey, kids, where are you? / Nobody tells you what to do, baby." It's

1993. Maybe that means something, maybe it's an illusion, I'm not sure. Time is a concept. Newspapers tell us what day it is and what's going on that's Important, but I don't trust newspapers. I do trust music. This is not a pledge of allegiance. It's simply an acknowledgment of what seems to work for me. I'm not necessarily looking for truth. I'm looking for pleasure. Melody, rhythm, and narrative. Tell me a story. Sing to me. Give me something to move to.

I'm still hearing voices. The purpose of this essay has been to talk with you about what I hear on these shiny round CDs (notice that they're mirrors? that they're prisms?) when I take them out of their square plastic boxes. New music. New messages. Somehow I think this keeps me alive, keeps me connected, keeps me healthy, keeps me reaching out for something. I need friends. It sounds ugly to say I buy them in a store, but that's only a small part of the process. The real connection begins when I give my attention, and discover (sometimes) that they, the artists, have been giving their attention to me. Have been waiting for me to come along and listen. Have something to tell me, to share with me.

And they do. Sometimes they do. This month they do. It excites me. I wanted to tell you about it.

Don't stop the music. Well, we *can't* stop it, can we? We can shut ourselves off from it, pillows over our heads and cotton in our ears, or we can search for it fervently in all the wrong places and then come back proclaiming bitterly and proudly that the source is dried up and things aren't like they used to be, but all the while the music keeps coming, extraordinary natural resource, the record companies can't believe their luck, turn around and there's some new kid or bunch of kids with a new sound, new vision, new open channel to the source, the magic. Bring a bucket, it's raining money. Better than that, it's raining spirit, raining honest and deeply felt emotion and insight, raining dissatisfaction and awakening, raining revolution. Co-opt it, package it, buy it off, give each kid a million dollars and the keys to the funhouse, but it does no good, knock one down and two more seem to spring up in his place. Amazing stuff. Indomitable and irrepressible, like the human spirit. Don't try to stand in the way of this flood tide.

Arrested Development is a great band and they've made an astonishing first album that people will be listening to and learning from for the next several decades. Never mind that you're not the first on your block (the album's been out for more than a year and has sold two million copies so far) or that you've never bought a rap/hip-hop album before (or you did once and you didn't like it). Run don't walk to the nearest entertainment emporium and pick up a copy of *3 Years, 5 Months and 2 Days in the Life of* . . . (While you're at, you might also treat yourself to their new videocassette, *Eyes as Hard as a Million Tombstones*, one of the few really satisfying long-form music videos I've ever seen.) You're gonna like this one.

Gershwin, Dylan, Hank Williams, and the Rolling Stones notwithstanding, twentieth-century music in the West belongs to black Americans. As the century and (one hopes) American domination of world popular culture come to an end, black America (source of jazz, gospel, blues, and soul/R&B) is making one more monster contribution to the evolution of universal language with the first new popular music that's come along in the last forty years that has not been (and will not be) assimilated and eclipsed by the durable umbrella called "rock and roll." This music is called hip-hop, and its most popular and recognizable form (at present) is rap. Arrested Development's music is more hip-hop than rap, I would say, but that's a matter of emphasis—they are certainly rappers, and a huge part of what makes them so important *is* their rap, that is, what they say in their words.

But their genius, their breakthrough, and their enormous impact is equally the result of their musical ideas. These ideas do not trend in the direction of rock or pop, like most crossover rap (but the rules are changing fast; check out Digable Planets). Rather, they are something truly new that at the same time is instantly recognizable as an extension of the spirit and the sound of hip-hop. World music in the twenty-first century will owe a lot to hip-hop, I suspect, for pioneering a form in which native or local music and culture can graft itself onto a world-accessible language (pop music, cassette CD jukebox radio fodder) without losing most of its own innate rhythms and values. This is big. This is revolution, transformation, grassroots paradigm and value shift. Hope for the planet. What rock and roll supposedly promised once upon a time, but much more broadly based. New music. New vision. Real alternatives. And so likable. Play it loud.

The journey into Arrested Development's first album of "Life Music" can begin almost anywhere. The act broke, as they say in the music biz, via a very unlikely number one single (and accompanying video) called "Tennessee." My own conversion (I don't watch MTV or any TV, hadn't seen/heard "Tennessee") came when my son Taiyo requested the CD for Christmas, I copied it and became captivated by "Mr. Wendal," not least because it was a (rapidly climbing at the time) hit single about a homeless person, a bum. Opened me right up—I'd already heard great things about "Tennessee," and yes they were all true, but I quickly discovered that I liked *all* of the very different, very articulate songs on this record, an hour of fascinating, inventive, substantial music full of valuable timely intelligent messages to black youth, black adults, world youth, world adults—all of us. Whoever's listening. Talking to ourselves out loud. This is some-

thing that has been desperately needed. The world in i
out for more sanity, more purposefulness, more love
spirituality, more community, more respect, and mo
resent a good beginning, and may a thousand more f
response to what they've (already) accomplished.

"Give a Man a Fish." Okay, starting anywhere
sixteen), this song with its relentless rhythmic riff, great to dance
to—but stop right there. This is not the beloved relentless rhythmic
riff of the Rolling Stones or the Velvet Underground, or for that
matter of Robert Johnson or Howling Wolf. This is not a riff or the
sort of riff you'll hear on any Motown record, any Stax record, any
disco record, any Beatles or Bob Marley or AC/DC or even James
Brown record. It's something radically new. You don't need sophisticated ears to hear this. What a neat sound, what a simple idea—why
didn't I think of that? Probably because your rhythm guy was pounding a drum kit, not scratching on a turntable. I mean the riff itself is
played on a keyboard bass (I think), and yes there is a drum back
there, and the actual sound of scratching (manual manipulation of
needle, disc, and turntable to produce repetitive and unusual sounds;
nonelectronic sampling) is not dominant on this track as far as I can
tell. But I believe—and I'm an utter idiot in this regard, so don't take
my word for it, it's just that I sincerely believe music in some ways
is meant for and is heard more clearly by those who have no comprehension of its technical aspects—that the sound of this track, with
its magic organization of "noise" elements that all work together to
produce a very pleasurable funky harmony, and particularly the ef-
fectiveness of that rhythmically odd naked bass line, is directly the
result of hip-hop being built around a DJ with his turntable and boom
box rather than around the Chicago blues model, popularized by rock
and roll, of a guy with an electric bass and a guy with a bass drum
creating a "bottom" between them.

Start again. I love this riff. I love the way it makes me feel. I
love the way the rap builds and builds in intensity, largely because of
the meaningfulness and humor and cleverness and intelligence of
what the man's saying, the way he's using (and playing with) words,
augmented by the tension as the unchanging riff repeats and repeats,
holding itself back briefly to emphasize a particular line and then
starting right in again, implacable—builds and builds and then breaks
wide open in the great release of the chorus: "Give a man a fish and
he'll eat for a day / Teach him how to fish and he'll eat forever."
Wow! Hey, it's not that we've never heard this thought before. But

we need to hear it again, and get it at a deeper, simpler, more basic level? You bet. And it's the job of the preacher, singer, rapper, testifier, to get us to hear it so we *feel* it, so it becomes part of us, so we possibly start to redefine our sense of personal identity around these simple truths of self-reliance, rather than around the lies perpetuated by those other voices we are constantly exposed to.

Content. That is what is most extraordinary about Arrested Development. (Didn't I just say it was the revolutionary freshness of the sound, the musical and rhythmic ideas? Well, maybe it could be both at once, inseparable, like the sound and message of rock and roll.) Listen to the words of this song, what they say, what they include, the territory they cover. I want to quote them, but when I try I discover how carefully they're knit together, each thought leads to the next and it's the flow as much as the individual thoughts that has the impact. We are inside a person's mind and feelings, starting from depression and poverty—"We're not sure where our lives are going, friends"—but from within the reality of these feelings and thoughts come respect for a companion who won't be defeated by the challenges ("Headliner's strong so he keeps his 9-to-5 / Cuttin' brothers' hair as a means of stayin' alive") and awareness of the source: "If it wasn't for the rhythm / I think we would have given up by now / This system has gotten the best of me / Now I pray for god to invest in me."

These four lines illustrate the complexity and fullness of the thought process: as performed on the record, they become a strong expression and celebration of the core value of rhythm (the role music plays in our lives), a powerful and uplifting statement, without taking away the impact of the acknowledged desire to give up, the political social and personal significance of sharing the very real (very common) feeling that "this system has gotten the best of me." Swoop, faith to despair, and back to faith again as the despair directly leads to prayer, and thus to awareness that we / I are not alone in this process. "Give me strength so I can finish the story."

This is not simplistic stuff, nothing anthemic about it. We are inside a man's heart. It's also a song about being a musician, being ambitious, and about having something one needs to communicate: "Keep on searching for the right way to go out / Cause going out is what it's all about / You can't be passive, gotta be active"—his thoughts naturally move into speechmaking, street politics, preaching, politician in the best sense, a man with something to say because he cares about and feels the anguish of his people—"Can't go with what looks attractive." The verse climaxes in a pledge of integrity, thought arising from the awareness that his ambition itself, while a source of strength, could also easily be his downfall, and so he articulates for himself the rationale for keeping one's independence no matter how hungry you get (for food and/or a podium): " 'Cause if they take away our contract [*love the way he sings that*] / We still got talent and we still got contacts / 'Cause we've worked real hard to get this far / We were catching the bus before we bought the car" . . . and with this brilliant likable folksy image the verbal flow, too, moves naturally into the funky folk wisdom of the chorus. Notice further that Speech (vocalist, leader, songwriter) plays with time as easily and subtly as Bob Dylan, as his verse moves from present tense poverty and feelings of despair about whether we'll ever get a record deal, et cetera, to present tense we're recording this song because we did get a record deal, but don't think that invalidates anything! As though the verse itself moves through time, perseverance and prayer bringing success right before our very eyes, but also perhaps awareness of how "success" can be its own sort of "smudged-up window." And then the second verse starts, "Gotta get political," and we're on to a whole further extension of the thought process.

Stream of consciousness. But Speech never allows his intelligence and hard-fought self-awareness to cause him to talk over the heads of the people he wants to reach. "Grown but can't hold my own / So this government needs to be overthrown." Simple statement: The system doesn't work for us, so we have to change the system. The next lines address themselves to the foolishness of brothers shooting each other when the system is the cause of their woes, and they do it in a way that brothers in the 'hood could possibly hear and identify with; it takes a lot of care to choose words that challenge people's present actions without simply making them defensive and closing down their willingness to listen. Speech (with Headliner, who co-wrote this one song) speaks to, not against, their macho feelings, and at the same time is ruthless in his attack on the prevailing mentality (in the 'hood and in rap lyrics): "But I tell you ain't no room for gangsters / 'Cause gangsters do dirty work and get pimped by mobsters / Some fat Italian eating pasta and lobster / Brothers getting jailed and mobsters own the coppers." (You can call this racism but that's crap; it's an accurate shorthand portrait of the power structure of the drug culture, expressed in a way that could actually help some of those trapped within it to rethink.) Pulling no punches: "Malt liquor got you licked, it's your powerful master / You'll never get out without much discipline / Raise your fist but also raise your children." This is great; it's as if the voice that was silenced when Martin and Malcolm died is returning, not in one person but to the community, at last. Speech addresses himself: "Direct your anger, love! / Nothing's ever built on hate instead of love / Love your life, tackle the government." Because we can hear him talking to himself, thinking out loud, we are encouraged to add our own thoughts to the process.

A splendid song. The verifying ends just past halfway through, and then the chorus is repeated, followed by an extended jam that is inspiring, joyful, intense, inviting the listener's thoughts and feelings to continue where they will, finally opening out into a verbal celebration of rhythm (picking up on that one early line, and on the rhythmness of the whole performance): "Rhythm makes your body move, rhythm makes your mind move, rhythm makes your elbows move, rhythm makes that behind move, rhythm makes the people move—" With this band, even the partying is political, and profound. "Rhythm makes your mind move." Exactly.

The album opens with an introductory jam—"Man's Final Frontier"—including the brag session that is obligatory for any new rapper on the scene, but with a difference. AD's first order of business is to invoke a higher power: "Man's final frontier is the soul / Guarded by someone more powerful than any human being / Someone felt, but never seen." And then this brag: "You will be surprised at what resides in your insides." Evidently this group presumes to give us a guided tour. Wild scratching and general fine funkiness follow (George Clinton's influence can be clearly heard), and a further promise: "With a rhythm as complex as life itself . . ." This album may not quite live up to that high standard, but it does indeed serve to carry a novice hip-hop listener like myself deep into a world of varied and subtle rhythms, a composite portrait of life (one of AD's monikers for what they do is "Life Music") in these black United States, which powerfully demonstrates that simple language and complex rhythms can be tools for communicating truth that are at least as effective as the complex language and monotonic rhythms of the academy, still the ruling intellectual and aesthetic power structure. Speech is visionary enough to be calling for (and attempting to carry out) a revolution in aesthetics as well as in street lifestyles and national politics. Iggy Pop once sang, "I'm looking for one new value / But nothing comes my way." This album would open his mind.

Example: "Mama's Always On Stage." Has there been a pop song before this that explicitly calls on young men to volunteer child-care time to single young mothers in their community? "Brothers talking revolution but leave their babies behind / Well sister he's a sucker just leave him be / The revolution is now up to brothers like me." This is one of the best dance tunes on the album, with a wonderful fresh straight-ahead rhythm, punctuated and indeed dominated by a gorgeous harmonica sound—I found myself wondering if that sound is created by a synthesizer, and finally realized, Duh! It's *sampled* (the whole concept of building sounds and songs by sampling is one I'm still trying to wrap my brain around), and that's why the fine print on the liner notes says "contains portions of the composition 'Snatch It Back and Hold It' written [and performed] by Buddy Guy and Junior Wells." A very hot track, and appropriately so, because the song is also about the young mother's desire to "attack the dance floor" ("Cool, I'll hold her, you have a good time"), which is to say, it's also about the conflict, especially for the young, between parenting and living out your own life. "Mama's always on stage" as a metaphor for what it's like to have the responsibility—not just conceptual but practical—of mothering. This song goes far beyond political correctness, guys trying to be cool by flaunting their "feminism." It addresses real issues, and makes us feel good while it wakes us up, maybe even suggesting that waking up would itself feel good if we'd only throw ourselves into it.

There are a thousand *moments* on this record that fascinate me. A powerful one comes at the end of the second verse of "Mama" when the beat and the riff and the solo vocal and the meter of the rap all pause or break, and a medley of voices chants (accent on every syllable, great double-time effect) "KEEP UP YOUR STRENGTH NOW CUZ WE MUST GROW SOMEHOW BABY MAMA IS ALWAYS ON STAGE!" What was that? Why does it work so brilliantly?

The third track on 3 *Years*, "People Everyday," was remixed after "Tennessee" broke, and released as the second single. Later pressings of the CD include this "Metamorphosis Mix" of "People Everyday" as a sixteenth track, and indeed it's fascinating to hear how much the song is changed and improved by the new mix (which includes newly recorded sounds and vocal accompaniments). Nevertheless, one of the few ways 3 *Years* could be improved on would be if the early track were simply replaced on the CD by the new mix—the transformation is so inspired that the early version sounds plodding by comparison, and besides, it would be nice to have the album close as originally intended, with "Washed Away."

In any case, "People Everyday" is itself a metamorphosis of Sly and the Family Stone's 1969 hit "Everyday People," and as such, an appropriate nod to one of the primary progenitors of AD, in terms of musical approach (James Brown was at least as groundbreaking in his musical inventions, but no one anticipated the musical gestalt of hip-hop half as much as Sly), in terms of outspoken political consciousness-raising, and in the whole concept of a "family band." Arrested Development presents an image of itself similar to Sly and the Family Stone circa 1969 as a group of people who live together like a family, at least onstage and in the recording studio and in front of the video cameras. The video of "People Everyday" is dominated by the marvelous image of the group sitting in back of an open truck, lip-synching the song while riding through the Georgia countryside. Have I failed to mention that another key to the image AD presents is its *Southernness*, indeed, at least implicitly, a kind of rural South-ernness? This could be considered misleading, since Speech grew up in Milwaukee, and I believe Rasa Don (the drummer) called out "Jersey!" while accepting his MTV Award. And the part of the South the group actually assembled in is Atlanta, one of the larger urban areas in the United States. And yet Eshe seems to be telling the truth in *Eyes as Hard* when she says, "Nothing about Arrested Development is fake at all." There is in fact a rural black Southern perspective at the heart (and in the soul) of Arrested Development's music that is a significant piece of what sets them apart from the image and reality of most other rap groups. And their sense of community as a band is also palpably real, though they have their separate lives when they have time to lead them (Headliner, twenty-five, talks in the video bio about his two young children). One of the many little surprises one encounters as one begins to learn more about Arrested Devel-opment is that one of the six basic members of the group is a sixty-year-old man ("the father figure") named Baba Oje. He doesn't rap or play an instrument, most of the time, yet he is credited on the album and takes part in their live performances. Beyond this unusual blow against ageism, it is clear from AD's recordings and particularly from their videos, that the gestalt of the different personalities that make up the group is a very important part of their impact. Taree's brief rap about horseshoes on "Tennessee" has become one of the group's signatures, precisely because it says so much and yet cannot be reduced to metaphor. Its power lies in its transmission of her per-sonality, and in Speech's and the group's willingness to put that per-sonality—all of their personalities—front and center, with no apologies, no explanations. We are who we are. It's a surprisingly fresh message.

The metamorphosed "People Everyday" starts with Speech spitting out a marvelous "diddy bop bop bop diddy bop bop bop diddy bop bop bop hey!" vocal riff over a strong (partially sampled, partially drummed) beat, with the turntable man announcing, "Yo, this is Headliner from Arrested Development, and right now you're in the midst of a celebration—a celebration of life, death, and the struggles of our ancestors," followed by a bit of Ray Charles–like call and response, then the chorus from Sly's hit song, and finally Speech rapping the story with constant repetitions and interpolations from Taree. Fabulous joyous sound; wow. The story, however, is a variation on the confrontation narrative familiar in gangsta rap, in which the poor narrator unfortunately has to blow away a few dudes, or maybe a few dozen, who cross him up. In this case the storyline is twisted so that Speech is the victim of a bunch of macho dudes ("drinking the 40-ounce, going the nigga route") who don't like his clothes or his hairdo and who sexually harass his girlfriend in a threatening manner that makes confrontation unavoidable, even though Speech knows "If I start to hit this man they'll have to kill me." For the sake of the story Speech whips their asses ("But he wouldn't stop and I ain't Ice Cube / But I had to take the brother out for being rude") and Eshe delivers the moral (much more effective than the earlier version, in which Speech delivers it): "It ain't even worth it!" Why be a nigga, when you could be an African, a person of dignity and pride and real inner power? The final vocal riff ("no brother no brother no brother no regrets," or something like that) sounds like it might be Baba Oje making a rare appearance. A wonderful performance from start to finish, and a brave attempt to beard the enemy in his own lair (the enemy being not the niggas, exactly, but the weak spots in the Africans' self-image that allows them—us—to act like that).

I have to interrupt now this rather leisurely progression through the wonders of Arrested Development's debut album to say something about their videocassette, *Eyes as Hard as a Million Tombstones* (seventy-five minutes long; available for rent or purchase at your local video store, and at some record stores as well). First, a warning: Do not confuse this with the videocassette of their *MTV Unplugged* appearance, which reportedly will be released soon. The CD of the show has already been released, and it is not of much interest. The band is proud of being the first hip-hop group to be featured on this popular program, and of having pulled together a very "African" collection of guest performers and acoustic instruments. But the vocals and the ambience and the overall "it-ness" just aren't there for me; great event and great concept, maybe, but not an especially good show. I'm sure they're a much better live band than this *Unplugged* album shows (and I hope the "professional music performer" voice Speech seems to take on for the evening is just a passing aberration). So the album, which is almost entirely songs that can be heard on *3 Years* in better versions, plus the same live tracks sans vocals to fill out the CD, is not recommended, although it has two good moments: the opening rap by Baba Oje, part of which can also be heard on the *Eyes* videocassette, along with the brief "Time" chant that follows; and Speech's heartfelt speech at the end of "Mr. Wendal," where he warns us that "A lot of people, you're under the big misconception that you come here tonight and you listen to a group preach to you all night, and you think you've done your part in this world . . . Sooner or later we gotta understand that it's time for real change, and that means it's time for sacrifice . . . Music cannot revolutionize anything, only the people can revolutionize. People like yourselves, people like ourselves, but not as musicians but as people. Let's not ever forget that, cuz that's the only way things are going to change, you understand what I'm talking about?" He's talking, again, about self-reliance, and not being suckered by the star system. Right on.

But basically my counsel is to avoid anything with the word *Unplugged* in the title, and curl up and spend some time with this amazing tape called *Eyes as Hard as a Million Tombstones* (title from a line in "Raining Revolution," in reference to the eyes of the suffering, discouraged people in the ghetto).

Eyes starts with a "video bio" called "3 Years . . ." made at the beginning of 1992 to promote the album. It was directed by Keith Ward, who obviously worked closely with Speech and shares or has assimilated his montage technique—the style is very much a visual version of what Speech does in assembling and juxtaposing words and rhythms and sounds. This kind of thing can go so wrong and turn out so dumb, but here it's a great success (and one must give credit to the director of the "Tennessee" video, Milcho, who presumably first helped AD discover and develop their unique and very striking video "style"). This is followed by a compilation of footage shot on-stage, backstage, and on a farm somewhere outside of Atlanta, presumably, between July and October of 1992. Included within this compilation are three MTV videos, "Tennessee," "People Everyday," and "Mr. Wendal," plus a previously unseen version of Spike Lee's video of the AD song "Revolution," written for the soundtrack of his Malcolm X film.

"People Everyday" (directed by Otis Sallid) and "Tennessee" are great videos, truly unusual works in this medium in that they carry the spirit and meaning and creative essence of each song further along its true path through their images and timing and the moods they evoke. They open up the listener/viewer's experience of the song rather than shut it down. "Tennessee" is particularly effective in this regard, with the moody impact of Speech sitting and rapping, and the evocativeness of the dancing, and most of all the stark images of (Rasa Don's?) drawings of lynching victims, nooses around their necks (certainly an unusual sight for MTV—violence okay, but consciousness-raising's a no-no—as of course it's unusual to have a number one radio hit song with the lyric "Climb the trees my forefathers hung from").

"Revolution," an important song not included on 3 Years (it's available on a CD single and on the movie's soundtrack album), is a good video—there are some powerful lingering images, of Taree and Speech singing and rapping and of the group members responding "No!" (like grade-school students to the question "Am I doing as much as I can for the struggle?"), of Baba Oje jumping into the crowd and righteously taking a bottle of beer out of the hands of the kid drinking it, and in general a good sense of rhythmic interplay between the images of people marching and the beat(s) of the music. But song is better than video (in the context of Eyes as a whole, the "Revolution" video works nicely, giving us more images of the group working together and some fine close-ups of their faces shot in a different—and thus contrapuntal—camera style). "Mr. Wendal," directed by Keith Ward who does such a terrific job with the semidocumentary material that makes up the bulk of Eyes, is more of a typical MTV video; not in the sense of cheap sex and violence, of course, but in its lack of content. The effect, as with most videos, is to narrow the listener's experience of the song . . . an effect, unfortunately, that lingers long after one sees the video. We listen to the record and tend to focus our minds on the memory of Speech's interesting hairdo and the bright orange-and-red mood of the video rather than opening ourselves to new images conjured up by words and music. Incidentally, this non-awful but distinctly non-great video is probably less the fault of the director than it is a reflection of Speech and the group's lack of energy after an exhausting year of touring. Which is a backhanded way of saying that the brilliance of the first two videos, and of this long-form tape, is a reflection of the group's unusual creative energy and vision, which extends itself very effectively into the visual medium most of the time.

Get the *Eyes* videocassette to feel the full impact of Taree's outrageous presence, to see Eshe dancing, to experience Headliner's shyness and sweetness (his comments about what he's learned from his father are particularly moving); get it for the delightful clips of the group onstage (their music, cut up in fragments like this, works so well as part of an aural and visual montage) and fooling around backstage before the shows; for Rasa Don and Dionne discussing what happens when they close their eyes and perform; for the great recurring shots of photos pinned to a clothesline; for the rhythm of the editing (sound editing is as important in film as picture editing, and the good filmmakers understand the musical interplay between sound and image); for the scene where Headliner talks about a twenty-two-year-old basketball buddy shot dead robbing another black man's house, and Taree talks about her uncle-in-law who's a crackhead; for the shots of the camera running through a field; and most of all to fall in love with (the 1992 video image of) Speech.

Speech in the video bio, telling the story of why he wrote "Tennessee" and what it means (his grandmother died, his whole family went to Tennessee for the funeral and he experienced their coming together as an intensely spiritual event—and then his only brother died a week later), is an attractive and intriguing presence (his hats, his posture) . . . but it is the friendship we are allowed to form with Speech in the later (summer/fall '92) interview segments that makes such an indelible impact. The setting is wonderful: rural/industrial, we see Speech running at us from within a large open shed (as though he lived in there), a visually unresolved structure surrounded by industrial tanks of vague content and purpose, colorful and dingy at the same time, much of the time Speech talks to us leaning against the huge tire of a blue truck (we never see the whole vehicle). The person we meet is open, easy to identify with, and absolutely compelling and charming. At one point he beats out a rhythm on his portable synthesizer/sampler (with his hands . . . the machine is turned off), and raps a new song (actually a very personal prayer; his sharing it is like a conscious act of fellowship) called "Allow Me to Introduce Myself." ("My Lord, my Lord, show Your path to me . . . / Wondering what city we go to next / Thinking how my life got to be so complex . . . / Now I'm living out of a suitcase / My nerves are so shot I break down over a shoelace . . . / I swayed away a bit but here I am again.") It's a riveting performance (partially filmed, partially superimposed on images of Speech sitting there but not singing), a magical moment. This is followed by him talking about how stressful it was to play Milwaukee, because of all the people he felt a responsibility to give some time to—except during "the celebration," which was a peak experience because he had the opportunity to share with all these old friends and acquaintances, through his songs, his "deepest innermost feelings" that he'd never express otherwise.

Segue from video back to album. "Blues Happy," a forty-six-second interlude (it is *so* difficult to make an interlude that works not just at first but every time you listen to an album), serves to introduce the band and help us shift gears between "People Everyday" and "Mr. Wendal." Speech charms us with his self-effacing self-confidence ("I'm the leader," he laughs. "My nose is stuffed up, though. Check it out.") and makes us feel like we're in the front row of a live performance; the sound of noodling blues guitar under the rap is strangely pleasing, a humorous tip of the hat to all sorts of musical memories, and it builds at the end into the perfect dramatic lead-in to kick off "Mr. Wendal" (BIG sampled beat, Speech's crazy laugh/ invocation) in the grand style it needs and deserves.

Every track on this album sounds different, and none of 'em sounds anything like "Mr. Wendal," but nonetheless this is the pure essence of Arrested Development, the heart of the critter, big beat, charming melodies, irresistible rhythms, great subject matter with words and performance to match, African chants and wails, a big fat hook in the form of a thirty-five-second pseudo-xylophone workout after the lyrics are out of the way, voices and sounds of family all around even as we are completely alone with the narrator as he puzzles out the meaning of it all in the privacy of his own mind and feelings. And a groove. Makes you smile. No, makes you grin, crazy grin, makes you get up and frolic. Makes you reconsider. " 'Be strong, serve God only; know that if you do beautiful heaven awaits' / That's the poem I wrote for the first time I saw a man with no clothes, no money, no plate." "Civilization, are we really civilized? / Yes or no, who are we to judge?" In my many writings about Bob Dylan's poetry, I've always contended that we don't hear the words without the performance, that this sort of poem is written on our minds with voice not pen and so we confuse ourselves if we try to judge it as page poetry. So again: This is superlative contemporary poetry, not the words on page but the words performed and heard by our ears. "Uncivilized we call him but I just saw him / Eat off the food we waste / Civilization, are we really civilized?" A contemplation. Not to be understood too quickly. Delightful and demanding. Listen again. That's what a single is good for: listening again. With ever new rewards. So much music happening on this song, so many different melodic/rhythmic/sonic elements in different places moving together with such dignity and playfulness and strength. "A human in flesh, but not by law." This is a demand, and as we listen it becomes (I hope it becomes) our demand, too. Happy childish sound, inviting, lovable, and why not? It's a song about freedom. And not a simple one. If I were doing the *100 Best Singles* book now, this would make the list for sure.

"Children Play with Earth"—one of the most interesting turntable effects on the album weeps through the tribal polyrhythms of this polemic addressed to the younger generation: "The way kids are living is one hundred percent European / African boys and girls, set down your Nintendo joysticks right now / Unplug the television, and make way for an older vision / Dig your hands in the dirt . . ." Speech is a back-to-the-Earther of a certain sort (and I agree with him that the key to education is unplugging from the hive and making contact with a more immediate and more powerful teacher), and in the next song, "Raining Revolution," he slides easily from the natural to the supernatural (and then makes his own patented sidestep from the supernatural to the political). I like the way Headliner says "rain." I like the interesting drone that gives the song its late-afternoon Southern thunderstorm atmosphere. I like, again, Speech's polemic (we got a street preacher here, a sincere one): "Every drop that hits me / Fills me with an unmeasurable amount of security / Knowing my God acknowledges me / As if each drop of rain is aimed toward me / My Lord thanks for life." I like the movement from this thought to the walk through the ghetto, seeing the eyes of the afflicted and feeling called to action. "I feel the rain enhances the revolution." I like the different voices in the song, their rhythms and textures. I like its sense of dramatic development: "Now the ceremony begins / Lord, let the heavenly rain cleanse." There is hope here, and a threat, and a sense of resolve.

Perhaps the most unlikely rap on the album is "Fishing 4 Religion," absolute proof of the authenticity of AD's Southern vision, as it calls on the black Baptist church to shake off its complacency and resume its historical role of leadership in fighting for the human rights and needs of its parishioners. Speech is wonderfully direct and wonderfully sly both at once: "The reason I'm fishing for a new religion / Is my church makes me fall to sleep / Praising a God that watches you weep / And doesn't want you to do a damn thing about it." His portrait of the lady who "prays and prays and prays and prays" just to "cope" ("The word 'cope' and the word 'change' / Is directly opposite, not the same") is masterful. And he probably realizes that when he raps, "Baptist teaches dying is the only solution" it sounds a lot like "Baptist teachers dying . . ." I like the percussive sounds on this track. Musique concrete. And the voices! Dionne's incredible open-throated gospel testifying near the end of the track . . . I don't know where you could go in music today to find a more radically experimental composition and performance. Or a more serious-minded, or funny, or successful one. Score a point for Southern-fried funk.

The next four tracks are very good and well worth inclusion on the album, but none of them hit quite as hard or as true as "Give a Man a Fish" or "Mr. Wendal" or "Fishing 4 Religion," and I think it's not a coincidence that they're all songs about relationships (except "Eve of Reality," a well-intended but forgettable interlude of sampled sounds from nature), whereas AD's most successful songs are about social and spiritual issues. When Speech shares with us his thoughts and feelings about social and spiritual realities, he is speaking as someone with a very active inner life in these areas, someone involved in a sincere, passionate, engaged struggle for understanding and right action. When he shares with us his ideas about love relationships and marriage, what we get are songs that are mostly mental in a realm that for most of us is primarily emotional. It's not a putdown to say these songs are naive—naiveté is a strength throughout this album, and in almost all of AD's work—but they do suffer from being two-dimensional. There are no real women here. The best moment for me is the haunting passage in "Natural" where a repetitive bed of sound is created, and the singer momentarily writhes in desire atop it, not in Prince fashion but vulnerable and authentic. "I wanna be inside you / I wanna be sleeping deep in you." Note that the feeling expressed is not entirely sexual. If this is intentional (and the music here suits the theme of womb-longing very well), it's quite brave. If accidental, it's still very moving.

Speaking of Prince, "U" seems to me a deliberate tribute to or send-up of the purple beatmaster. As such, it is charming and fun (I like the fast rapping and the dance beat, but the best part is the off-the-wall intro), but it is also I think a demonstration of why Prince's music is a bridge to hip-hop but is not hip-hop itself: it's rooted in a rock/soul beat, and for all its rhythmic inventiveness and indeed genius (I'm talking about Prince now, not "U"), it doesn't have hip-hop's freedom of structure, its sense of being built on a flowing and reworkable foundation. I'm not saying this makes hip-hop "better"— just different. Anyway, "U" is no masterpiece but it is a remarkable sharing of a young man's daily process regarding desire/love/sex/marriage, incorporating pressure from family and peers as well as those old inner feelings (there's a moving reference in here to his brother's death, in relation to his parents wanting a grandchild; but this is easier to connect with reading the lyrics than listening to them). I can imagine a reworked live performance of this song someday that would be magnificent.

"Dawn of the Dreads" is rhythmically the most interesting of these "love" songs. Makes me smile. It's a narrative, written like a movie based around a triple play on words: dawn as a time/event; dawn as the beginning of a new era; Dawn as the name of the girl the narrator meets or hopes to meet. The title is like the title of a zombie flick. "Dread" for Speech is a name for members of his "outcast tribe" (as he explains in the song, "The dreads symbolize the natural growth / Of not just the hair but also of the mind"). Song begins with the sun setting and ends at dawn, and in between there's a rejection and an acceptance, courtship as metaphor for the narrator's relationship with society. All very charmingly executed, with great breaks in the beat and vocal moments that stick in the mind: "Things beyond my reach don't exist for Speech." "Rejection is a fear of mine . . ." "Put both feet up in the air and swing 'em back and forth to the music!" Just monkeying around. The beat is silly but it grows on you. I like it.

Finally, two more knockout punches—"Tennessee" and "Washed Away"—two more examples of the originality and power that make Arrested Development the best new band of 1992, rap or otherwise. "Tennessee" is obviously a very unusual hit song; but let's start with the fact that it's a prayer, and a very unusual prayer. Listen to that beat! Best beat I've heard on a prayer (leave out all those love songs that might or might not also be addressed to a higher power) since U2's "Gloria." And equally sincere, with that special soulfulness that seems to have something to do with being young and courageous, full of fire and doubt and lack of doubt and energetic outspoken devotion. "Lord I ask you / To be my guiding force and truth / For some strange reason it had to be / He guided me to Tennessee."

And then these words, which have already made a difference in my life (and I know I'm not the only one): "Take me to another place / Take me to another land / Make me forget all that hurts me / Let me understand Your plan."

That beat. White people over the age of eighteen aren't supposed to be able to relate to a beat like this, but try this track out on them and somehow it's different, they make a connection right away. This is real education. I remember the first time I heard Wilson Pickett's "In the Midnight Hour." How to learn a new language in four minutes. You will never be the same.

Another candidate for the *100 Best.* I guess the single isn't dead after all. That's Dionne Farris ("extended family member") singing so beautifully at the end of the song. And of course Aerle Taree cracking, "Speech's hair? Don't it look like the roots of the tree my ancestors were hung from? / But that's okay, get it, 'cause it's down to earth." What a song. "Now I see the importance of history / Why my people be in the mess that they be / Many journeys to freedom made in vain / By brothers on the corner playing ghetto games."

Speech and Arrested Development have some new ideas (I'm not saying they invented all of them, but they sure are popularizing them) about melody and how to use it, about singing and the ways human voices can be used to communicate, and about what needs to be taught and how popular music can be used to teach it. "Washed Away" is a song about the struggle between God and the Devil, an image I tend to be very uncomfortable with, because of the way people use it as an excuse not to listen to their own hearts. But Speech is coming from a place I can relate to very well: recognizing the struggle, recognizing temptation and the perils of giving in to it, as the means and motivation for self-reliance. "We can stop being washed away." What a message.

Given the reality of the ghetto, given even mothers being lured away from their babies by the power of crack cocaine and the horror of life without some kind of illusion-maker, given the deaths of so many young men (and women) through violence and drugs and drug-related disease, given the ravages brought on by the temptation to make some quick money, to get a quick hit of feeling good, to look sharp or tough or successful in front of one's peers, the evidence everywhere of how a wounded or weakened human spirit

makes things worse for itself, or anyway, does when there are predators all around, allowed free reign (and many of these predators
are not of the community; some are mobsters, but even more work
for the government) . . . Given what Speech has seen and what he
tells of in his songs, I can hardly fault him for believing there's a
Devil. And when he talks about revolution, I guess what that means
to me is that he wants to go after the real devils, not the imaginary
ones the preacher loves to box with, when he's not telling us to
"cope."

"Washed Away" is a little sonic masterwork, a portrait in music
of the subject of Speech's parable: a sandy shore being washed away
by the persistence of the ocean. Arrested Development create the
sound of this image, accurately and lovingly, imaginatively and with
great beauty. How many bands or individuals out there are conducting
this sort of musical experimentation these days, with such great results? Oh, I asked that question already. But anyway. This is a beautiful montage, a remarkable musical creation.

As for the parable: listen to it. You may think you've heard it
already. You haven't. I'll quote a few words, but they say even more
in context: "Most of the people follow the serpent / Cuz the serpent
preaches all for self." "Why do we let them wash it away? / Why
won't we teach our children what is real? / Why don't we collect and
save what is real?"

First album. You can't stop music like this. It comes up out of
the ground; it rains from the sky. I thank God, and I thank the
musicians, too. "Going out is what it's all about"—and it certainly
has its rewards, but it has its risks, too, and it's very very hard work.

Anyway, my message to Speech is the same as what Mama Win-
bush said. (The reference is to the enigmatic liner notes on the videocassette package.) Stay thirsty, man. Stay thirsty.

So here's another very successful first album. *Ten*, by **Pearl Jam**, has
sold four million copies since it was released at the end of 1991, and
is still being discovered by enough stragglers like me to keep it near
the top of the charts.

I'm writing about it now because these essays are, among other
things, directed by curiosity. I'm curious about what people are listening to. I'm curious about what's going on out there. I'm curious
about what new music might really interest and inspire me if I opened

myself to it. And then if it does catch my attention or push my pleasure buttons in an aesthetically acceptable way, I'm curious about why I like what I'm hearing.

Do you like Pearl Jam? If so, do you know why you like them? Or perhaps do you dislike them without ever having heard them, suspicious of their very popularity? I sympathize. I tend to be automatically (and probably unfairly) suspicious of any band or artist that is currently very successful, even when it's a band I championed for years, like U2. *Achtung Baby* is a surprisingly good album for a band that's been through what U2 has (too much attention), and it contains a couple of songs that may turn out to be real keepers ("One," "Who's Gonna Ride Your Wild Horses?"). But I don't love the album as a whole; a lot of it is, um, subtly tiresome. U2 is one of those groups you want to be able to love, or forget it (admittedly, that's a lot to ask after all these years and all this embarrassing success). I love those two songs but I don't love the group that made this record. Why am I going on about U2? Because that is the question about this Pearl Jam debut album. I admit it's perfect, a gem, an instant classic hard-rock teenage-angst album. But do I love it? I don't think so. But I'm still not completely sure.

Youth is an advantage in rock and roll. That went without saying at one time. Nowadays there seems to be some confusion on the point. But seriously, I can think of one rock-and-roll band that's aged well: the Grateful Dead (as live performers, of course, not as recording artists). Who else is there? A few individuals: Bob Dylan, Neil Young, Van Morrison. Among the younger dinosaurs, R.E.M. is holding its own very well. But for the most part the great groups and individuals come on in a burst of glory, and either die young or dim their vision. Lou Reed is a serious artist with a respectable body of work, but I'm sorry, his place in the pantheon of rock-and-roll immortals is almost entirely due to his work with the Velvet Underground. His kid stuff. Same for John Lennon and (more obviously) Paul McCartney. Mick Jagger has done very little of consequence since 1972. John Lydon you can take or leave, but you can't take or leave the Sex Pistols. Most really powerful rock-and-roll music has been made by the new kids on the block. Most of the The Who's best work was pre-*Tommy*. Or maybe I'm wrong. Maybe I'm just a reactionary still clinging to the idea of rock and roll as quintessentially teenage music, listened to and created by natural revolutionaries. Maybe. But I don't think so. So I check out Pearl Jam because if rock and roll is still alive, stuff like this and Primus and Fugazi and Pavement is probably where it lives. Probably. Not necessarily. I told you this is about questions, not answers.

A terrific hard-rock album. It has the *sound*. You'd think this would be easy to accomplish, but it absolutely isn't. These guys are a group, a band. I mean what's the big deal? Electric bass, drums, rhythm guitar, lead guitar, vocalist—generic rock-and-roll ensemble, precisely the makeup of the Rolling Stones and almost every punk and heavy-metal group. This many years down the road, surely there are smart producers who can tell a group of reasonably accomplished young rock musicians exactly what to play when in order to make a sound that will maximally stimulate teen hormones (male and/or female, mainstream, alternative, or heavy metal, select your demographics) and light up cash registers. Maybe. But the stuff those producers and their groups turn out is garbage, even if it does occasionally sell like hotcakes. Pearl Jam is something else. If anyone could do what they do, everyone would. Instead, records like this come along very very seldom, and then (look at Led Zeppelin) get listened to over and over forever.

It's the sound. Eddie Vedder has a very special voice, but what makes it so appealing is the sound that his voice and Mike Mc-Cready's lead guitar, Jeff Ament's bass-playing, Stone Gossard's rhythm guitar, and Dave Krusen's drums make together. Rick Parashar's production (and occasional keyboards) deserves some credit for how magically the sound comes across on record, but I suspect that this sound was created not in the studio but live and in the rehearsal room, and that to a certain extent it was not created but discovered, a happy accident, even—that *this* voice and this unusual and dominant bass-playing style and this very classic (very difficult to achieve) rock-and-roll electric guitar sound are, like, pitched to each other in some way, they vibrate together, they become something. And then on top of that there's a lot of skill and soul involved in the way Vedder has learned to sing into what his buddies are doing, and the ways they've developed of leaning up against each other sonically, building a wall of sound full of subtlety and detail but never losing its raw forcefulness. Take that! This is kick-out-the-jams music, the sound of rock and roll that grabbed me when I was a frustrated confused adolescent male, and I don't wonder that it is apparently inspiring the sort of loyalty and enthusiasm that I once felt for the Who, the Yardbirds, the Stones.

Is it as good? Well, that's a complicated question. For one thing, it's just one album, not a body of work. And critical opinions are utterly subjective, let's not forget that. Basically I'd say Pearl Jam have yet to demonstrate the greatness as songwriters that would put them in a class with the Who or the Stones in their glory days. On the other hand, *Ten*, in my opinion, is a better album than anything the Yardbirds did. And I loved the Yardbirds when I was seventeen. I was hungry for music like this. They were the hardest thing around, and they had those wonderful blues chops, the sound of that voice with those instruments. Most of their songs weren't that good, but I sure liked the feeling I got when I listened to them.

Ten is a great album with no great songs on it—just eleven very very good songs that work together brilliantly, sustaining a mood and sound and intensity extremely effectively for fifty-three minutes (and you can put it right back on and listen to it again when those fifty-three minutes are over). (I like the clever circularity, the way the album opens with a hypnotic riff that is abruptly interrupted by the first song, that ultimately returns and resumes what it was doing, halfway through the final track. Idea okay. Execution magnificent.)

There isn't a payoff song, nothing to deliver on the extraordinary promise made by "Once" and "Even Flow," the opening tracks (and my favorite tracks on the album, not for what they say but for how the music, including the vocal music, feels). But maybe a payoff song (though I'd love to hear it) would be a distraction on an album that flows into itself so successfully, that is so remarkably consistent in its overall sound without ever getting boring (unless, of course, this wasn't what you felt like listening to today in the first place). These guys don't have a big message. Instead they have the classic message, maybe the only one that matters: WE EXIST! This is what it feels like. This is the sound of what it feels like. And yes the words convey it, too, not in full story-songs but in graffiti that jump out at you here and there: "Once, I could control myself. Someday he'll begin his life again. I'm still alive. Why go home? All the pictures have been washed in black. Clearly I remember picking on the boy. Hold on to the thread. There ain't gonna be any middle anymore. I will walk with my hands bound. Can't touch the bottom. I'll open up—release me." This is what it feels like. We listen, and we know they know.

Mind you, I'm forty-five, and I'm not so sure they know. But I love the way they sound when they make music together.

There's a crescendo thing they do that's really striking. It occurs at the end of "Jeremy" (the background "woop-woop-woop-woop" vocals, wonderful pulsing feeling, the way all the sounds rise in intensity together); the last two minutes of "Black," with the repeating keyboard-and-voices figures, is another favorite moment for me. Another sort of crescendo is the delightful two-minute guitar rave-up that caps off "Alive." You gotta like this stuff.

A weakness of the album is that they (actually, Eddie Vedder, who apparently wrote all the lyrics) don't have their Disjointed Narrative Technique as well developed as it might be. Songs tend to get dumb if you can figure out what they mean, and pure nonsense or double-talk is equally irritating most of the time. So (see R.E.M. discussion last chapter) a songwriter uses misdirection of various sorts to tell a story that you can't quite follow but you can't quite let go of, either, out of which strong images and feelings emerge. Pearl Jam's lyrics do evoke strong feelings and images, mostly of males (men and boys) tormented about various kinds of loss that they (the characters in the songs) obviously think about too much for their own good (except for the guy in "Even Flow," who chases the thoughts away before they get too close). And the words are very good as riddles that pull you in to listen more closely. My complaint is that, once pulled in, I'm not adequately rewarded for my effort. " 'You're still alive,' she said. 'Do I deserve to be?' " is an inspired bit of dialogue, but I am more frustrated than charmed by the fact that I can't get a handle on what it was the woman did that left him unable to see. (And I'm worried that if I did know the answer, it would be too linear for me, like the answer to "Jeremy" which I guessed and my daughter confirmed by describing the video. Too specific a situation. I want my mind opened to possibilities, not closed down into the contentless images of television news.)

Narrative lyrics I like a lot: "She scratches a letter into a wall made of stone / Maybe someday another child won't feel as alone / As she does, it's been two years and counting since they put her in this place . . . Why go home?" A teenager of my acquaintance hadn't seen the lyric sheet and spent days worrying about whether they're screaming "Why go home?" or "Why go on?" Makes a big difference. I'm glad it's a song about bitter anger rather than despair.

Strengths of the album: eleven songs, eleven attractive rewarding melodies. Every song with a memorable hook, not trivial but usually at the core of the feelings being expressed in the performance, often but not always connected to the title of the song. Song titles themselves very conscious and clever, one short word or maybe two. Pithy. Evocative. Consistent. Satisfying. And the album title (what's it mean?) the shortest word of all. Some sweet implicit mysterious order there.

These guys are a group, a band. Rock and roll is bored by great vocalists, but it loves great vocalists who are truly submerged in a group, part of a collective identity and sound. Jim Morrison, for example, is not the story. The story is, always was, the Doors. The group, the sound, the gestalt. Listen to the straightforward intelligence in Pearl Jam's music, throughout this album. Each instrument is speaking, making an original and often very smart contribution to the total sound. The rhythm guitar inventions in "Garden" (and throughout the record). The subtle interplay on so many of the tracks between bass and rhythm guitars. The tapestry of sound made by the bass and guitars and drums on "Release," four moods blending into one mood that then both counterpoints and merges with the mood of the vocal. And oh the singer does so much with the sound of his voice, plays it like a cello or a tambourine (well mostly, appropriately, he plays it like a voice); and hooray finally for the lyrics that give him the freedom and foundation to do this, and of course for the music that animates the words and the singing. Music written by Gossard or Gossard and Ament most of the time, couple of songs by Ament alone, one by Vedder alone. Vedder is given credit for all of the lyrics, which makes you wonder which came first, music or lyrics? They seem so well married to each other. Group mind at work. May or may not happen on the next album. But for this moment, writing/performing/recording *Ten*, these guys functioned as a collective creative entity, a beast (ten hands; ten ears) with a strong, distinct sense of its own identity and purpose.

The gestalt of the rock group has always fascinated me. If you meet and talk to the artists you'll learn nothing, as a general rule—to get any insight into the mystery, you have to watch them work together, and the best place is on a stage. The next best place is watching with your ears as they interact fiercely and complexly and with affection and spontaneity and fiery inspiration, performing a record. You can feel the group personality, you know and identify with and are befriended by this entity. Not Jim's band, or Eddie's, or Paul's or John's. The entity. Band name. Individual personalities felt as part of a collective presence.

Pearl Jam is, for this moment anyway, an identifiable entity, a personality, a sound. It's like a new friend who is deeply attractive in an unusual way, and really seems to understand you, and has an attitude you can't help but connect with. This, I believe, is a significant part of rock and roll's (music's?) purpose: to provide friendship and human contact particularly at those moments in our lives when we most need it and are most cut off from it.

It is a music for the alienated, and we rightly feel that there's a contradiction in having it be so damn successful. But the alienated are common as flies in this country, especially in a certain age range. Pearl Jam, I would say, serves up a very mainstream sort of alienation—and that's not bad. If you've ever liked the Beatles, then you understand that there is something very appealing about the universality of rock and roll. We are everywhere. It is possible, at giddy moments, to feel this way. It's even possible that it's true.

We are everywhere. But am I on this record? Some days, yes, I identify with it and draw joy and energy from it, and release rage and frustration through it. It stimulates and soothes me. And yet I hold myself back. I'm ready to admit, I think, that kids today could have a hard-rock album that speaks for them and for whoever wants to embrace it just as loudly and just as fulfillingly as the Who singles and Stones albums I loved when I was the kid. I'm willing and indeed eager to give up the myth that the past is always somehow better than the present. But I also have to report that, talking from my present moment which is always the only place I can talk from, this Pearl Jam album doesn't speak to my heart the way *3 Years, 5 Months* does, or the way *Automatic for the People* does, or *Ragged Glory* or the Waterboys' *Fisherman's Blues*, to name a few of my favorites from recent years. The fact that I feel a need to make this distinction should indicate just how much respect I have for what Messrs. McCready, Vedder, Gossard, Krusen and Ament have accomplished. You can even tell, perhaps, that I feel a little regret at not having been seventeen years old when this album came along—damn, that must be a good feeling.

Check it out. Straight-down-the-middle, joyous, intelligent, richly musical rock and roll lives. It breathes. It has nothing to apologize for. You may or may not fall in love with this album. It has its limits. It is perhaps for those moments when we want spaces inside ourselves filled, not for moments when we want those spaces opened up. Different strokes for different folks, or for the same folks at different moments. Whatever. But on the other hand if you're one of those people who thinks they just don't make the stuff like they used to, this is your chance to find out whether "they" have changed, or you have.

Ten is the sort of record young people discover rock and roll—

and, to a certain extent, themselves—through. "I will walk with my shadow flag into your garden, garden of stone." Yes. This is the sound that first awakened me, and it's lost none of its power a generation later. I'm glad I know where to find it when I need it.

Pearl Jam is rock and roll. Arrested Development is not. Neither is *The Juliet Letters* by **Elvis Costello and the Brodsky Quartet**. Subtitled *A Song Sequence for String Quartet and Voice*, it is exactly that, and may be properly identified as classical music, I think, although it is a sort of classical music that is exceedingly rare. Turns out, composers almost never write for voice and strings alone. Well, they should. Elvis and the Brodskys have demonstrated this quite convincingly, which is a remarkable accomplishment.

And they've made a very likable record—more likable the fewer expectations you bring to it; which is to say, Elvis Costello fans and string-quartet fanciers are most likely to have difficulty warming to this one. My wife and my daughter, neither of whom is familiar with Costello or string quartets, are both really fond of it.

For myself, I admit to mixed feelings. I do very much like what *The Juliet Letters* tries to do, musically—and I believe it succeeds quite well at what it attempts. And yet ... well, I guess my problem is I think most people are only going to listen to a few new albums at any given moment in their lives, and so in my writing I feel a need to make a distinction between records I believe you could love deeply, versus records that are rewarding to spend some time with, but are ultimately (in my experience; these are subjective reports) limited in how much they have to offer.

In an odd way, *The Juliet Letters* is like Pearl Jam—what is most appealing to me is the sound, and specifically the sonic relationship between the singer's voice and the other instruments. Very different sort of sound on the two albums, but quite pure and thrillingly realized in both cases. If there's a difference, it's that I think Pearl Jam have found what their sound is good for, and Elvis and the Brodskys haven't quite, not yet. But they have certainly opened the door to a brave new world.

In the BBC-TV documentary released as a videocassette in the States (same title as the album), Costello and his collaborators are at pains to explain that this isn't a vocalist backed by a string quartet but rather a quintet in which one of the instruments is a human voice. Along the same lines, Costello was not content to write songs and have the quartet help arrange them; instead he seems to have conducted a songwriting workshop, setting a theme and having the five work together to create songs that might fit in the cycle. Costello (under his real name, Declan MacManus) shows up somewhere in the writing credits of eighteen of the twenty tracks on the album (and the ones he's not on are instrumental passages), but twelve of these eighteen are collaborations—with the Brodskys working on the words as much as the music—and according to the liner notes, Costello was often not the originator of a song's primary musical or lyrical conceit.

The general idea is simple, and smart: Write an album in which all the songs are letters. There's a suggestion of a more specific context, having to do with the discovery that people over the centuries have been writing to "Juliet Capulet" in Verona, Italy, as though she were a confessor–advice columnist rather than a deceased fictional character—this is charming, but since few of the letters on the album are actually addressed to Juliet, the concept serves mainly to provide a title and something to chat about with interviewers. In the liner notes to the album, Costello suggests that one purpose of the song cycle is to capture the ways people speak in letters. Musically, I think this is achieved at times, and with quite a bit of wit and inventiveness. Lyrically, however, the songs tend towards the superficial: well-written and clever, but repetitive in tone and frustrating in their inability to move past the conscious realm into the world of the unconscious where most of the significant interactions of music and words, and of listeners and performers, take place.

The value of the musical inventions—all of which derive from the fact that these are songs, with words and other elements of musical structure peculiar to songs—should not be underrated. I am not suggesting that this unusual musical collaboration was a failure. Quite the contrary—the album represents a surprisingly successful coming together of two seemingly very different musical languages, in a union that is no hodgepodge or exploitation but a modest and brilliant step towards new languaging, new possibilities for both musicians and listeners. There have, of course, been light operas or operettas or, as we call them in the States, "musicals," for several centuries, and these *Juliet Letters* songs are not unrelated to the sort of songs and the style of composition—pop mixed with classical—found in *The Marriage of Figaro* or *The Pirates of Penzance* or *Guys and Dolls*. But the specific characteristics of the string quartet and of Costello's unusual vocal approach and talents, and the ways the two are joined herein, make this album more than a rediscovery of a familiar form. It is, I suggest again, a door into new possibilities, and I think it will turn out in time to have been an influential, maybe groundbreaking, work.

Listen, for example, to "Damnation's Cellar." Melody and lyrics, though both fun, are familiar Costello fare; but the sounds made by the instruments, and especially the rhythmic and harmonic interplay between voice and instruments, are full of unexpected pleasures. I want to hear this expanded on somehow. This is followed (last track on the album) by the sensuously textured vocal-instrumental inter-action on "The Birds Will Still Be Singing," overdone in places per-haps, but the first verse and the final chorus are exquisite. Am I ridiculous to praise this album so extravagantly and then be so stingy in picking out the bits that please me? But the bits are everywhere: the rhythmic backdrop in "Jacksons, Monk and Rowe" (and the lilt-ing melody it plays against, and the way Elvis sings words like "com-plicate"), the outrageous lyrical and musical humor of "This Offer Is Unrepeatable" (a Gilbert and Sullivan send-up, among other things; the vocal performance is alternately teeth-grating or side-splitting, depending on the mood you're in when you hear it), the attractively dramatic instrumental passage that opens the album and the way the voice arrives, and the sound of Elvis's voice and the rich layers of melody and rhythm and silence—musical space—on that opening song ("For Other Eyes"). And lots more. And things that bore or irritate me one time through that just pull me in (the tune and the singing on the chorus of "This Sad Burlesque") on other listenings. There's so much here. I wouldn't want to have missed this music, nor am I ready to put it away and stop playing it.

Yet at the same time I can't tell you I like it.

I'm picky, that's what it is. This is a daring, ambitious project, brought off with love and imagination and hard work and a sincere commitment to pushing the envelope of what modern music (and for that matter creative collaboration) can be. But I want more than that. Great language *and* a great story and something to say, besides; beautiful cinematography *and* a script and acting worth driving down-town for. In a musical performance I want, in addition to everything I'm getting here, some kind of message from heart to heart, soul to soul, that touches me intimately and at least momentarily expands my awareness of what is real. I want connection. Music-and-words is a form uniquely suited to this kind of passionate communication (and "Elvis Costello" a brand name that has brought me great satisfaction in the past, not consistently maybe, but quite spectacularly when the wind was right).

These people—Costello specifically, but I don't mind directing my complaint to the quintet as a whole—are hiding. Song cycles don't have to be abstract, but this one is: a meditation on letter writers, oddballs of all shapes and sizes. So what? I'd rather get to know these people. These are vignettes instead of stories, and they don't have to be. The problem is not the form but the intent.

This was brought home to me when I realized that the song and performance on the album that touches me most deeply is so carefully hidden I have to work at listening to it. It's the fourth track, "Expert Rites" (dumb title), and after the one-verse vocal it segues into an instrumental called "Dead Letter." But in order to hear it, I find I need to punch the "backwards skip" button as soon as the vocal ends, replacing the instrumental with a repeat of the vocal passage. As I do this, the singing and the violin and even the words (it helps but I think isn't entirely necessary to read Costello's explanation of the song, as well as the printed lyrics) get a chance to sink in, and they sink deeper for me than anything else on the album. It's shocking, in fact—here is a human being talking compassionately and earnestly to another human being, utterly in contrast to all these other people talking to themselves and the dead air, alone (and obsessed with themselves) in an uncaring universe. "I live with my regrets / Don't despair, my would-be Juliet." I love this brief track, and the person who sings it to me. I want more.

Bone Machine by **Tom Waits** is a magnificently inventive album. This must, after all, be a very healthy time in the history of Western music—look at what it's possible to get away with! The range of different sounds and musical ideas that are being experimented with is staggering, and what's more, people are listening. Tom Waits is certainly not for everyone, but I feel sure this album has sold at least one hundred thousand copies—probably a lot more, but my god, one hundred thousand is a lot of people. This is not academic experimentation here, where (especially in the arts) only a handful of people are listening, and most of them are thinking obsessively about the politics of the situation. This is public. This is instant promulgation of new language, ongoing revolution that has an impact. It's alive. It's scary. It's wonderful.

It's dirty. Waits and his co-writer/associate producer Kathleen

Brennan have clearly set out to create and convey a truly dirty sound and state of mind here, and I suspect they consciously chose to avoid the sexual as subject matter in order to get to that less obvious and more pervasive source of psychic dirt: death, fear of death, awareness of the cruelty of life, oneself, others, God, and the dissatisfaction and discomfort that arises from this awareness. This is not even primarily an angry record—one of its many breakthroughs; since anger can be close to a dead end for rap and heavy metal and rock and roll, what do you do when the fans are waiting for you to smash your guitar again tonight? Tom Waits has been described as having a gritty voice, and a gritty perspective on life. This can be romanticized easily enough, and the general direction of romanticizing is to wrap that which is dirty and desirable in a safe and pretty package. I think Waits has successfully resisted that sort of pressure here, and he's done it, clearly, through his loyalty to music. The sound he set out to create grabbed him and ran, showed him that it wanted to get a lot earthier than anything he'd imagined, and showed him how to do it. And he listened. "Follow me down . . ."

Great music is most often created by following, I believe; following something one hears in one's inner ear, a sound that can't be described but must be created, and all you know as you pursue is that you haven't quite got it yet, and you have to reach further.

I'm not ready to say this is a great record, but it's certainly a candidate for that stature. Ask me a year from now. Meanwhile, I can't even promise you it's a record you'll like. The first, most obvious obstacle is Waits's voice. I don't know why I'm so comfortable with voices like this (Leonard Cohen, Dylan—though my friend Cindy says Waits's voice makes Dylan sound like Michael Bolton), but anyway I won't make fun of you if you find the raspy gargly atonality of Waits's voice utterly unendurable. He's got a permanent frog in his throat, and sometimes it sounds like you could get warts just from listening to it. But—it's got something. The melodies and words and personalities of the songs reach through to me in spite of the voice and I want to listen more closely, hear them again, and then suddenly I realize that I can't imagine them sung in any other voice, song and voice are symbiotic with and indeed have invented each other, and then pretty soon I'm hearing all these expressive (and melodic!) subtleties in that gargle, it still sounds weird but perfect weird, beauty like the bark of an ancient tree or caked clay at the bottom of a dry lake. I stare at it hypnotized. I'm a goner. Sounds better, sounds different with every song. And I hear more each time. I love this voice!

I won't make fun of you for thinking I'm out of my mind, but hey. Come listen. I wish you could hear what I hear.

Next obstacles: the words and the noise. The words are like, heavy, man. Creepy, even. "The earth died screaming / While I lay dreaming." Some other era that might be funny, but in 1993 it definitely has an edge. "We're all gonna be just dirt in the ground." Cheerful. And then this song which would be so sweet, "A Little Rain" (never hurt no one), except that it seems to be about a teenage girl running away from home to see the ocean and getting murdered. ("The last thing she said was, 'I love you, Mom.'") Eek. Too close to real life. I don't want to think about this. And more songs about murder and decapitation and the seductions of evil and kids seeing the five o'clock news and not wanting to grow up. Hey, man, good art maybe, but not my idea of entertainment. And yet there's a tone here that's so different from anything I'd expect, not righteous, not exploitative, sincere and subtle and such wonderful choices of words. . . . Maybe I could just skip the songs that make my skin crawl (no, they're starting to pull me in, too).

And the noise. Tom Waits discovers percussion. Get outta the way or you're gonna get hit. This stuff is crude, demented, rising periodically to shrill cacophony. I'm not sure how my dinner guests are going to feel about this.

Track one: "Earth Died Screaming." Wonderful. Three voices: guttural for the verse, hoarse and frenetic and doubled over on itself for the chorus, and then a baritone's version of falsetto for the little tag line, "Dreaming of you." Unique, exquisite percussion sound from the outset, Waits, Brennan, and Joe Marquez on sticks, joined soon by Larry Taylor's inspired intuitive upright-bass playing (Taylor is on twelve of these sixteen tracks, and makes a tremendous contribution to the sound Waits achieves here), plus, for this track only, Les Claypool of Primus on electric bass. Big band. The sound of the room is important here, too, as it often is on our favorite records. The sticks set up this brilliant, simple, richly textured beat, and right away I hear the echoes or something; anyway, I feel the space. Great transition as the title line bursts in (temporarily separating the beat from its foundation, but it hobbles back quick enough). Amazing words, so full of their own rhythms, like a duet between voice and sticks: "And the moon fell from the sky / It rained mackerel / It rained trout." And weird music at the end which I adore, like from an old radio drama, only an artist who's really listening to what the music tells him can do something as outrageous and as eerily effective as this bit. Wooo.

Track two: "Dirt in the Ground." This is a truly beautiful song. There are three or four others on the album: "Who Are You," "Black Wings," "Whistle Down the Wind." I know you think I'm just Mr. Enthusiasm, but I have high standards for beauty. It has to have staying power. It has to make me feel special when I see it or hear it, it has to draw me in and touch me more deeply the more I open to it. It has to be truly itself. It has to surprise me (again and again). It has to earn and keep my respect.

"Dirt in the Ground" is a terrific melody married to irresistible words, with a vocal performance and an ensemble sound and a "feel" to die for. That about says it. The piano-playing! The buzz of the sax and/or clarinet or however they do that. The tones in Mr. Waits's voice (not so atonal after all, it reeducates you if you give it a chance). The way he sings each phrase in all of these verses and choruses, but especially the last one: "Along a river of flesh / Can these dry bones live? / Take a king or a beggar / And the answer they'll give / Is we're all gonna be . . ." The way everything my ears hear is tuned to the piano and the voice, not just pretty good, but glorious eccentric and perfect. The way I know for certain that the singer, insofar as he has put on a persona, has become that persona privately as well as publicly, and truly means every word he's singing to me. Preach it. Tell it like it is. That's beauty. You can't fake soul. I mean you can I guess, but it's a worthless activity. A performance like this gets under the skin. This is what a real spiritual sounds like. (You can tell your kids you heard one.)

"Such a Scream" is confrontive, funny, the subtle perfect sweet thread of percussion in "Dirt" transformed aggressively into hot noise, the outside of the Pompidou Centre rendered in sound, a maze of pipes and the hot hiss of escaping steam. (Jesse Dylan's photo in the insert is just right.) Wild words. Ralph Carney's brass another link to the totally different-sounding previous track, and then I am thrilled (when I can stand it at all) by the transition into "All Stripped Down," these noises are old friends (albeit from nightmares maybe) that I don't remember being introduced to before.

Hot, hot sound. And again, hear the preacher: "All the sinners know / What I'm talking about / I want you all stripped down." Can't get this across in lyrics alone, but put sound words melody and performance together and you've got something. Every song on this album communicates something, has something to communicate. Not that Tom Waits has a message for us, not at all. The song does. He is its humble but eager servant. Working with sounds, working with words, all this stuff is a quest for spirit.

"Who Are You" is a love song, of the "not one more kiss" variety. It intentionally reminds me of Dylan in '66 singing "Sad Eyed Lady" ("your sailor's mouth") and "She's Your Lover Now" and Springsteen in '73 singing "Sandy" and "For You." Hey, I'll pay good money to reencounter this vocal texture, this particular bittersweetness, anywhere, anytime. Words worthy of comparison to "She's Your Lover Now" also (and to Rumi)—now who can you say that about lately? Yes, it's a derivative song (I like the way he says "red house"!) just as much as "Dirt in the Ground," but you see that's part of the form. Dylan did the same thing on *The Basement Tapes*. Parody/pastiche can be the most direct ticket to true originality. Because what we're really doing is exorcising ghosts, musical ghosts, the ones that live in the backs of our minds and whisper to us like memories of how certain songs felt so long ago we're not even sure of their names. The beats, too, are from old, old memories; possibly from dreams. But (this is the thing about rhythm) collective dreams. Like, there are rhythms out there, and we hear them through dreams. And then in records like this one and *Kiko* by Los Lobos we discover that we aren't the only ones who've heard these sounds.

I don't actually want to untangle the web this *Bone Machine* album is weaving in my mind. I do need to say out loud how much I appreciate the salute to Ennio Morricone (spaghetti-western music man) in "Black Wings." Just the right sound for the song, and perfectly realized. What spooky words. I like this sort of thing, that dances just out of reach of identification—who is the person/creature he's speaking of? Never met the man. (But yeah, he's a little like any of the three stars of *For a Few Dollars More*.) Great lyrics again (note recurrent words and themes): "When the moon is a cold chiseled dagger / And it's sharp enough to draw blood from a stone / He rides through your dreams on a coach and horses / And the fenceposts in the moonlight look like bones."

The music of the song. The melody. The sound of every instrument, especially that simple percussion (shaker) in the background. The sound of the guitars. The timing. The vocal, again. Beautiful.

"Goin' Out West" and "Whistle Down the Wind" are a fabulous pairing, same story told so differently (different personalities, different kind of music) but so interrelated, and ultimately so compassionate in both cases. "Goin' Out West" makes me think Springsteen's the cynic, with his lack of irony in "Working on the Highway," and Waits the one who really loves his characters (not that it's a mutually exclusive category), the one who wears his heart on his sleeve. Good beat, huh? That jangly guitar. Joe Gore is another musician I never heard of who does brilliant things all over this record. God, I love the sound of the room those tom-toms are being struck in.

And "Whistle Down the Wind" (piano again, and my god, that voice) is the vulnerable ballad version, and hey, I surrender absolutely. "I can't stay here and I'm scared to leave." Tell the story. (Listen to the way the accordion comes in! This is my favorite kind of music. Every wrong note in place, every fumbling beat a revelation.)

I haven't told you half of it. And everyone will have different favorites. (Jonathan, for example, first mentions "I Don't Want to Grow Up," Tom and Kathleen's Disney tune, and the line from "The Feel" about "I cross my wooden leg / And I swear on my glass eye.") There aren't any tracks here I dislike, though for quite a while as I worked my way into the album I believed it was too long. Now I think that was just one manifestation of my resistance, a resistance that the record actively courts, while it seduces me brazenly at the same time.

Got to mention "In the Colosseum." Quintessential *Bone Machine* noise, I have hated it and loved it, and will do both again. And rightly, because it's a funny song about the genuine horror of, not the ancient Romans methinks, but our own Congress, our economic structure, our infotainment media, our participation. Funny beat. Ugly (excellent) words. Ugly vision. Honest, un-angry portrait. It is the way it is. Are we afraid to look at that?

I am. But I can't resist this album. It's scruffy. It comes at you from all directions. It's demanding. And it pays off big. It's a keeper.

And so. Here's what I notice. I still have a sense of wonder; I mean that an Arrested Development could come along and have *so much to say* to me, musically and politically/spiritually/socially, that Tom Waits's record could turn out to be as good as people say it is and that I could find myself crazy about it, even though I'm not familiar with his most acclaimed work—idiot again, there's too much out there and I haven't gotten around to it all. But I find it's not too late to start.

Sense of wonder: that I like the Pearl Jam album so much I'll probably buy the *Singles* soundtrack just to hear a few more songs of theirs. Like a kid! This pleases me. Curiosity begets curiosity. I feel awakened.

And I feel connected. There's other stuff I wanted to talk about, but my enthusiasm for Arrested Development has gotten in the way; I babbled too long and so I have to wrap this up now. But I'm not apologizing. Just these four albums is more than enough for me to feel connected to the moment I'm living in, 1993. I'm ready to sit down with anyone from age fourteen forward and probably find some common ground for talk, sharing, turning each other on (hey, I've found some stuff I like; I'm ready to believe there could be more out there), communion.

"Brothers and sisters. Turn off the television. Make way for an older vision. Which will now be a new vision. Yes."

In my lifetime, it sometimes seems we see most clearly with our ears. Music has a way of being honest with us. This is one good reason why we listen.

3

I BELIEVE YOU ANYWAY

Life is imperfect. And so endlessly filled with blessings! In Lewis Shiner's new novel *Glimpses*, an alcoholic stereo repairman whose marriage is falling apart discovers he has a mysterious ability to imagine famous unfinished recordings in such detail that he and others can hear them and reproduce them as bootleg albums. He starts with a Beatles track and goes on to "trick" Jim Morrison into completing the Doors' *Celebration of the Lizard*, and then tackles the most legendary unreleased rock album of all time, the Beach Boys' *Smile*, with mixed results (immaculate babe born, world rejoices, mother lost in childbirth).

Meanwhile in the summer of 1993, coincident with the publication of *Glimpses*, Brian Wilson's legendary *Smile* recordings have finally arrived at your local record store after twenty-six years, not with a bang but a whisper.

They're part of a new box set (hey, every time you turn around there's a new box set; who even notices anymore?) called **Good Vibrations: 30 Years of the Beach Boys**. Sixty is a lot of money, but my advice is, eat peanut butter for a month if you have to, the music will sustain you. Hog heaven, at least for this unrepentant Beach Boys lover: five compact discs, 141 tracks, more than six hours of music, and only two or three tracks in the whole shebang that don't make me grin at least a little bit. When I retired from *Crawdaddy!* the first time, end of 1968, and moved to a cabin in the woods in Mendocino, one of my dreams was that I'd systematically listen to the Beach Boys' entire catalogue, immerse myself in it for months, and come out with some kind of summing-up essay and a much deeper understanding of this beast called music and my heart relationship with it.

Never happened, and I'm not going to try to live out my childhood fantasies now. I think. But certainly one of the best aspects of the boxed-set craze is the opportunity it gives us listeners to reexplore, in depth, a body of work that we've mostly experienced in album-sized chunks up to now. (Imagine a Who box set featuring all the singles from the sixties, properly mastered so they sound like they're played on a 45-rpm phonograph, if that's possible on CD, with the best B-sides and alternate takes and live fragments, plus "A Quick One" and "Rael" and the other genuine high points. Death to *Tommy* revivals!) Putting aside the sonic advantages (and occasional limita-tions) of CDs, there's no denying the usefulness of being able to listen to so much music with so little effort. On the surface it may seem just a matter of convenience—but if, in twenty-five years, a passion-ate BBs fan like myself has never quite managed to surround himself with their music as thoroughly as he's always wanted to, until this box arrived, then I think we must acknowledge that form sometimes is almost as important as content in terms of what we actually do get around to experiencing.

(Turned my CDs into cassettes and listened to the entire six hours and twenty minutes in one sitting, driving the California in-terstate from San Francisco to San Diego. Wow. A hundred or so years from now, when there are no cars or freeways anymore, people will be spending their life savings for the opportunity to have such an experience.)

Life is imperfect, but something in us longs for perfection. *Pet Sounds* and "Good Vibrations" (album and single created by Brian Wilson in 1966 at the height of his powers; vocals by the Beach Boys) are as close to musical perfection as can be found in modern rock and roll or whatever you wanna call it, but Brian, like Icarus, saw a higher place to fly towards. Stunned by the beauty of the aforementioned discs, I found my way to Brian's mansion at Christmastime 1966, smoked grass with him inside the Arabian tent in his living room, listened to acetates of unbelievable, heavenly music from the *Smile* album in progress, attended a recording session, traded jokes and in-sights in the heated outdoor pool at four A.M., the lights of L.A. twinkling far beneath us, and eventually made my way back to New York to spread the word, like other journalists before and after me. Present at the creation of the myth.

The *Smile* album David Leaf, Mark Linett, and Andy Paley have compiled for this box set (building on the efforts of Carl Wilson and others before them) is not perfect, of course; not the mythical beast he and we fantasized and promised. But—and it shocks me to be saying this, after all these years and all this hype—neither is it a disappointment. It's a tour de force, a thrilling, charming, revolutionary piece of work, obviously unfinished but still worthy to nestle beside *Pet Sounds* and the rest of the best of what contemporary musicians have accomplished. We weren't crazy after all. Listen to this. Listen.

The way to listen to the new "Child of *Smile*" album, I suggest, is to put disc two of *Good Vibrations* on the CD player and start with track eighteen. Let it play to the end of the disc. Twelve tracks, thirty-two minutes of music. (About the length of a typical Beach Boys album from that era or any other, although *Smile* like *Pet Sounds* was conceived of as a more extended work.) Don't include "Good Vibrations," or the 45-rpm version of "Heroes and Villains" that opens disc three. Don't think about what did or didn't get included, or any other might-have-beens. Listen, over and over, like you listen to any record that lands in your hands: as a fait accompli. This is the album that is. Do you hear anything in it?

I hear a lot. Let me back up for a moment and say that this thirty-two-minute *Smile* album, as exquisitely pleasurable and historically significant as it is, does not overshadow the rest of this box. It's not a 600-pound canary. It fits in. This is a box full of astonishing, earthy, complex and simpleminded and gorgeously beautiful music. I don't always reach for disc two. I don't find myself dodging disc four, the one with the later, seventies and eighties, material. I enjoy the whole package (how many box sets can you say that about?). Disc five, the "bonus" disc containing recordings of recording sessions and miscellaneous live performances and songs split so you can hear vocals without instruments or instrumental tracks without vocals, is the one I don't reach for quite as often—it contains some incredible treasures, but lacks the sweet flow of the other CDs. For particular occasions.

The box rises very successfully to an unusually difficult challenge: It has to satisfy two quite different constituencies of Beach Boys fans, who can be described roughly as those who might go see the band play live if they came through town, and those who bought copies of Brian Wilson's 1988 solo album. Messrs. Leaf, Linett, and Paley have succeeded at this daunting task by arranging the songs on the four CDs in chronological order, packaging the fifth CD semiseparately as a "bonus bootleg disc," including all the BBs' Top 40 hits up through 1988's surprise non-Brian hit "Kokomo," and at the same time including much of the long-awaited *Smile* material and a tremendous number of other unreleased recordings from throughout the Beach Boys' career. The rewards of the box set are substantial; in other words, whether one is inclined to view the Beach Boys as pure pop (nostalgic or newly discovered—one testament to the quality of this music is how enthusiastically it is embraced by each new generation of subteens that encounters it, almost regardless of cultural context) or as vital and remarkable semi–high art.

Lotsa good stuff. Disc 1 opens with a track that should delight both constituencies, even though its purely musical value is questionable: It's Brian Wilson's piano demo of "Surfin' USA," sung with tremendous heart and spirit in a flat, breaking, painfully raw voice. Brian was twenty, and he had not yet sung lead on a Beach Boys single. "Surfin' " (November 1961), "Surfin' Safari" (August 1962; their first Top 20 record), "409," and "Ten Little Indians" were all Mike Love vocal leads; as was the released version of "Surfin' U.S.A." (March 1963; the peculiar *"30 Years"* in the box-set title apparently refers to this single, because "it was their first Top 10 hit"). Brian was shy. His idea of how to write a song in those days was: write an anthem about surfing (a nod to brother Dennis who first suggested the idea and perhaps made all this possible). He did it on the first two singles, the third flopped, now he'd thought of a way to do it again by writing new lyrics to Chuck Berry's "Sweet Little Sixteen" and his excitement is evident and infectious. (He would soon do it yet again on "Surf City," a song he wrote and gave to Jan and Dean, who made it a number one hit.)

So where is Brian on this song? We hear Mike's voice on the final version, and Carl's charming Chuck Berry guitar riffs; we hear Berry's melody and arrangement, with words ostensibly written by Brian (most of them, he acknowledges, were a kind of found art, in that he asked his girlfriend's brother to write down the names of all the good surfing spots he could think of). Brian is there in some of the flourishes ("inside outside U.S.A."), but the demo calls attention to a deeper truth: he's there everywhere in the song, not because he produced it but because *he thought of it*, it's his vision, he pulled all the parts together out of his inspiration and enthusiasm and will. Musically, this is expressed on the demo in the lilt of the sloppy vocal performance, the freshness and fierceness of the piano rhythm (actually a dumb/brilliant evolution of what Berry created, although the finished song sounds more like the Berry version), and most of all in the unearthly beauty of the brief falsetto parts: "Everybody's gone surfin' . . ." This is the essence of the matter. This is what those of us who've fallen in love with this music listen for, I suggest. I call it a mysterious spirituality, because of the effect it has on me. Cindy speaks of an irresistible sadness in the voice. Whatever it is, it's there in that falsetto, not the product of genius in the sense of some kind of studio mastery or compositional talent but rather a direct, crude gift for the expression of feeling through voice, music, melody. "Everybody's gone surfin' . . ." A very psychedelic moment. This man knows something (whether he admits it to himself or not). Like all great American singers and music makers, he has seen (heard, felt) the glory.

Disc one, which takes us to the beginning of 1965, is roughly the equivalent of the excellent 1974 compilation *Endless Summer*: it sums up the early, surf (cars, fun) era of the Beach Boys. (It does offer quite a few tracks that aren't on *Endless Summer*, including such gems as "Don't Back Down," "Please Let Me Wonder," "When I Grow Up (To Be a Man)" and "Why Do Fools Fall in Love?") I know there are people who regard *Pet Sounds* as the greatest album of all time who don't appreciate the Beach Boys' earlier recordings, but such a position is indefensible, probably the result of cultural prejudice. It (music, art) doesn't get any better than "Don't Worry Baby," "I Get Around," "The Warmth of the Sun," or "Fun, Fun, Fun." The musical ideas, groundbreaking then, are still full of revelation today. The sonic beauty of the recordings is unsurpassed. This is the rock-and-roll aesthetic, compressing the meaning of existence (and all the feelings such contemplation, conscious and unconscious, stirs up in us) into a two-minute performance, totally present and in your face and just as suddenly gone again, except for certain melodic or verbal or rhythmic hooks left behind. What was that? Play it again. Reexperience it. Drink it in. Still full of all those stirred-up feelings, but no longer alone with them.

(One caveat. I would like to believe that sonic perfection is forever, but in fact it's as much a will-o'-the-wisp as the rest of our supermodern reality. Mark Linett has done a superb job massaging these tracks into digital CD-encoded form, but this whole milieu of ephemeral hardware that allows and requires endless remastering of earlier recordings is treacherous. No one can really say how these recordings should sound, except possibly Brian Wilson, and if able, he's certainly not willing to direct the proceedings. The problem is, when we're talking about magical sounds, relationships are everything. I believe the "oooo-weeee"s at the end of "Fun, Fun, Fun" are the defining moment of the record (bookending and trumping the perfect son-of-Johnny-B.-Goode guitar intro). But in my mind and memory they should soar free, dominating the record's fade while everything else slips to the background, not swamped into the chorus like one more special effect. The song *is* that triumphant falsetto swoop, and to my ears it's lost here, at least on the various CD players I've tried it on—a very great loss indeed. I know that if I go back and listen to a variety of earlier cassette and vinyl copies of the song, what I'm wanting to hear may be elusive there as well, depending on the pressing and other factors, notably the nature of the equipment I'm listening on (one phonograph's not the same as another, by a long shot). And the kind of 1960s AM radio Top 40 transmission and compression that these singles were designed for simply does not exist anymore at all, no more than the cars and transistor radios that received the signals. Lost in time. Anyway, I guess I'm acknowledging that there is no objective truth in such matters, but still I feel certain that if I were standing next to the sound engineer with a bomb in my hand, this CD version could sound a lot closer to a certain subjective ideal I happen to feel rather strongly about.)

I like the guitar sound on "Surfin' Safari." I like the haunting melody of the twenty-second unfinished fragment called "Little Surfer Girl." I have always loved "Shut Down" and "In My Room" and still do—the former appealed to me when I didn't even like rock and roll, and I certainly wasn't into cars or drag-racing, but there was something about the unique sound and structure of the song, that *tautness*; never heard anything like it. As for "In My Room," I guess I'm a sucker for Brian's terrifyingly honest confessions and expressions of feelings most folks never even talk about ("Don't Worry Baby," "In the Back of My Mind," "Please Let Me Wonder"). That is the key to *Pet Sounds*, just as much as the extraordinary arrangements and melodies. I'd even argue that the quality of Brian's melodies is also due to a kind of honesty. And courage. I love the vocal, the harmonies, the hypnotic pace of the thing, the high "ooo" in the middle of "room" at the end of the track ... And oh yeah, I've always been fascinated by the lyrical and philosophical similarities between "In My Room" and the Beatles' "There's a Place," recorded six months earlier, but how likely is it that Brian or Gary Usher imported the album from England? "There's a place/world where I can go ..."

John's was his mind, Brian's his room, and there you have it, sports fans.

I like "The Surfer Moon" 'cause I never really listened to it before. "Catch a Wave," a gem I'd overlooked or underrated (layers of sound!). Crank it up. "Don't Back Down" a shining example of Brian at his best I hadn't really connected with till now. Or I did, and forgot, and this box is the occasion of a happy reunion and rediscovery.

And more. Fascinating to listen to "Surfer Girl" and realize Brian wrote it at the same time as or before "Surfin'," the very beginning. How it contains the essence of all that was to come later. Recorded it again and released it as a single with his own lead vocal just as soon as he got his dad and the Capitol guys out of the studio, their first ballad single, and second Top Ten hit. Those harmonies. He may have been thrilled and inspired by the Four Freshmen, but this is something different. His own little discovery/invention. A vision of harmony. How we (each appreciated for his own special qualities) could be together.

And lots more stuff. Fount of creativity. Listen. Listen. Listen.

The imperfection in disc two is simple (and unavoidable): Listening to selections from *Pet Sounds* is like listening to an edited version of your favorite song. Eight *Pet Sounds* songs are included here, and it's either too many or not enough. Immediately and every time, I find myself missing the other five songs: the astonishing and underrated "Here Today," "Don't Talk (Put Your Head on My Shoulder)" (some days my favorite Brian Wilson song), "Let's Go Away for Awhile," "I'm Waiting for the Day," and "That's Not Me." The compilers have a seeming prejudice against Mike Love lead vocals, which I don't share. Mike's leads on "Here Today" and "Sloop John B" and "I Know There's an Answer" are an important part of the magic of *Pet Sounds*—much as I love Brian's vocals, the sound of the album would be thinner and a lot less perfect without Mike's voice. Along the same lines, it's wonderful to be able to hear Brian's draft vocal for "God Only Knows" (included with other pieces of the session on disc five), but gorgeous as it is, it can't touch the finished version and Carl's extraordinary vocal performance. The point is that Brian is a painter, and the sound of the Beach Boys' voices is the most important part of his palette. His process is not precisely to create sounds, but to find them and put them together. At the time of *Pet Sounds*, even though he was making something that could easily have been called a solo album, he was at the peak of his creative powers partly because he still had complete and unself-conscious access to the palette of sounds, vocal and instrumental, that he had worked with over the years, along with all the new sounds he was discovering and uncovering every time he walked into the studio.

Anyway, I'm not saying the compilers should have done it differently. But the real Beach Boys box set is the one you have here, plus the *Pet Sounds* CD (exquisitely mastered by Mark Linett). Some things can't be excerpted.

Disc two starts with two of the Beach Boys' biggest hits, "California Girls" and "Help Me, Rhonda." Both songs have always bugged me—they get old for me much faster (I get tired of hearing them) than most of the Beach Boys' oeuvre. I'm not sure why this is. I don't care much for the lead vocals on either song (Mike on "California Girls," Al on "Help Me, Rhonda"), and the lyrics of "California Girls" are irritating for their cuteness as well as their double chauvinism. But I think there's an irritation factor in the music as well, by which I guess I mean the arrangement of both songs. Is it possible that Brian the eternal innocent is displaying a bit of cynicism here? He does come up with some fresh musical ideas in these songs (I wish the compilers had put the two songs in their proper chronological order, instead of yielding to the temptation to put the eternally popular "California Girls" at the start of the disc), but finally there's a shallowness for me, a slickness, maybe an absence of that mysterious spiritual quality that's present even in songs like "Wendy" and "The Girls on the Beach." I don't know. I do like the long keyboard intro to "California Girls," and I notice that the chorus of the song introduces the "round" effect that is used so well on *Pet Sounds*. But I can't feel the "warmth of the sun" in either of these songs, or not as strongly as I want to feel it. Brian's salute to Phil Spector, "Then I Kissed Her" (sung by Al again; a Beach Boy who seldom sings lead), is fun but nothing special. What I really like amidst this strange miscellany (Brian seems to have been floundering about a bit in 1965, trying on different styles, looking for something and tossing off records—always under pressure from Capitol and others to produce, make us some more money kid—the way other people write postcards) is the one-minute a cappella snippet "And Your Dream Comes True," and the playful, atavistic "Barbara Ann." Pure essence of Brian, even if there's no studio whiz kid anywhere in evidence.

The transition into *Pet Sounds*, on the box set and as a matter of historical fact, is another odd experiment, a cover of a folk song previously popularized by the Kingston Trio, "Sloop John B." At Al's suggestion, Brian recorded an instrumental track for this song in summer 1965, while "Help Me, Rhonda" and "California Girls" were dominating the charts and before he and the group made *Beach Boys Party* in response to record-company pressure (their third album of new material that year). In October "The Little Girl I Once Knew" was recorded (need a single!); in November the instrumentals "Pet Sounds" and "Trombone Dixie" (outtake included on the *Pet Sounds* CD) were laid down; and then just before Christmas Brian brought the group in to do vocals for "Sloop John B." Two other events are significant for this chronology: Sometime in 1965 Brian took LSD for the first time, and was profoundly moved by the experience; and in late autumn the Beatles released a record called *Rubber Soul* that threw down the gauntlet as far as what a rock-and-roll *album* could be. Brian, like the Beatles, had previously thought of his work in terms of single songs, but he was ready and eager to rise to the challenge.

"The Little Girl I Once Knew" is an inventive recording, but certainly not an ambitious one. "Pet Sounds," the instrumental, is very ambitious: you can hear the arranger/composer/producer trying hard to capture something, a sound he hears in his head, a feeling, a whole set of sounds and feelings. "Sloop John B," reportedly only on the album because the record company insisted (but an integral part of it nonetheless through the miracle of fait accompli), splits the difference, a routine instrumental track with a delightful opening, but something happens to the vocals at the end of the first chorus and through the second verse and chorus that is transcendent. A door has been opened, and love and beauty and musical magic are flooding in. Specifically I'm talking about the dumb angelic "doot-doot" backup vocal that starts after "I wanna go home," quickly joined by a wonderful density of sound, "oooh"s, and bells and a soaring feeling of musical intensity and momentum, that patented Brian Wilson "saturate the track with music" effect, building up and bursting into the climactic a cappella "Let me go home / Hoist up the John B sails" vocal break in the second half of the second chorus, just amazing. Brian was ready. He wrote and recorded the rest of *Pet Sounds* between January and April of 1966.

So even as we're sitting here, someone is listening to the box set, her parents' copy, or he got it for his birthday, and hearing "God Only Knows" for the first time, really hearing it. And nothing will ever be the same again. Wow. Even after all these years and all the hype, I find the power of this art form awesome to contemplate. How does it do that? Why does music mean so much to people?

I have spent my life trying to answer this question, and still I don't know where to begin. What happens when I hear "God Only Knows"? I get feelings. Deep feelings. This matters because these feelings don't pass unnoticed. They have an impact. They bring about some kind of awakening, or a renewal, rediscovery, of faith. A sense of my own existence.

This is not achieved by anything that could be called "meaning." It's not about the meaning of the song. Nor is it about its musical innovations. It's about what it says, through its sound its performance its totality its presence, to our hearts.

Pleasure is an important part of it. Good music brings pleasure, like good sex with someone you love, or a walk in the woods. My pleasure in "God Only Knows" begins with the first note, the sound of it, the ways it makes me feel, the way it comes full-blown out of nowhere, the melody that already seems implied in this first note or chord (I guess it's a bunch of notes at once), its personality, its intelligence, its warmth. Then the intro that follows, the orchestral sound (I could never guess what combination of instruments this is, but I love the feel of it, like the texture of a piece of rare cloth), the rhythm that's immediately established, the moment when the bass comes in, and the sweetness of that bass line, and the moment when the other instruments drop out. I could just listen to these seventeen seconds over and over, like a cat lying in the sun. And then the heightened pleasure of the eighteenth second when the voice comes in, that transition, the purity and the beauty of the singing, the way the music and voice go together, the connection felt with another human being (music is spirit that becomes flesh when it's vocalized: Hey, that's a person, like me, I have a voice, too), the way the melody he's singing keeps ascending, moving upward, and the power of *this* voice and *this* melodic progression speaking/sending these words:

> "I may not always love you
> But long as there are stars above you
> You'll never need to doubt it
> I'll make you so sure about it
> God only knows what I'd be without you . . ."

I don't want to say any more, except to acknowledge that I'm just as excited and fulfilled by the other verses, and the amazing little musical transitions between them, and the instrumental/vocal bridge in the middle of the song; oh, and most of all the ending of the song, the repeating ascending round of individual voices, one atop the other in an ecstatic loop, the most heavenly forty-seven seconds in contemporary music, what does it arouse in me? I feel accepted. I feel forgiven. I feel called, and better yet, I feel the energy and the will and the self-confidence to answer. Inspiration. I feel full of the breath of life.

Hey, it's just a song. Yeah. Wind me up and I can wax just as enthusiastic about "You Still Believe in Me." And "I Just Wasn't Made for These Times." And *Pet Sounds* as a whole. The sound of Brian's voice, of all the voices, of those incredible live in-studio orchestras (no instrumental overdubs!). David Leaf's liner notes (in the box set, and the more detailed notes he wrote for the *Pet Sounds* CD) provide a great deal of fascinating information about how the album was recorded. But all you need is ears. And an open heart. There's no other album like this one.

But Brian couldn't help trying to top himself anyway.

"Good Vibrations" is a record I don't get tired of. I screen it out sometimes, deal with its omnipresence by ignoring it or taking it for granted, but whenever I do choose to give it my attention I *always* find myself richly rewarded. Most spectacular collection of transitions in rock-and-roll history (take that, Mr. Spector). This is the three-and-a-half-minute symphony every marijuana-dazed sixties rocker dreamed of recording, and no one else really came close. Some kind of miracle. The sound of those voices! No way it would sound half as good if all the parts were sung by Brian. Real genius is more than conceptual. It gets its hands dirty. It shapes deathless sculptures out of clay found in the artist's backyard.

"Good Vibrations" took six months to record (April–September 1966) and huge quantities of money and studio time, but there are indications that this had more to do with self-consciousness than creative necessity. The engineer on the project feels that Brian had ninety percent of the song the first time he recorded it, and that the lengthy and complex process he went through in the months that followed ultimately served to bring him back to something very close to his original inspiration.

"Good Vibrations" began during the *Pet Sounds* recording sessions, but Brian correctly (intuitively) perceived that it was not meant for that album, that it had a different flavor and character and required a different approach. It was his greatest juggling act: See how many balls I can keep in the air without losing the great-hearted vulnerability of spirit that makes my music worth listening to. He did it. And then . . .

The *Smile* album that's been cobbled together for inclusion in this box set, twenty-six years after the fact, starts with a timeless a cappella invocation (stark and soothing and startlingly beautiful) called "Our Prayer." It's a wonderful wordless beginning for a record that for the most part uses words the same way it uses strings and keyboards—for their sounds. This is in sharp contrast to *Pet Sounds* where most of the songs have titles and lyrics that evoke specific situations and feelings. *Smile*'s radicalism begins with and centers around the fact that it is abstract, whereas all previous Beach Boys records and most rock-and-roll songs are concrete in their imagery. They have words, and those words generally tell a story. Van Dyke Parks's impressionistic *Smile* lyrics resist literal comprehension, but I think it would be a mistake to think it was Van who led Brian down this bold and risky path of abstract expression. Rather, Brian chose Van Dyke as a writing partner because his peculiar (and magical) way with words and ideas and images seemed perfectly suited to the vision that had already powerfully seized Brian's imagination. (Earlier in the year, I suggest, Brian chose Tony Asher as a collaborator because he needed someone square and articulate; now he grabbed Van Dyke Parks because he needed a co-writer who was, so to speak, inarticulate, and hip.)

The primary abstractions on *Smile* are not lyrical but musical. This is evident as the second track on the album ("Heroes and Villains," unreleased version) spills over into the third track, "Heroes and Villains (Sections)." The "Sections" track is six minutes and forty seconds of pleasing, intelligent, highly experimental music, with an important couplet at the beginning ("Bicycle rider, just see what you've done / Done to the church of the American Indian") and then no other identifiable words except "heroes and villains" and once, delightfully, a climax to an out-of-nowhere doo-wop chorus, "How I love my girl!"

In 1964 when he wrote "Don't Worry Baby" (with help from Roger Christian) Brian was, mostly unconsciously, breaking through the limits of language, so that a song about a teenager challenged to a drag race became something hugely more immediate (and unspeakable) for both singer and listener. Now he wants to break through the limits of language consciously, wants to apply to his new album not only what he's learned from "Good Vibrations," but also what he's learned from "Barbara Ann." The communicative power of the human voice singing, for example, "Ba-Ba-Ba-, Ba-Barbara Ann." What is that? "Everybody's gone *surfin'* . . ." Those "ooohs". He's built a career on those "ooohs". Knows they touch people, knows how to touch people with them, feels fulfilled when the connection is made. Brian, like any great performer/producer, has always spoken in tongues, "imitations of speech," more powerful than speech itself. Now he wants to speak in tongues more openly, less hiding behind narratives, no surf anthems, no teenage love songs or even cool songs of existential angst. Just, um, sounds that I like. Tripped-out sounds that I like. In the form of music, of course. Rhythmic, melodic, stimulating, seductive, reassuring music. With trippy funny important (relevant) stories and images encoded in the lyrics and/or in the choice of vocal and instrumental material. (It seems fair to say, listening to these tracks, that Brian Wilson was one of the earliest pioneers of sampling.) Hey. Listen to this.

Does it work? Gotta kill history to get an honest or fair answer to this question. Forget the drama, forget the expectations, forget if you can the context of all this, forget even that this work is unfinished and that its creator has not actively participated in its preparation for release. Forget that there's another "Heroes and Villains" (which happens to be one of my favorite records of all time). Forget the confusion created by the bandying-about of that meaningless word "genius." Listen naked. And listen and listen. Are you getting into the rhythm, the sense, the feel of the album? Is it taking on a form of its own? Do you like it?

I do. Very much. But because of the way the album has been built up over the years, I feel a need to point out that you should not feel dumb if you don't enjoy it. It's not a work of genius. (*Pet Sounds* probably is, but that's another story.) It's a passionate experiment that both succeeds and fails. As a failure, it's famous. Its success, now that we all can hear it, is likely to be much more modest. But these words of mine are mixing up artistic success and public recognition. In hindsight, it may in fact have been impossible for Brian, even under the best of circumstances, to pull together *Smile* the way he envisioned it. There's no way to know. It's easy to imagine that the man who could pull together "Good Vibrations" could pull together anything. Maybe. Anyway, he didn't do it, and maybe in fact there was no way to take all these endless excellent snippets and alternate sections of "Heroes and Villains" and many other songs and merge them together into a single unified work of music that would provoke immediate recognition and pleasure in its listeners the way all Brian's songs (and his one great album) had done until now.

But we have the sessions. And the best or most coherent of those sessions, more or less, have been assembled here and released to the public, in an arbitrary but well-thought-out and highly gratifying (sez me) sequence. Child of *Smile*. I've been listening to it a lot. And it amazes me.

Putting aside the myth (which David Anderle and I certainly helped create, in our published conversation way back a long time ago) of the genius artist frustrated on the brink of his greatest masterwork, these tracks are clearly the work of someone very stoned, a powerful creative artist very much under the influence of marijuana and amphetamines. He was also stoned on power, the power of having the money and the reputation, the intelligence and the talent and the fear/respect of the people around you, that allows you to do whatever you feel like, whatever you think of. Amphetamine makes the user imagine he has such power; in Brian's case, at that moment, he really did have it (almost). Look out, world.

And of course the people around him, the witnesses to his "genius," David Anderle, Van Dyke Parks, Derek Taylor, the journalists like myself, were also very stoned. This could possibly have had some effect on our assessment of what was going on.

I don't mean to sound cynical. History is subjective, and I just want to take this opportunity to remind you of the subjectivity of the historians. Brian Wilson is an artist whose achievements are truly substantial (as evidenced by the box set); but for twenty-six years now he has been judged not on his achievement but on his potential. This is unfair and misleading. *Pet Sounds* is one of the greatest albums of our era. Why should it be eclipsed by the "even greater album" that turned out to be a pipe dream?

Being stoned definitely promotes original and unusual ideas in creative people, and it also serves to make one less inhibited about exploring and using those ideas. This is genuine, this is a plus. On the minus side, being stoned often makes dumb ideas seem terrific; it makes you laugh at things other people wouldn't see the humor in (not a problem unless you've decided to record an album that includes "lots of humor"); and while (especially fueled by amphetamines) it gives you plenty of energy to start things, it very often leaves you without the energy to finish them. A more subtle aspect of being high on marijuana or hashish that many people have noticed is that it stimulates the "head" (mental ideas) but suppresses the heart, the responsive, "feeling-based" side of the personality.

There are moments of great sensitivity and deep feeling on these *Smile* tracks (notably Brian's vocal performances on "Wonderful" and "Surf's Up"), but in its overall character it is not at all a "heart" album (as *Pet Sounds* certainly is); rather it is, and was clearly meant to be, a sort of three-ring circus of flashy musical ideas and avant-garde entertainment. Many of the tracks contain brief segments of truly extraordinary beauty and musical originality (it was hearing some of these tracks, as acetates, that got me and other visitors so excited). The presumption that Brian was working on a masterpiece and would pull it off was based on the obvious ambitiousness and fecundity of the work in progress, and on the astonishing model of "Good Vibrations," which seemed to prove that in the end Brian could take all these fragments and miraculously sew them together into a whole even greater than the sum of its parts. Maybe. Maybe not. Ironically, I think the 45-rpm version of "Heroes and Villains" that Brian put together with fresh vocals near the end of the *Smile* period, which has been criticized as an abandonment of the *Smile* vision, is the best example other than "Good Vibrations" of Brian's ability to unify a thousand working drafts into a brief, coherent, magnificently heartfelt finished statement. But by creating an actuality, we put an end to all the fantasized possibilities. The moral is: Don't let anyone watch you paint. They'll always feel (and sometimes be brash enough to say) that the canvas they thought they saw emerging halfway through was oh so much more beautiful.

("You never knew what I loved in you / I don't know what you loved in me / Maybe the picture of somebody you were hoping I might be" —Jackson Browne, "Late for the Sky")

Goodbye, sweet genius. Could we have the hardworking guy back now, please?

What *Smile* has, instead of the radical but intuitively ear-pleasing structure and irresistible spirit of celebration found in "Good Vibrations" and "I Get Around," and instead of the unearthly beauty and oh-so-human emotional nakedness of "The Warmth of the Sun" and *Pet Sounds*, is an enthusiasm for life (what I saw when I came out of my room, and before I got scared again) and a love of music in all its possible forms, a love of the human voice in all its myriad manifestations, a fascination with the relationship between music and voice, and a veritable eruption of musical and sonic insights, new language, new combinations. It compresses half a dozen different songs into one ("Cabinessence"), and at the same time it repeats a single melodic and rhythmic theme (the "Heroes and Villains" chorus) in otherwise separate songs, breaking down the walls that give songs identities without ever offering conceptual ("rock opera") explanation or resolution. It is a series of visions, some muddied but tantalizing, others breathtakingly clear and full of a beauty that is itself the pure product of wonder. *Smile* has sense of wonder. Beyond humor, it expresses awe at the entire human and natural universe, and reaches out unself-consciously to capture the sound of that awe and amusement in music and voice. It sparkles.

It is also perhaps the story of the unnatural love affair between one man's voice and a harpsichord.

"Heroes and Villains" runs everywhere and remains elusive. David Leaf tells us plainly (in the liner notes to the reissue of *Smiley Smile*) that the original eleven-minute single that Brian almost released in January 1967 has yet to be found; that if it had been located it would have been included on that reissue, and this one. And there's lots more "Heroes and Villains" lying around. But there's also this confusion as to where one song starts or stops. "Do You Like Worms" was a separate enough song-idea to be included on the jacket Capitol printed for the ill-fated album, and yet the track included here is full of "Heroes and Villains" choruses, along with the wonderful "Plymouth Rock roll over" refrain (nothing about worms). Who's zooming who? "Vegetables" has a strong tune and verse identity all its own, but it's at its best between verses (and in the long coda at the end) when it bursts into pure *Smile* vocalizations, manifestations of a higher reality, unmistakably music that belongs to the album as a whole rather than to any one song.

I love the two discrete, narrative (verging on the abstract or even the fractal, but still distinctly narrative) songs Van Dyke and Brian managed to write together, "Wonderful" and "Surf's Up." I am amazed at the beauty and grace of "Wonderful," "Wind Chimes," and "Vegetables" in contrast to the awkward raw goofiness of the *Smiley Smile* versions. I like "Cabinessence" even better in the supportive company of these other performances than I did when it was first released (on *20/20* in 1969). I am pleased and tantalized by the "words" version of "Heroes and Villains" here, very visual narrative like the start of a film that then trails off as though the words have either been forgotten or the camera's pulled so far back you can't hear them, like the whole album's the continuation of the narrative. Listen. I love not most of all but equally with "Heroes and Villains" (verbal) and "Wonderful" and "Surf's Up" the nonverbal vocal/instrumental presence that weaves its way throughout the album, overtly on "Our Prayer" and "Heroes and Villains (Sections)" and "Heroes and Villains Intro" and "Do You Like Worms" and "I Love to Say Da Da" (and on "With Me Tonight" if you include that on your *Smile* album; I do because I like it a lot and because it's there, fait accompli, I don't want to jump up and stop the CD just because I know it was actually recorded a couple of months later), and covertly absolutely everywhere, I mean the nonverbal embraces and almost swallows the verbal even in such delicately articulate and word-centered moments as "a boy bumped into her" and "canvas the town and brush the backdrop."

There is no other album like this, no music like this. "Wa wa ho wa." Myths die hard in Auld Lang Syne but— Come about hard, already, okay? Find your way in, dear listener. You're going to truly delight in this record.

So: After a disc one which contains most of the great early singles that made the Beach Boys famous and which speak so immediately and pleasurably to all innocent listeners in any era, and a disc two which contains "Good Vibrations" and much of *Pet Sounds* and the first release of the legendary *Smile*, what's left? Why, it's the third era of the Beach Boys, the secret era, the not-popular, not-legendary era that encompasses their last four Capitol/Brother albums and their first two for Warner Bros. 1967–71, a time when Brian and his brothers and extended family quietly and awkwardly produced some of their most enduring and most endearing music. At the big science-fiction gathering I attended this past weekend I met a number of people who have been listening to this box set as hungrily and happily and perpetually as I have, and several of them volunteered that disc three is their favorite, the one they find themselves drawn to most often and insistently. Me too. I love disc three. The post-ambitious period. Here as much as anywhere is the real genius of Brian Wilson, the real achievement of Brian and the Beach Boys. Here as much as anywhere is the music for which they will be remembered well into the next century.

First of all, of course, here is "Heroes and Villains," the original single, which I have already described here and in my book *The 100*

Best Singles as one of my most beloved records of all time. In a sense Brian went back into the studio and recorded all of *Smile* in three and a half minutes. This truly is genius, and it went unappreciated in its time and still today, as people waited for something more obvious and pretentious (and they got it, too, in the form of *Sgt. Pepper*). If there was indeed a conscious creative genius somewhere inside Brian, I think it withdrew in a pout when this single went unheralded, silent with the egotistic fury usually associated with French chefs, vowing never again to cast its pearls before such swine. Harumph. Well, that's the pop-music biz. Live by the sword of mass popularity (and critical worship) and you'll die by the sword. It's still an inexpressibly beautiful piece of music.

And there are at least two other recordings on disc three worthy of mention in the same breath, two other masterpieces worth the price of the box set all by their lonesome selves: "Can't Wait Too Long" (1967/1968) and the reworked "Surf's Up" (1966/1971).

"Can't Wait Too Long" is a delicious surprise. It first surfaced a few years ago as a bonus track on the CD "twofer" of *Smiley Smile* and *Wild Honey*. The box-set version is an alternate edit and mix, and while the first version is a splendid find ("the single best piece of unreleased music in the Beach Boys archive," David Leaf wrote in 1990), this new version is hugely better, thanks to a welcome abbreviation of the repeating chorus in the middle (eight repetitions instead of sixteen; works much better) and a different mix that reveals the spoken/sung section just before those repetitions, a brief, possibly accidental segment that gives me gooseflesh and unending pleasure equal to the closing movement of "God Only Knows" or my favorite Bob Dylan performances. I must say, however, that comparison of the two versions requires me to mention another of the very few flaws in this box set: the last forty seconds of "Can't Wait Too Long," a bass-driven instrumental break reminiscent of "Shortenin' Bread," is inexplicably missing from version two, and the song is the poorer for it (instead we get a clever, but frustrating, segue into "Cool, Cool Water"). In other words, for the perfect "Can't Wait Too Long" one must tape the box-set version and then add the ending from version one. A regrettable error. But it embarrasses me to be even slightly critical of the gentlemen who are responsible for the fact that we have this exquisite bit of "unfinished" music in the first place.

"Can't Wait Too Long" is truly mysterious in both its complexity and its simplicity. Like "Good Vibrations," like "Heroes and Villains," it's one of a kind; there really is no other piece of music quite like it. The man who later in 1968 would put out an album entitled *Stack o' Tracks* seems to have been dreaming on tape here, stacking up instrumental and background vocal tracks into a snippet of music entirely outside of normal song structure, yet as certifiably ear candy (listener-friendly) as any of Brian's early pop creations . . . and for all its ethereal abstractness the song has a brilliant and haunting lyric of extraordinary cleverness, as "been way too long" slips into "can't wait too long" and back again. The opening line, "I miss you darling, I miss you so hard," is also a striking bit of language, especially as sung here, and along with the earlier choral fragment "Been . . . so . . . long" it easily carries an opening minute and forty-two seconds in which these are the only words. There is no way of knowing now whether this gloriously successful use of a few words to flavor and give emotional specificity to a long, complex, deeply expressive nonverbal passage (remember that, with Brian, nonverbal doesn't mean nonvocal; when background vocals become part of the foreground like this, what shall we call them?) is intentional or simply an example of a track for which lead vocals were planned but not completed.

The mystery deepens, and the power and beauty of the song increase almost unbearably, in the next twenty-three seconds, as Carl sings again, "Miss you, darling, I miss you so hard" and Brian, speaking, echoes "miss you so hard" and seems to be teaching Carl (and others?) the rest of the words while the track is playing. He says/sings: "Now, 'Come back, baby, and don't break my heart.'" The idea that this is an instructional or guide vocal is my assumption, and may be all wrong, but in any case the musicality of Brian's (it is Brian, isn't it?) spoken phrase, the way it leans into each beat of the track, is magical, and if the effect were consciously planned would certainly be deserving of the g-word. I believe Brian then mutters, "And it goes [break]"—and we hear this sparkling keyboard sound and a heart-stoppingly beautiful bit of speaksinging: "And now I'm alone lying down looking up at the stars" (Carl echoes, adding melody and more heart, "stars") "Reliving the" (melodic fragment from Brian, I think, as a reference, then right back to speaking without missing a beat) "Reliving the times we shared with the moon and stars and the music we love," split-second breath and then I'm guessing it's Brian and Carl singing together live but who knows, anyway a classic majestic Brian transition into "Been way too long, been way too long, baby . . ." Wow. That moment, that two-line epic poem of Brian's about lying down looking up at the stars, reliving the times we shared, is a complete stoppage of time, quick trip to eternity; sexual love and the Grand Canyon and modern computer technology are wondrous things but no more awesome than this fragment of music, what is that, where did it come from, how did it get here? What are these feelings it evokes in me? Whew. I won't walk you through the rest of the track, but it's not a letdown. Some kind of place where conscious genius and accidental, spontaneous genius meet ... and the track we're left with is like a photograph someone took who happened to be standing there at that magic moment.

"Surf's Up" is another kind of magic; in its finished form it's a masterful nostalgic evocation by Carl of a time gone by, that moment when Brian like Dennis before him ran into the surf, full of excitement and wonder and a youthful sense of immortality, hanging ten all smiles on the crest of a tidal wave ... I believe Van Dyke and Brian wrote this in an evening, the day they first got together; if it's not true, it's mythologically appropriate anyway, pure collaboration, Brian inspired by God and Van Dyke inspired by the divine melody and rhythm and presence coming through Brian's fingertips and vocalizations, and out spilled these punning word-sounds so exquisitely evocative not just of the communal fantasies and promises of 1966 in LSD-enhanced California/America but of that moment in any person's or generation's life when the power and promise of the future seems to open up before us without limits, so that even sadder-but-wiser (actually very fin de siècle) lyrics are experienced as that delicious predawn sadness, part of the awakening, a farewell toast to the old world (blind class aristocracy, columnated ruins) and also perhaps smug youthful celebration of our own wisdom, our ability to see the grand sweep of the past and (implicitly) the future. Am I babbling? This song does that to me, reduces me to pure feelings with millions of specific images loosely attached, floating by, all contradictory and all true at the moment that I see and feel them.

The box set contains Brian's complete rough vocal with piano from 1966 (disc two, *Smile* section) and the instrumental track from 1966 (disc five) that Carl sings to in the first part of the 1971 version (Brian '66 takes over with "dove-nested towers"). So we get the pieces of the puzzle (except the *Smile* section doesn't offer the original "Child Is Father to the Man" track that Carl et al brilliantly reworked as the ecstatic conclusion to "Surf's Up"), but of course the whole is more than the sum of its parts. There is a grace to the finished "Surf's Up" that is positively otherworldly. When Brian's held note on "song" explodes into the group singing "the child, the child, the child," it is for me one of the happiest moments in contemporary music—and even so, it's not my favorite among this wonderful compilation of amazing transitions. That honor belongs to the moment when Brian sings the words "Surf's up! (mm mm)"—and why does it move me so much more deeply in the later version when it's the exact same track? It must have to do with the greater piquancy Brian's vulnerable solo vocal takes on in the context of the fancy wild inventive music on the opening track and the patented "Beach Boys" feel of Carl's opening vocals—universal, collective, omnipresent. That "Surf's up!" moment, then, is not just a transition from what Brian was singing in the previous verse but rather a pivot on which everything that's come before in the song wheels and turns, and maybe not just everything that's in the song but everything the Beach Boys and Brian have sung and played and done up to this moment. The lyrics overtly refer to the Beach Boys' musical legacy at this point; indeed, although it's Brian singing we can hear Van Dyke speaking *to* him, with love and compassion, more so even in hindsight than could possibly have been true when the lyrics were written. Mysterious (I said that before) the workings of songs and lyrics and performance. Magical (another much-used word) the impact all this has on us the listeners, moving far beyond the conscious and unconscious intentions of composers and performers (and after-the-fact assemblers) and into the private realm of our own feelings and personal histories. Singing to me. He's singing to me. And with tears in my eyes I thank him.

But carrying on about these three masterpieces only scratches the surface of what disc three has to offer. "Darling" sounds better every year, wow. "Breakaway," a long-lost favorite I can't get enough of. *Friends* and *Wild Honey* and *Smiley Smile* and *20/20* all deserve to be listened to over and over in their entirety (so get the twofers), but the selections chosen here are intelligent and so pleasing: Dennis's "Little Bird," "I Went to Sleep," "Let the Wind Blow," "Time to Get Alone," "Do It Again," and the sublime fragment "Meant for You." "This Whole World" from *Sunflower*. " 'Til I Die" from *Surf's Up*. And some top-of-the-line unreleased tracks: "Games Two Can Play" (Brian, where do you get these melodies? How do you speak so directly and unself-consciously?); "San Miguel" (Dennis again—why didn't he write more?); and the 1967 version of "Cool, Cool Water." These are not lesser works. The third era of the Beach Boys is every bit as rewarding as the first two. Brian gave up his crown but could not (yet) escape from his talent. The more time passes, and the further we get from the commercial and critical expectations placed on the Beach Boys at the time, the better this music sounds. What a triumph, how American, how Emersonian, to be able to be so disconnected from what's hip, what sells, what's fashionable. It's true, sadly true, that if it were not for what went before, no record company would ever have released any of these albums. Are there other Brian Wilsons out there, then, who never had a string of hits and whose idiosyncratic creations, however brilliant, are therefore unreleased and ignored? Maybe. Probably. But right now that's not the question. Instead we celebrate the accident or grace of God that has brought us wacky delights like "I Went to Sleep" and "Busy Doing Nothin'," and we listen not just with pleasure but fascination to the melodic, chromatic, harmonic, structural insights and innovations hidden within these seemingly simplistic creations.

Melodies. You'd think that there were only a handful of melodies in the world, especially given the way folk and country and rock and pop and jazz musicians continually borrow and recycle them, and then you listen to Brian Wilson, and can't stop listening, and wake up in the morning with the tune of "Games Two Can Play" or "Breakaway" playing in your mind, irrepressible, and you have to think that here's a guy who's tapped into some larger musical universe. And you can complain about his problems and his laziness and the people who've exploited him and what we've lost, perhaps, but who among us can say they've come anywhere close to absorbing what he *has* recorded and released? Melodies. This is a man who built almost an entire album around one melodic riff ("Heroes and Villains"), who can just as easily include enough separate melodic ideas in one song to last most rock groups their entire career. Mystery. Magic. Listen. I think perhaps the post-ambitious period represented on disc three is the most rewarding because it is such a direct linkup with the child consciousness at the heart of this (and every?) great musician. Music for music's sake. Just fooling around. Just trying to talk to you.

Disc four is the "wilderness" era: the Beach Boys don't know who they are, Brian doesn't know how to make records or if he wants to make records or who he is, and the years roll by. The first three discs take us from 1961 to 1971; the fourth goes from 1972 to 1988 (and it might as well be 1993). Brian's 1988 solo album is not represented here, since this is a "Beach Boys" collection, so we can leave the successes and failures of that effort to be discussed another time (basically it's a very listenable disc full of wonderful Brian moments but almost every track is crammed with co-producers trying to help Brian finish what he's apparently lost interest in). The live Beach Boys, who were so wonderful in concert in 1974 when *Endless Summer* put them back on top for a little while, are unfortunately not represented here, and what we get instead is selections from the relatively few albums the Beach Boys made over this twenty-year period, only one of which was truly memorable . . . Brian's charming return to form, *The Beach Boys Love You*, which went unnoticed at the time and has yet to be issued on CD as far as I know.

And yet, perhaps just because the good bits have been so carefully selected from a long dry period, and maybe also because these later Beach Boys explorations and evolutions deserve more attention than we tend to give them, disc four is surprisingly rewarding—not close to the quality level of the first three, but still a pleasure to listen to again and again.

This confuses me. If I love discs one through three because they're full of great recordings (Brian's medium was not the song or composition or arrangement or performance but the *recording*; that was what he saw himself creating), why do I waste my time with disc four, which contains no major works and very little to compete with the long list of disc three wonders? I'm not sure. There are plenty of good melodies here, including some oddball unreleased tracks that are still growing on me, notably "Still I Dream of It" and "Our Team." The best songs from *Carl and the Passions* and *Holland* are here and well worth discovering or rediscovering: "Trader," "Funky Pretty," "Marcella," "You Need a Mess of Help to Stand Alone," and "Sail On Sailor." (The two albums have been switched chronologically on the disc, for no apparent reason.) I also like the spacey "All This Is That," and it's quite nice to have Brian's "Fairy Tale Music" without the narration. Nice, but not a major event: it's a composition by a man who clearly doesn't have the energy to write a soundtrack or compose a concerto or record a "Good Vibrations." And there are a couple of Brian tracks here I actually would rather not listen to; I've never liked his hit arrangement of "Rock and Roll Music," and "That Same Song," which he sings, is equally irritating. But still there are moments all over this disc that do pull me in, particularly the four songs from *Love You*. "I'll Bet He's Nice," for instance, seems to me as fine an example of Brian's crude, inventive musical exuberance as "Friends" or "Let Him Run Wild." And "Airplane" to me is irresistible. But I wouldn't start a new Beach Boys listener out on this stuff. A disc for fans.

And disc five is a fan's disc of quite a different sort, weird and wonderful and full of revelations. Would you like to have been standing in the studio while Brian supervised the recording of "I Know There's an Answer," "God Only Knows," or "Good Vibrations"? Now you can be, and the experience is anything but a disappointment. I know of engineers and musicians who have been studying these session tapes like holy writ ever since the box set came out. On "Hang On to Your Ego" ("I Know There's an Answer") and "God Only Knows," we hear Brian conducting a roomful of first-rate orchestral musicians, coaxing performances out of them ("Do you think we could hear a little bit more harmonica in that instrumental break? I don't know," he asks, and the solo that results is one of the great dadaistic moments in modern music), complaining about a rhythmic phrase that isn't going down to his liking and then getting a suggestion from a musician and incorporating it immediately with exhilarating results. We hear him trying on musical phrases and combinations of instruments and alternate angles of incision on fifteen minutes of "Good Vibrations" takes, and although it's a bit much for casual listening, when you can give it your attention it's absolutely riveting—more than an education—more like a personal tour of one of the wonders of the world conducted by the architect/contractor who built it. Best of all, for me as a listener, is the quality of the music itself, "Hang On to Your Ego" just gorgeous before as well as after its brilliant and imaginative transformation into the piece of music it was meant to become. There are parts of "Good Vibrations" not included on the finished track that are pure treasures, the "hum de ah" chorus being my personal favorite, at least this week. And although there's no talk, it's wonderful, in terms of listening pleasure and mental stimulation both, to have pieces of tracks from "Heroes and Villains" and "Cabinessence" and "Surf's Up." Certainly Brian's most beautiful and inventive instrumental excursions were created to serve as framework and backdrop to foreground vocals.

Along those lines, I am very pleased with the seemingly gimmicky set of five songs on disc five that can be heard as pure vocals or pure backing tracks as you switch your stereo "balance" knob back and forth. *Stack o' Tracks* was a fine album and a great idea, but now at last we have "*Stack o' Vocals*" as well, and the only thing is, I want more. Listen to that backing track for "When I Grow Up"—outrageous! And then those vocals, and then the amazing ways they both come out so different when they're put together. I find the vocals for "Wouldn't It Be Nice" particularly intriguing (and at times hilarious). "Wendy" and "All Summer Long" are also tasteful choices for this "toy microscope" section of the box. (Kids! You be the producer! What would you have done?) And I tip my hat to the pointed sequence of tracks from "I Get Around" and "Dance Dance Dance," the former sounding remarkably similar to the latter, something you'd never begin to guess from listening to the finished records. What it shows is that the revolutionary structure and sound of "I Get Around" is entirely in the vocals and in their relationship with the music; it can't be heard on the track at all. "Dance Dance Dance" (the first tracks for which were laid down a month before Brian cut "I Get Around," and then put aside until six months later) is much less of a song in my opinion, but the track as heard here is far more lively and musical. (It would have been nice to have had more information on this disc five stuff, particularly as much identification as possible of the different segments of "GV" and the *Pet Sounds* tracks in terms of which takes we're hearing, and from what dates. Obviously we were going to listen like detectives; throw us a few clues . . .)

The demo of "In My Room" is a delightful touch. The live tracks that close the box set are well intended, but too brief for the listener to really get into (three tracks from a 1964 show, one each from concerts in 1966 and 1967). "Interesting" stuff (i.e., the first live "Good Vibrations" and the last live Brian appearance with the original group), but the compilers of the set don't seem to be fans of (this kind of) live music, and, I think, don't really realize that an earnest search of the Beach Boys archives and fan's tapes would turn up some superb concert-length performances (which ideally would be presented to us listeners with most of the between-song patter cut out). If we had to be limited to a few samples of live Beach Boys, I would have preferred more emphasis on the beauty of the voices (the 1967 "Surfer Girl" *is* quite special) and the enthusiasm and inventiveness of the band, on a good night before a responsive and intelligent crowd. Oh well. It's an absolutely fantastic six hours and twenty minutes of music, and the further good news is that it's selling well, which means Capitol may be encouraged to release some of the other unreleased Beach Boys/Brian Wilson material in their vaults; i.e., a collection of BW productions of other artists (released and unreleased), a complete set of *Pet Sounds* session tracks, a lot more *Smile* tracks, and other assorted riches. This could be fun. Is fun, is magnificent, is an embarrassment of riches already.

So the moral is, life is imperfect, but an American kid with a CD player and a roof over his or her head doesn't have a hell of a lot to complain about. And even the Beatles only lasted seven years, so why do you keep asking Brian what he's done for us lately? But what an amazing story! And leaving aside the hype and confusion over the *Smile* stuff, how can we listen to the *Pet Sounds* studio sessions or even *Pet Sounds* itself and not believe that this guy, somewhere inside, still has this kind of music flowing through him, and could even still have the ability to walk into a studio, under the right circumstances ("no pressure"—hah!), and get talented players to perform their hearts out for him? The thing about Brian (and I think Lew Shiner's novel does capture some of the poignance of this, although his book is really about us fans, not about musicians) is, as long as he's alive, at any moment he could awaken from his nap and saturate our ears with great music again. I don't think he will, necessarily; for one thing, I think his loss of self-confidence is just about absolute (where do they grow that stuff?), and the precious unself-consciousness that made possible all his great work in each of the Beach Boys' "eras" might also be very difficult to resurrect (although the one track I've heard from Van Dyke Parks's forthcoming album, featuring Brian not as composer or producer but simply as guest lead vocalist, is extremely encouraging).

Uh, where was I? Where am I? Which disc is this? I don't want to stop listening to this album (I know, I don't have to stop, but it's such a great excuse to be working on a "review"). It's disc three, actually, in my headphones again right now, and I am ecstatically listening to "Let the Wind Blow" and "Cool, Cool Water" and "Little Bird" and, and . . .

And no, I don't feel satisfied that I've found or expressed the secret of what this music means to me. I can do a good song and dance when I'm talking about a lyric, but what can you say about a melody? Or the sounds of the voices and instruments in "Cool, Cool Water" (1967, one minute and eleven seconds) and the ways they echo off each other? I surrender. I admit my helplessness. (Now I'm listening to "Do It Again." God, it's wonderful.) I shall go back and consider the matter (what can you say about a melody, except that you worship the air it vibrates in?) for another thirty or forty years. In the meantime, I leave you with the words of another fan, a Mr.

John Cale of the United Kingdom, who wrote/sang in his great 1975 song "Mr. Wilson" (not about a British prime minister):

> I believe you, Mr. Wilson, I believe you anyway
> And I'm always thinking of you when I hear your music play
> And you know it's true that Wales is not like California in any way
> And when I listen to your music you're still thousands of miles away . . .

There are many stories still to be told. At any given moment in history people will dispute this claim, and I question it myself often enough— isn't it just the same old stories in new costumes, "rearrange their faces and give them all a different name"? I ask, I doubt, and then every time (so far) I eventually decide that the problem is not that the universe's supply of new wonders has been exhausted but rather that I need to de- wax my ears, break my addiction to a handful of familiar plots (and, in some cases, tired storytellers) and open my listeningness to that which I have not yet heard, from any voices new or old as long as they're sin- cere and awake.

Why? Because I need the nourishment. I need to feed and renew my own vision.

And at the same time, I have to tell you, "too many choices" doesn't work for me. Record stores make me crazy. We are a consumer culture, I think it's fair to say, and one of the challenges I find in writ- ing/editing my magazine is that there is considerable pressure on me, most of it coming from the chatter of my own inner voices, to be a good consumer and, as a public commentator in this realm, to encourage (and even pressure) others to consume as well. The argument in the paragraphs above ("open my listeningness") can certainly be heard as a rationalization of energetic consumption of new product. But that's not what I wish to communicate.

There are alternatives. The most obvious one is quality not quan- tity. We can open our listeningness not necessarily through buying more new albums but by listening more deeply to what does catch our attention. Contemplation. And ideally, although I really do find the language involved quite slippery, I would like this chapter to be less about evaluating the six albums under discussion and more about sharing the fruit, such as it ·may be, of my contemplation of them. Six mysteries. Yes of course there are albums released that don't do anything for my sense of wonder, but I try not to spend too much time with them. My subject here is stories and storytellers. I want to report on some tales that have recently caught my attention.

Bob Dylan's been telling friends how enthusiastic he is about his new album. That's unusual; and so is *World Gone Wrong*. In one respect, however, it fits the classic concept of a new Dylan album: it's a Rorschach test. A gorgeous rich heartfelt splatter. Be careful. What you hear is what you've got.

I hear death, desire, compassion, humor, integrity, fascination with the simple deep lives and emotions of human beings, love of music, and an older person's awareness of the complex patterns of work, suffering, loneliness, failed ambitions, and small pleasures that life is mostly made of. I hear presence, depths of feeling, and subtleties of feeling. I hear intense concentration on performance, and I feel a friendship or camaraderie that that concentration somehow implies. This singer/player cares passionately about getting something across to me. The record overflows with warmth. I am moved.

World Gone Wrong is so warm, in fact, that it makes Dylan's previous album (*Good As I Been to You*, which I praised in chapter one for its unusual intimacy) seem cold and distant. It wasn't, but it is an indication of the extraordinary power of this new set of performances that they set a standard that, unfairly but inevitably, diminishes prior efforts in the same direction. Of course, the creative process is a working-out, involving a great variety of internal and external considerations. *WGW* very probably could not have come into existence without the personal and public breakthrough that *Good As I Been to You* embodies, and one can further speculate, from the comfortable perspective of hindsight, that that album was the fruit of a variety of frustrated earlier efforts, including the relatively unsuccessful (personally, aesthetically) *Down in the Groove*. Perhaps Dylan's inability in the early 1980s to get or create record-company support for such projects as his collaboration with Clydie King also laid the slow groundwork for this 1992–93 reassertion of self.

For that is what it is. Reaching back twenty-three years to a still earlier attempt at recording an album made up mostly of cover versions, we can recognize *World Gone Wrong* as the REAL *Self Portrait*, the one Dylan wasn't willing, able, or ready to perform and share until now.

Being literal won't get you anywhere. What Dylan was trying to say in 1970, and what he succeeds in saying now, is that a self-portrait moves from the inside out, not the other way around. It's not a peep show. This album does not reveal that Dylan killed a lover, was killed by one, patronizes prostitutes, or died of the plague on the way to a Crusade. All the songs about death on his first album did seem to indicate that, like most twenty-year-old kids, the singer was scared of and fascinated by the idea of dying; but all the songs about death this time out don't even tell us that. There's more personal fear, it seems to me, in the chorus line from "Delia" ("All the friends I ever had are gone") than in any of the death stories told here, even though "Two Soldiers" does capture the terror and despair of the two protagonists with astonishing immediacy. What comes across instead is that death for the singer is a narrative focal point, awakening him as listener (the self he's portraying here is, in every case, the listener in him awakened by hearing these songs) to the poignance and humanness of these life stories—murderess mocked by a parrot (if she could eliminate all witnesses, her vanity assures her, the event would never have happened), murderer haunted by his victim (Stack A Lee, whose bullet created rather than destroyed his tormentor, and Cutty, who still yearns pathetically for Delia's attention even after he's done the one thing he could think of to prove his own existence). Dylan shares with us his empathy for these characters (and for the characters he inhabits as first-person narrator, ragged, hungry, bloody-eyed, broke down, abandoned, and yet mysteriously enduring, even indomitable), not to boast of anything (he ain't philosophizing disgrace here) but, I think, to confess and share his humanness, which is ultimately no more or less than ours, or theirs. "What good am I?" That 1989 song asked the bones of a question: "If my hands are tied / Must I not wonder within / Who tied them and why / And where must I have been?" This album puts flesh on the bones.

You can hear it in his voice.

And of course you can also hear it in his guitar-playing. The two—voice, guitar—work together so closely it seems inappropriate to speak of one as accompanying the other. They are inseparable partners in the act of articulating the mood of the performer, a mood as multifaceted and full of subtle intricacies as a tidepool at sunset, half-moon rising over the observer's shoulder.

My notions about the primacy of performance in Dylan's art are well known at this point. Ben Edmonds, in a recent review of one of my Dylan books in Detroit's *Metro News*, summed them up efficiently: "Dylan's genius is, Williams contends, as a performer. The act of composing the song is only preparation for the moment of its performance. At that moment, the artist is telling us everything we need to know about his art and his life." Everything we need to know . . ." That's a lot. The point is, a great artist is one whom we experience as being almost inexplicably articulate. A measly brushstroke speaks volumes; and speaks them not just to the critic/scholar who has some grasp of the technique involved, if there is such a person, but direct to you and me as we look at the painting, ignorant perhaps of painterly technique but one with the artist in terms of human experience. We've seen and felt the movement of a man's shoulders as he receives news of a great disappointment and pretends it makes no difference to him. We know, even if we could never describe or paint it, the look in a woman's eye as she persuades whomsoever stands in her way ("It would not make me tremble") to let her go to the aid of a loved one. And when we hear or see the artist's representation of this truth, we *recognize* it. Magic word. We know it to be true, not through persuasion but because it matches our experience. Indeed, the moment of recognition is a moment of reexperiencing. Art would have no power if life itself did not open our hearts at times (more times, perhaps, than we care to remember or admit). Art reopens our hearts, and the greater the art, the more simple and mysterious the process. Why does Delia's song turn out to be about Cutty? Because it is. Because that's the way Dylan *heard* it. In 1963, in Cambridge, Massachusetts, I fell hopelessly in love with Jackie Washington's performance of a variant of this song, different melody, different words, all I remember or ever heard is the incredible chorus, I could sing it for you if this weren't print: "Delia gone, one more round / Delia gone, *one more round* / Delia gone . . ." Maybe that song was about Cutty, too. It was certainly about someone not gone, about his feelings of pain and loss and something regretted and inescapable. Thinking about it, intimations of my own response as a fifteen-year-old to . . . something—words? chords?—stir deeply in me. And this new (to me) version hits me almost as hard, but somewhere different. New story. No end to them. No limit to the power of performance.

But some of my friends feel cheated that Dylan hasn't written any great songs lately.

He obviously hasn't needed to. But that doesn't matter; if you're a fan you just want what you want, and Dylan understands that, and so—a further expression of his enthusiasm for *World Gone Wrong*—he reaches in his pack and plays a trump he's been saving so long it's grown whiskers: liner notes, genuine 1965-style liner notes, funny and crazed and rhythmic and earnest, and on top of that an absolutely gorgeous cover photo—those colors! that angle!—evocative of and satisfying as *Bringing It All Back Home*. Is that his own painting? The placement of the title is impeccable. Latest rumor is he played a club in Manhattan and the *New York Times* gushed and Sony got it all on film. It just doesn't sound like the recalcitrant (mumbling, shambling) public Bob-face we've grown so accustomed to. (Not that anything he does, however welcome, is likely to make the album sell any better than any other disc he's put out in the last ten years—one week at number 30, then off to oblivion. But you can look at it another way, which is that this will almost surely be the best-selling collection of traditional blues and ballads released this year by any American artist.)

World Gone Wrong sounded good to me on first listen ("Blood in My Eyes" jumped out) but took a little getting used to—the rawness of some of the recording, the succession of violent deaths in the story-songs. Two months and many listenings later, I can fairly confidently guarantee that it will amply repay as much time and attention as you choose to give it. It has legs. It passes the one real test: it gives pleasure, and goes on giving (still fresh, in other words) on listen after listen after listen. Of course, I can't tell you now if I'll lose interest next week, but I suspect not, and anyway it's been a great ride so far.

So much for evaluation. But what is the story he's telling? What is the story I hear? Well, first of all, of course, the world's gone wrong. This is not a sudden occurrence. We've heard this report from this particular weatherman before—and it's always been correct. But what a delightfully off-kilter song, written well before Bob Dylan was born, and as timely and up-to-date as Pearl Jam or the poems of Rumi. Strictly a relationship song, but with Implications (roughly the inverse of "Everything Is Broken," now that I think of it, which is ostensibly about the state of the world but sneaks in a couplet suggesting it could be about a relationship after all). There's a nice pronoun confusion, B. Dylan specialty: *Who* is it who can't be good no more, who's gonna quit whom anyway, and why? If her, then is he being all sarcastic about her "world gone wrong" excuse? Well maybe. But it's surely gone wrong for him. Way I hear it, she's given him walking papers, probably because the world's gone wrong in the sense of money tight and she can't afford to house the bum like on previous occasions. Wounded pride, he responds that she can't throw him out, he's just leaving before he does something nasty, and "No use to ask me, baby, 'cause I'll never be back." By way of bonus, we get this memorable and highly useful bit of advice (women substitute the word "man" please): "If you have a woman, and she don't treat you kind / Pray to the good Lord to get her off your mind." I love the sandpaper-sweet texture of his voice throughout, the easy beat and that astonishing little melodic hook on "world gone wrong"; vocal first and then the guitar goes on to twist the endpieces and leave you with this indefinable physical feeling that includes among other things gratification and regret. Opening guitar-strum and notes and first words of song/album are pretty devastating, too; how does he do that? Expressive. We got a master at work here. "These are just as good as it's possible for me to play them," he told an interviewer recently, and yes, I believe it's true.

"Love Henry." Notice how there's a very successful unity of sound on this album and yet the guitar-playing and vocal approach are so different on each song. We can listen again and again because so much more is communicated than meets the conscious mind. This gal is arguably the only unsympathetic female on an album full of men beseeching women for something (and frequently getting turned down), but, as Dylan's notes suggest, Love Henry himself is one of only two wholly unsympathetic male characters on the record, the other being the wealthy merchant father in "Jack-A-Roe." Dylan the liner note writer doesn't like men with power and money. Okay. Incidentally, there was a murder trial recently in northern California where the defense attempted to introduce, indirectly, the testimony of a parrot ("No, no, Richard!") who was at the murder scene. (Richard was not the name of the defendant.) The judge was not amused.

"Ragged and Dirty." I find this one strangely attractive, even though there doesn't seem to be much to it. Must be the riff. The right blues riff at the right moment has a totally mysterious, hypnotic impact on me. That little lick he plays, combined with the sound of his voice, tells me everything about the mood of the narrator, everything he feels about the way his life is at the moment. And the low notes that drive the song along. Rhythm section. Pulls me in. "I'm broke and hungry, ragged and dirty, too." That says it all, and the meter (Dylan's phrasing) is irresistible. "If I clean up, sweet mama, can I stay all night with you?" Rest of the song's a lyric blur, she won't let him stay (this is "make me a pallet on your floor" territory) but he still threatens that he's "leaving in the morning." She's got a man, he's got a woman, maybe he's singing to two different women in different (alternating) verses, they both mistreat him, everyone mistreats him, he's outta here. 'Bye.

"Blood in My Eyes." Early favorite, and still intoxicating. Dylan is one of the few contemporary male singers who can sing about desire without trivializing it. (Prince is another; his poses on the subject get tiresome, but his performances remain the real McCoy.) A more devastating or sympathetic portrait of a dirty old man would be difficult to imagine. Dylan captures the shabby dignity of the narrator with great relish: "I tell you something, tell you the facts / You don't want me, give my money back." The story of the power women have over men is told four times in a row on this album, without rancor—on the part of the singer. The persona he inhabits in "Ragged and Dirty" is definitely peeved, and Cutty's anger at Delia has turned into a nightmare for himself and every other character in that narrative. But Dylan never suggests, at least to this listener, that the women in these songs are deserving of criticism or judgment. They are human beings, dealing with life as it is, and with the evident imperfections of these men they're involved with. To the men, however, they are almost forces of nature—certainly they hold their fates in their hands. Sexual power—not societal, but personal—is the subject here. Or one of the subjects. The singer in "Blood" has at least a little money (and a room to keep his tie in), the singer in "Ragged" has none, but they are equal in their powerlessness. Cutty, who makes the greatest show of power (shoots her down), is not coincidentally the most powerless of all (the woman in this song, Delia, is least like a force of nature and most like a character in her own right—she even has a name—this is presumably because it is the one song of the four told in the third person).

Conversely, the one character in the four songs who does not in any sense blame a woman for his troubles, the narrator of "Broke Down Engine," is easily the strongest, most attractive, most manly and vibrant of the lot, even as he begs on his knees for the Lord to bring him his woman back, even as he pounds futilely (but oh-so-musically) on her door. This song today strikes me as the hidden tour de force of the album (maybe I warmed to it slowly because I so love Dave Ray's very different 1965 version—don't even know Blind Willie McTell's original but will seek it out, box set coming soon). This man has no money and he tells us why—lost it gambling—takes responsibility, ain't necessarily feeling sorry for himself. Neediness don't have to be wimpiness, or self-pity. Listen to that guitar talking! "Feel like a broke-down engine, ain't got no whistle or bell." Dylan tells us in his essay it's a song about trains, but that's misdirection— beyond the title simile, repeated several times, there's no trains here. It's not about variations of human longing, either, sweet though the phrase may turn, or dupes of commerce (which of course we all are), or Ambiguity, but somewhere in there he nails it okay, song and performance are most certainly and precisely about "revival, getting a new lease on life, not just posing there" (in the bare-mattress room I envision the "Blood" narrator living in). This hero (he is a hero, him and Jack-A-Roe might be the only ones on the album; oh, and the lone pilgrim, I guess) embodies the reawakening human spirit, viscerally not intellectually; I mean listen to that guitar talking, listen to that singer singing, "Lordy Lord, Lordy Lordity Lord, Lordy Lord, Lordy Lordy Lord." Feel like I ain't got no drive at all, and that surely is how he's been feeling, but in the very announcing of it exactly the reverse becomes true. Lordy Lord. What an extraordinary perfor- mance. She don't open that door, half the other women in the neigh- borhood will, 'cause authenticity rules. In the praying is the answer to the prayer.

I've said a lot about "Delia" already. Its sweet sadness is the heart of this album; the gentleness that's there in the first strummed notes of the performance, and never lets up for almost six minutes. New voice. New voice for every song. Same uncanny vocalist. He makes me care about people and situations I'd rather not even think about.

Dylan suggests in the liner notes—and I don't think it's misdi- rection—that "Stack A Lee" is about reputation. "All about that John B. Stetson hat" is gently ironic; Billy in any version of this song didn't care about the hat, he was a compulsive (gambler, cheater, thief, whatever), and "Stack A Lee" was "bound to" take his life because his treasured rep as a "bad man" was at stake, plain and simple. After you make a fool of a man, don't walk into his favorite barroom. Dylan calling this a "monumental epic" is also ironic; it's the least of the performances on the album, which I think is why the harmonica's brought in to add some color. Nonetheless it's well worthwhile, full of little riddles ("Harlan Alley"? "on an alley"?) and bursts of humor and pathos. If only these guys *were* dupes of commerce, their fates might make more sense, but life was less simple, once.

"Two Soldiers" is the longest tune on the record, and even so, it's all compacted like a New York School poem or a *Reader's Digest* novel. You have to fill in the part where the tall guy gives the Boston boy a message for his girlfriend; the climactic nondelivery of both messages presses them up against each other so close that if you're careless you might think it a song about incest instead of about war and loss and duty and bad luck. Over *apfelwein* in Sacksenhausen last Frankfurt Book Fair, I watched the advance tape and the Walkman being passed back and forth amongst the cream of European intelligentsia, and I had to ask what part it was that everyone kept rewinding to. It was the end of the vocal of this song, without a name or any knowledge of subject matter, just something in the sound of his voice that transfixed even those who weren't sure how they felt about the album as a whole. Months later I've decided this was unconscious fascination (on the part of true fans) at the arrival of Dylan's "old man" voice, previewed perhaps on some of the *Basement Tapes* tracks, but now here it is in the flesh, on the tape, in our present reality. Scarily beautiful (de gustibus non est disputandum).

In the notes to "Jack-A-Roe" we find what may be taken (indeed, may be intended) as an epigraph for this album: "Are you any good at what you do? Submerge your personality." Is Dylan boasting? Certainly the persona and personality of the songwriter is submerged on *World Gone Wrong*, no easy thread of autobiography may be found at all; instead, the storyteller's professional, theoretically impersonal selection of good stories to tell (picked to get a response). And yet this submersion leads paradoxically to a suffusion of personality, in which the performer might feel, at least for the moment, that no album he ever made has come closer to telling the truth about his private world. Self-portrait. I like the tense strumming in this song, always suggesting that something exciting's going to happen (he strums more quietly when important events are actually taking place), and the abstract moodiness of Dylan's voice with extra reverb on it. ("My kind of sound is very simple, with a little bit of echo, and that's about all that's required to record it."—Dylan to Greg Kot, 1993) Speaking of echo, how about that great third line in each verse of this song, always starting "Ohhh . . ." and then repeating the last half of line two? Simple, and full of mystery. Singers are drawn to songs by such curlicues, and rightly so. Hints of the inner structure of the universe. Wonder why Dylan likes songs in which a woman passes herself off as a male (ask Lou Reed if the phrase sounds familiar to him?) sailor. In addition to "Jack-A-Roe" and last album's "Canadee-I-O," he did a song in concert last year called "Female Rambling Sailor." His own answer is the "submerge your personality" line (oh, and traditionally in American Lit we go to sea for discipline and freedom). Maybe it has something to do with his relationship with the Muse.

I see from reading other reviews that disagreements might arise as to which songs on *WGW* are third person or first person. I think of "World Gone Wrong," "Blood in My Eyes," "Ragged & Dirty," and "Broke Down Engine" as true first-person, the form Dylan most often writes in. (Of these, "R&D" is directly addressed to another person, or maybe two of 'em. "Broke Down Engine" is a kind of soliloquy, sometimes addressed to the man's woman and sometimes to God or us or whomever's presumed to be listening. The two Mississippi Sheiks songs are addressed to a collective audience, with choruses that quote a line said by one person to another.) "Love Henry" is third person, omniscient narrator, told largely in dialogue. Interesting form. "Delia" is a third-person narrative with a change of protagonists partway through. (The first-person chorus phrase might throw people off. The narrator is quoting it. This is also true of the last two verses, in which the narrator seems to become the protagonist. Fascinating form.) "Two Soldiers" is third person, omniscient narrator, with some dialogue. "Jack-A-Roe" is a narrative told in the third person by a first-person narrator—the singer takes on the persona of a storyteller, as opposed to just telling a story. This is communicated in the first verse—"The truth to you I'll tell"—and pays off in the last verse, with its bizarre, unexpected moral, a sort of advertisement, albeit an unconvincing one. Dylan definitely likes eccentricity in songs. Hence a version of "Stack A Lee" that omits gambling and seems to focus on the hat. Speaking of "Stack A Lee," it's the same as "Jack-A-Roe," although the first-person narrator is extremely unobtrusive—I think I hear him refer to his own existence in the line "I heard a bulldog bark," but Dylan's diction in this song is elusive. It's also possible (but unlikely) that there's a reference to "our police."

Finally, "Lone Pilgrim" is a first-person narrative (first verse) that quotes a first-person monologue (the other three verses). This actually is closer to the third-person narrative form, in my opinion, than it is to the first-person songs listed above, in which the story being told is a personal one to the character the singer inhabits. But the point is quite arguable. I guess I'm saying the first-person narrator of "Lone Pilgrim" is just a framing device, related therefore to the form of "Jack-A-Roe."

(I like examining such matters because they point, ultimately, to the question of who the person singing the album is, or claims to be. Who is he, anyway?)

I like "Lone Pilgrim" a lot. It's different, as a good last song should be. A country spiritual, while everything else on the album's a blues (the "first-person" songs on my list, hmm) or a ballad (all the third-person narratives). It's beautiful and eerie, like "Rank Stranger" on *Down in the Groove*—always a good trick for an older artist to end an album with a song that could be about his own death ("Weep not for me now I'm gone"). But "Rank Stranger"'s eerie beauty was bleak (loss of friends, as in "Delia"), whereas "Lone Pilgrim" is ecstatically serene. And how fitting, after all these songs of murder and death and guilt and haunting, to close with a character speaking of his own death with an acceptance beyond forgiveness ("The lunacy of trying to fool the self is set aside") and a simple need to pass on to those he's left behind the news that all is truly well with him. Great adverb images in this song: "pensively stood," "sweetly sleep," "kindly assisted." The guitar-playing and lyrics and vocals communicate an extraordinary stillness, filled with comfort and deep insight. You could say, though obviously it's just a reviewer's conceit, that the album progresses from the implied atheism of "World Gone Wrong" through the fierce agnosticism of "Broke Down Engine" to the simple faith of "Lone Pilgrim." You could say all kinds of things. It's an album that allows you to have this kind of fun.

Just two more comments, then. One: It's a classic Dylan album, listenable and quotable. If I were writing a book about the effect that big-money dominance of the news media and the entertainment industry has on individual writers and reporters and artists, I'd certainly call it *The Doors to Your Cage Shall Be Decked with Gold* (the phrase is from "Love Henry"). And, two: Dylan, by ending his liner-note rant/essay with talk about "the Never-Ending Tour chatter" (delightful!) makes a rare and welcome (if implicit) acknowledgment that Bob Dylan fans exist and make up a significant segment of his record-buying, concertgoing audience. Who else would hear chatter about the Never-Ending Tour? Who else would have access to playlists? (His dates are off a little, but what the hell. New Rising Sun Tour, anybody?)

In Utero, the title of the new **Nirvana** album, means "in the womb." It's the sort of title that rock stars who've recently become parents give their records, and as such it's not quite as rich in multiple implications as the Pretenders' brilliant *Learning to Crawl*. But there is a grace to it. The womb is a very private place, and what properly takes place there is gestation. Something is in gestation, something is being formed, something has been initiated and is getting itself ready to come forth, be born.

But the very phrase "in utero" is a medical (and legal) phrase, and tends to remind us that the womb-space has been politicized in our culture, with questions raised and battles raging over the individual's right to interfere with the gestation process and the state's right to interfere with the interference. And the privacy of the womb is routinely invaded (not necessarily to its detriment) by the voracious information-gathering that is so characteristic of our era, as radar and other devices examine and report on the sex and health (and, if possible, buying habits) of the inhabitant. All this, plus the obvious possible consequences of a sharp blow or a fall downstairs, points towards an underlying feeling communicated by the image of being "in utero": vulnerability.

This is a raw, noisy, tough-talking album, aggressive and unapologetic. It tries to sound dangerous, and in many way it succeeds. But its real strength is that, like other rock-and-roll albums before it, it successfully creates a womb of noise within which listener and singer can feel and express their own insecurity, frustration, vulnerability, anger, self-doubt. The basic principle of rock and roll since its inception, I think, is that this is a noisy invasive world and we have to make our own noise back to assert and reclaim our integrity and independence. When I like this record, which is a good deal of the time, I find myself screaming along with it. That says a lot.

Kurt Cobain is the singer, songwriter, guitarist, and designated star-figure of Nirvana (twenty-six years old in 1993, half the age of Mr. Dylan). His strength and his weakness is that he is a terrific whiner. He also has a great sense of humor, and some of the best moments on this album (as on the last) are when he mocks his own bad attitude: "Hey, wait, I've got a new complaint . . ." (chorus to "Heart-Shaped Box") and, "If you ever need anything please don't / Hesitate to ask someone else first" ("Very Ape"). He's as good a snotty kid as Gordon Gano was at a much younger age, and the future of his talent and his trio may be as problematic.

Cobain irritates me—but not, I'm happy to say, on this record, which for me is much more listenable as a whole than *Nevermind*. It doesn't reach the peak of "Smells Like Teen Spirit" and doesn't have the exciting feeling of breakthrough that surrounded that album, but it hangs together better; when you're in a mood to hear it, it fits and feeds that mood from start to finish without letdown or letup. It's good music and it's true to itself, never trying to fit someone else's menu. The screams and the singing are first-rate, the *voice* of the singer and of the vocal/instrumental unit is unique and attractive and timely, there are lots of good melodic hooks and fascinating noise harmonics, and the lyrics jump out and grab you a phrase at a time, not necessarily adding up to much, but they're smart and provocative and funny and twisted and they do their job.

Where he irritates me is a place that I normally avoid as much as possible: the world of talk that runs parallel to rock and roll and promotes it and feeds on it; the world, when you have the kind of success Nirvana and Cobain have had, of celebrity. Cobain complains a lot about the unwanted attention he gets, and then he gives interviews to every magazine in sight to promote the new album. You can't get away from the guy, his face is everywhere, and he's encouraging it, you see him and his female partner in photo opportunities as blatant as presidential-campaign stuff. He invades his own privacy, to the point that even I find myself reading some of this stuff to find out what all the hoopla is about. And then I don't like what I read. He threatens to kill a woman journalist for writing something about him and his wife that even his "official biographer" strongly intimates is true. And he repeats the threat, and says it with the intent of making it as believable as possible. When the *Nevermind* album is a big success, he changes the split on the songwriting so that it reflects more accurately his huge contribution. That would be okay, I accept that the purpose of giving the other guys co-credit in the first place was to help out when it looked like there wouldn't be any other money, but then he insists, over strong objections, that this new deal be retroactive—he takes away the money his colleagues have already been paid! He's a pig, basically, is the impression that comes through even when you read very critically to try to separate the journalistic slanting that inevitably goes on. He's extremely righteous about other bands that don't meet his idea of coolness, slamming Pearl Jam for supposedly trying to jump on his bandwagon when they weren't "true" indie-record people (he later apologized, partly, but only because Eddie Vedder was characteristically such a patient guy about it). He whines about how people don't understand that the only reason he became a heroin addict was he had these *very bad* stomach pains, and he sounds for all the world like a rich celebrity who has some real problems with which one can sympathize, but who has not the slightest notion that there are other people in the world whose difficulties might be as great or greater. Wow. I don't usually go on like this. But Kurt Cobain is a genuine rock star/celebrity for our place and moment. And the more I read, the more he represents an aspect of our moment that I am very unhappy about. And then he turns around and records a song like "Rape Me" that expresses the contradictions in himself and the moment he represents so perfectly, that I delight in it, even feel in some way enlightened by it. So okay. He's a kind of a mirror, I mean for me as much as anyone. He's doing his job.

Journalism needs celebrity, and in the 1990s the feeding frenzy is nonstop. *In Utero* is, among other things, a report from this front, songs like "Serve the Servants" and "All Apologies" letting us know how it feels to be the eaten. And Cobain is smart enough, at least in the songs, to see through the press-persons to the vast hungry public that pays the pipers. In "Rape Me" he follows the sarcastic/resigned "Rape me, my friend / Rape me again / Hate me / Do it and do it again" with one of his patented chanted choruses (certainly a significant contribution to the rock singer's lexicon): "Am I the only one?" For the abused child, we are told, attention is love. This is a provocative song. I can't imagine how it would feel with a woman singing it (and I don't think I want to find out). Cobain's and Nirvana's performance (rock music just doesn't get this good without a terrific rhythm section) is one of the more powerful things I've heard this year, with just a handful of words and a wonderfully familiar yet fresh sound (a variant on "Wild Thing," from the "Louie Louie" family) that work together to spin me off in new directions, emotionally/intellectually/viscerally, every time I hear it.

Another song I like a lot, for its melody, its overall sound (vocal-rhythm-drone), and the chanted chorus, is "Frances Farmer Will Have Her Revenge on Seattle." The chorus is, "I miss the comfort in being sad," which can and must be taken ironically and literally both at once, and again spins all sort of thoughts and feelings from this listener when I hear it. The word "sad," and the last word of each verse line, feature long, long extended vowels, full of spirit and mystery, a little taste of Om Khalsoum emerging unexpectedly in (North)western pop music, each long vowel like a little verse or chorus itself, so there are at least two songs here: one with words, and a far more expressive one with pure vocal sound. The rhythm of the songs builds it towards these vowel epiphanies with remarkable efficiency. The second verse may be about Frances Farmer (it's a blur, even when you know the words, until the lovely line about, "Come back as fire, burn all the liars, leave a blanket of ash on the ground"), but the first verse certainly sounds to me like it's about K. C.'s resentment when his bandmates won't roll over and give him their share of the loot. Oh well. I still love the sound of his voice all through it—"It's so soothing, to know that you'll sue me"—maybe the gossip that's stuck in my brain just increases the contradictory tensions he loves to inject into these things. Got me. Good guitar-playing, too.

Sing along with me: "I think I'm dumb." And I do (sing along), all twelve times that he chants it at the end of "Dumb," another song that highlights Nirvana's wonderful gift for structure. Listen to that melodic hook spiraling up to (in words) and down from (bass line) the word "happy." Makes it more than a word somehow. Great bridge. Fine verse-chorus-verse-chorus-bridge-verse buildup through the song, and then amazing payoff with the final chant. Am I the only one who hears R.E.M. when he sings like this? It's twelve years since "Radio Free Europe"—Buddy Holly's voice had only been on the radio five or six years at the most when the Beatles started doing great things with what they'd learned from him. This stuff is meant to be passed along.

The second half of the album is more gnarly than the first, although "Scentless Apprentice" provides a good burst of chaos early on, and none of these songs are what you'd call "adult alternative" fodder (well, I guess the remixes of "All Apologies" and "Heart-Shaped Box" might squeak by, which is why they were remixed in the first place, but they're not what I'd ever call tame). And, I hasten to say, this gnarliness is not gratuitous, letting their punk flag fly or something. That may be, but also the noise of this record clearly expresses the musical soul of the band, and it has a unique soul, one well worth contacting. So kick out the jams, and much praise to Steve Albini for recording these guys in a manner that encouraged so much spontaneity and life. There are times when I'm listening to this album, especially "side two," and all the lyrics drop out and I'm just sing-screaming along pure melodic voice sounds, intense sophisticated droning spirit music, ahh-ahh-ahh-ahh-ahhhhhhh! Totally caught up in it. Other times it's part trance (or ennui, if my mood's not in synch with it), and then great snatches of lyric/sound jump out at me: "What is wrong with me?" (the chant from "Radio Friendly Unit Shifter") or the adrenaline rush of the "sit and drink pennyroyal tea" parts of "Pennyroyal Tea." Lyrically, "Pennyroyal Tea" plays nicely into the In Utero mythology—it's a tea used for inducing miscarriage, and the other line of the couplet is, "To still the life that's inside of me." Cobain plays with the image of himself as pregnant throughout the album; here as elsewhere he shares (or rubs our noses in) his reluctance, his distrust of whatever it is that's gestating, or maybe just his uncertainty about accepting responsibilities for it. His conceit is that he's been raped by the Muse, and he doesn't have to like it. Maybe he doesn't even have to go through with it.

Repetition is instant ritual. "Serve the servants, oh no!" is repeated seven times in the climax of that song; "Go away!" seven times at the end of "Scentless Apprentice"; ". . . your advice" three lovely times after the last repeated chorus of "Heart-Shaped Box," "What is wrong with me?" and similar phrases (same chant sonic) eight times at the end of "Radio Friendly," and the title word—most compact chant of the album—seven times at the end of "Tourette's." This is not your typical song-ending rave-up, as exemplified (probably the platinum standard, best ever) by the Rolling Stones on "Last Time" and badly imitated ever since. These hypnotic rhythmic fiercely rocking chants are in fact the carefully crafted climax of each of these songs, the moment everything else has been leading up to, the moment when "meaning" is most firmly injected into all this hedonic hollering, the moment that gives most pleasure, for whatever mystifying reason, on repeated listenings—and the truly surprising thing about this album for me is how many repeated listenings it can stand. The dumb words (and there are enough of them) fall away, and a kind of pure white noise stays steady and glows, gives light, gives some kind of nourishment not precisely to be found anywhere else I know of. (If Sonic Youth's *Dirty* is a bold visionary stab in this direction, *In Utero* for me is the more satisfying and enduring realization of—of—whatever. Hopefully next time out S.Y. will again do what they've done best for years, which is up the ante.)

Repetition happens without words, too, of course, usually in the form of that most basic weapon in the rock-and-roll arsenal, the riff. Nirvana execute fat ugly satisfying wall-of-sound riffs on this album with unusual flair, notably on "Very Ape," "Milk It," and "Radio Friendly Unit Shifter." The latter song, particularly on the bridge ("Hate, hate your enemies"), also heightens the normal repeating pulse of a rock rhythm section to a fine intensity so pure it vibrates— not a groove so much as a scarily regular, hysterically rapid shudder. This is the essence of punk (ever experience X live?), and it does live on in whatever you want to call this present wave.

And then there's the normal (in song) repetition of entire song parts, acknowledged in a performance I haven't heard that was once to be the title of this album, "Verse Chorus Verse." Nirvana (Cobain) likes to call attention to this structure by repeating the first verse of a song at the end (saves wear and tear on the lyricist, too). "Heart-Shaped Box," "Frances Farmer," "Dumb," and "Radio Friendly" fit this pattern. And pattern it is. You can read the words to these songs and rightly feel that not a lot's being said here. But when you *listen* to the songs, the craft that's gone into the meticulous, inspired assembly of all the patterns that make up these performances is striking, inescapable. Instant ritual is the goal of the screaming auteur. James Brown was not being unimaginative when he fell down and got up again (fell down and got up again) all those nights after nights. He was invoking something. And provoking it as well. You take a simple riff, simple song, simple action, and repeat it, and play with the natural building-up of energy that repetition provokes. You push your audience until they're screaming, too.

Of course, if they're screaming "Kill the Muslims/Croats/Serbs!" or "Bitches ain't shit but hos and tricks," civilization as we've known it is in for some hard times. Nirvana's variation on this is to come dangerously close to "Kill all racists/sexists/homophobes!" and I believe Cobain may find, like others before him, that when you sing, say, "Born in the U.S.A.," fans don't always hear the irony. Nor is having contempt for your audience likely to do much to enlighten them. "Hate your enemies"? Yeah, I think maybe I understand how you mean that. But I'm a little concerned that my enemies might take the message literally.

Anyway, the whiner-in-chief effectively answers any complaints I might have about him by apologizing in advance. "Everything is my fault / I'll take all the blame." Big of you. "All Apologies" is another masterfully constructed song: melody, lyrics, sonic structure. "In the sum, In the sum, In the sum— Mary!" I don't know how many times they sing/chant "All in all is all we are" (sounds to me like " 'Oh no!' is all we are" in places, and I've heard other hypotheses) at the end of the song and album, since it's buried in the mix before we actually start noticing it, but I hear at least twenty repetitions. Hail Mary full of grace. Who are we, anyway? I think the question needs new asking at regular intervals, and new albums by relatively new artists with new constituencies and new musical vocabularies are an excellent continuing source of updated answers. Uh, but don't get me wrong. I don't listen to this album to try to find out what's going on with kids these days, except insofar as that kid is me. I listen to it to scream along with the questions. I listen to it to get some clue as to how I feel about what's growing in my womb, and what I should do about it. I listen because I admire its artistry. I listen because it gives me a lot of pleasure. I also like the sound of Bob Dylan's voice. No accounting for taste.

"There were giants in the earth in those days . . ." These days will be those days soon enough, of course, but meanwhile *Live* **MCMXCIII** by the **Velvet Underground** (get the two-disc version; don't leave the store until you're *sure* you have the two-disc version) is one of the first genuine rock-and-roll *objects of mystery* to fall into my hands in a long time.

What is this thing? A very long time ago there was a rock band called the Velvet Underground. They recorded four studio albums—one with Nico, two with John Cale, two with Doug Yule, and all four with Lou Reed on vocals and rhythm guitar, Sterling Morrison on lead guitar, and Maureen Tucker on drums (er, except that Maureen didn't actually play on the fourth album, being too pregnant at the time). Their era was 1965–70, they never had anything remotely resembling a hit record, and they are one of the half-dozen greatest and most influential rock-and-roll bands ever to come along from and go away to wherever such beings come and go from and to. I loved them then (well, not at first . . .), I heard them play, my life was altered by their music and by the music of so many others inspired by them, and hey—that's all history and ashes and legend and the dim past.

And now this!

Summer 1993, quite unexpectedly, the four original members of the Velvets got back together and played a Europe-only tour. This album is close to the taper's ideal of a professionally recorded, mixed, and mastered CD of one entire concert—it was actually compiled from three concerts, June 15, 16, and 17, 1993, at L'Olympia Thèatre in Paris. Twenty-three songs on two discs, more than two hours of music, excellently recorded, and, as it happens, a splendid performance. There have been two previous officially released live Velvet Underground albums, *1969*, which is terrific, and *Live at Max's Kansas City*, which I don't care for—and this new one seems to me as worthwhile and pleasurable and quintessential as *1969* even if it doesn't reach the ecstatic peaks of the *1969* versions of "Ocean" and "Heroin." It comes close though. Wow. How can this be?

In my "Ticket to Ride" piece in *100 Best Singles* I asserted that the gestalt that is a rock band is not only a group of persons functioning as a whole that is greater than or other than the sum of its parts, but such a group in and at a particular historical moment. Twenty-three years later, that the world is to some extent ready for the Velvets comes as no surprise to me or anyone else who ever discovered new realms of existence through their music. But that these four individuals can get back together and talk and rehearse after all the changes in their lives and values and self-images and musical tastes and situations and whatnot, and then step onstage and *be* the Velvet Underground, no better, worse, or essentially different than who they/it ever was— This astonishes me. I can't begin to explain it. Simple and straightforward as it is (We decided on these songs, practiced, wrote one new one and some bits of business, and went out on tour), I have no idea where this album came from.

Listen. There will be people who don't appreciate these 1993 performances, just as there are Velvets fans who think it all ended when Cale left after the second album (but don't they have *ears?*), just as there are people who haven't discovered or connected with this body of work at all. (Still not voted into the Rock and Roll Hall of Fame, which is just as well—creepy sort of idea, isn't it?) ("Inside the museums . . . voices echo . . . this is what . . . salvation will be like . . . after a while.") But don't be distracted. Just get the discs and listen. The truth will hit you smack between the ears, probably sooner than later: This is the real thing. This is more of that same stuff I haven't wanted to take off my phonograph in however many years it's been since I first encountered it. Just like the dream of a new first-rate Brian Wilson album, except that (*a*) I never expected this, and (*b*) it's actually happened.

On second thought, and when you examine the history and the circumstances, *every* Velvets album is inexplicable. The recording of "Sister Ray" (which without any possible argument is as far as rock and roll has ever got to in several significant directions) in 1967 is a good example. Sterling Morrison: "We would not accommodate what we were trying to do to the limitations of the studio. We kept on saying we don't want to hear [about] any problems . . . There would be a big brawl over which take to use. Of course, everybody would opt for the takes where they sounded best. It was a tremendous hassle, so on 'Sister Ray,' which we knew was going to be a major effort, we stared at each other and said, 'This is going to be one take. So whatever you want to do, you better do it now.' And that explains what is going on in the mix. There is a musical struggle—everyone's trying to do what he wants to do every second, and nobody's backing off. I think it's great the way the organ comes in. Cale starts to try and play a solo. He's totally buried and there's a sort of surge and then he's pulling out all the stops until he just rises out of the pack. He was able to get louder than Lou and I were. The drums are almost totally drowned out." Okay, that's hip. (Actually, the drums may occasionally be drowned out but I never stop *feeling* them. Three raging male egos and one cool indomitable extraordinary woman banging on her trashcan with true joy, holding it all together at every moment.) But what excuse is there for the fact that it worked so well? Why have so few other musicians, equally crazed, equally talented, ever come close to this, hungry as they must have been for it? What *happened* in that room? No one knows. Or everyone knows. Whatever it was that happened, it was recorded; that's all we know for sure.

And that's also all we know about this 1993 Paris compilation.

It's too soon to say whether this record stands as another miracle in and of itself (as each of the four albums plus 1969 does). But it is unquestionably a substantial addition to the canon. What is most striking about it, apart from its out-of-timeness, is its consistency: one fresh first-rate muscular alive and likable performance after another; not a clinker in the lot in my opinion.

And on the other side of the ledger, nothing that's truly transcendent. "Coyote" comes closest, and "Some Kinda Love," and maybe the feedback rave-up "Hey Mr. Rain." And moments everywhere, like Cale's percussive keyboard on "I'm Waiting for the Man," and the place in that song where the vocal (also Cale?) becomes a whisper. Lotsa delights like that. But not quite transcendent, except maybe sometimes when I'm in just the right mood, which isn't the same as the inevitable awesomeness of "Heroin" on VU1, "Sister Ray" on VU2, "Pale Blue Eyes" on VU3, "New Age" on VU4, "Ocean" on 1969, or "Foggy Notion" from the outtakes album. A lot to live up to. MCMXCIII is not one of those Velvets albums that ends history and forces the world to start over again—not that we expect it to be, but wouldn't that be something?

So what is it? It's jazz, man. It is from-the-heart wide-awake performance. "Cast the first stone." It is an affirmation. Rising to the challenge, not of living up to a reputation, but of making music together. Here and now. This is the mountaintop.

Somehow they never sound for a minute like they're *trying* to be the Velvet Underground. "We're Gonna Have a Real Good Time Together," opening track, immediately and effortlessly finds the groove, that mysterious easy untouchable syncopation of guitar and drums and vocals that is at the heart of the band's identity, nothing to do with their public image, a sound that Lou Reed for example never quite captured on any of his solo albums in my opinion; maybe 'cause he was dodging it or didn't know how wonderful it is for his voice, but probably just 'cause he never had the right rhythm section. Joyous. It appears again on the delectable "Guess I'm Falling in Love" (only Lou Reed and Neil Young can sing lyrics this dumb, this nonsensical, and make me want and need to hear them as ultimately cool and meaningful), and in between is "Venus in Furs," classic Warholian Velvet decadence, slow drone, ugly and exotic on its surface but actually just painfully beautiful, performed exquisitely this particular evening. Found this groove, too, while any imitator would have been still searching for the right neighborhood.

"Afterhours" next, and I love the way the crowd goes crazy when Maureen takes the microphone. Utterly appropriate, because this concert and this album belong to Moe Tucker and Sterling Morrison, the unsung Velvets, whose contributions in terms of both music and personality (sometimes it seems to me that music is personality made audible) are absolutely central to the Velvets' greatness, and whose name recognition in the rock-and-roll pantheon is about on a par with (the equally worthy) Doug Clifford and Stu Cook. And of course Moe, who apparently did much to keep the group on track during this 1993 reunion, is also as pure an example as there could be of a woman in rock and roll making great music way outside of such gender-specific contexts as "chick singer" or "all-girl band."

"All Tomorrow's Parties" is another drone riff, wonderfully played, and given unexpected richness by John Cale's singing, the sound of his voice. (Nico sang this on the first VU album.) Silly words, but the dignity of the melodic and rhythmic structure makes them profound. Cool segue (the sequence of these performances is excellent throughout) into "Some Kinda Love," the powerhouse performance of the set, "Sister Ray"–like drum snap and guitar heroics to die for. Nice amp sound. Call and response between Lou's vocal and Sterling's lead lines. (I assume he's playing lead—guess I could buy the video and check, but you know even if it's great I'll only watch it once. Audio for this kid.) Nine minutes, and after I've heard it I want to turn the volume up a little more and listen again. Ragged glory. Wish they'd write/perform more songs with this groove (different from "Real Good" or "Venus," this is Velvet groove number three). Can't get enough of it. If they ever perform live again, how about a two-hour version of "Sister Ray"? (God, what kind of exercise regimen would it take—at age fifty-plus—to be able to do that?) The only thing that keeps me from playing it over endlessly is that it segues into a deliciously sweet and ragged version of "I'll Be Your Mirror," with Lou's most heartfelt vocal until the encore, and all kinds of wonderful musical moments, particularly the big fuzz guitar after "I see you," and the closing vocal bridge. Oh, those vocal bridges at the ends of Velvets songs! I'm not satisfied with the '93 rendition of the next song, "Beginning to See the Light"; it's fun and I may learn to love it, but for now I'm still too attached to the original version, just wanna hear that phenomenal closing vocal bridge done "right." Well, you know how fans are.

"The Gift" is extremely well done, and I do get impatient with it. How many times can you listen to the same spoken narrative? It's kind of a Velvet tradition to put at least one brain-stopper on each album (*Loaded* the exception), one of the many wrinkles that helped protect them from commercial success, and you know while I like "The Gift," I *love* "The Murder Mystery." And even so it interferes with my listening pleasure, often as not. It's supposed to. We're not meant to get too comfortable here.

"I Heard Her Call My Name" could possibly stand to be a little more uncomfortable—I guess that's a comment on the mix. The drums sound great, though. And in many ways this is a better version than the one on the second album. The structure of the song is reclaimed, without sacrificing the gnarliness. Cool. I have the feeling that if I had a set of tapes from the summer there'd be versions of this as fierce as "Some Kinda Love." Swell "Femme Fatale" (first album very well represented in this show) to close disc one; I like those flat harmony vocals. Same arrangement as ever, and hey, it sure is a good one.

Disc two opens with fifteen and a half minutes of "Hey Mr. Rain," which already had this basic sound back in early '68 when Cale was still in the group (two versions show up on one of the outtakes records). Unlike ten and a half minutes of "The Gift," it seldom makes me restless. Super workout for the Cale attack-the-riff theory of (a)harmonics. As the first successful recording of a major Velvets work (you can't judge 'em by the length of the lyric sheet), a notable event, and once again an intelligent, gutsy, inspired choice. I can't think of another instance where a reunited band (or eternally touring old fogey) has explored their own catalogue so productively. Unfinished business? Hey, let's get to it! I'd like to play this for a young Primus or Pumpkins fan who's never heard the Velvets. Is it as cutting-edge and universal-language as I think, or does everything depend on context? I like the false ending just past the ten-minute mark. This is a very rewarding, very original piece of (unscripted) music.

Not the best "Sweet Jane" the Velvets or Lou Reed have ever done, but it sure sounds good anyway. Closing vocal bridge restored. I guess this is a number three groove. Irresistible. Basic test of a rock-and-roll band (and singer). What makes this song so special? Dunno. Play it again.

"Velvet Nursery Rhyme" an effective koan (Is Lou serious? Is he putting down his fellow band-members? the audience? himself? all of the above? nobody?); good breather in this heavy-hitting sequence, and a fine lead-in to a sparkling performance of "White Light/White Heat," groove number one all the way but with subtle undertones of groove number two (drone riff) playing against it somehow. Chuck Berry's in there, too. A high point. (Love those harmonies.) And then for those really ready for the finer points of the Velvets aesthetic, a truly marvelous "I'm Sticking with You"—Maureen, Sterling, audience participation, soulful Lou, extraordinary climax (love that guitar!), a winner all the way. A lesser group would have left this kind of sloppy inspired magic way behind them or maybe would have tried to recapture the old silliness with predictably dismal results. But the Velvets just act like they can turn it on and off at will. Like time don't exist. It's just a matter of getting in the mood. Spectacular. Mystifying.

The hits keep on happening, as "Black Angel's Death Song," dissonant arhythmic room-clearer from the first album, sweeps in and erases memory, provoking audience gasps and cheers, now a "greatest hit," no less, and yes, it is wonderful. How did they ever have the guts? How do they still? And a first-rate version of "Rock and Roll," still right in the groove. God, I like the way these musicians play together, expressive looping guitar as good as Dickey Betts or Jerry Garcia, that's in one section, fat fuzz progressions somewhere else, Lou scatting until the whole band is with him and it becomes a chant—"It's all right now," way cool—and then before you catch your breath we're in the middle of "I Can't Stand It," with more fabulous guitar/drum tricks, grooves one and three neatly and modestly merged; this one could go right by you, but go back and listen, it's full of wonders. "I'm Waiting for the Man" is similarly excellent (listen carefully, there are wonderful sounds everywhere on this album, new accidents and conscious inventions on every track) (kudos to

Mike Rathke, Roger Moutenot, and Bill Fertig for the mix). "Heroin" sounds okay but I guess something has to be the crowd-pleaser that the singer has trouble getting it up for—I'd say this track is closer to going through the motions (for the band, too) than anything else on the album.

I like the viola on "Pale Blue Eyes," which can't help being beautiful even if the vocal is not exactly the way I want to hear the song performed—lacks sincerity, I think, or else it's just me resisting the reinterpretation. Anyway, all is forgiven, because the final track, "Coyote," newly written by Cale and Reed, offers the best singing of the album (". . . starts to *howl* . . ."), not for any technical reasons but simply because Lou is so extraordinarily present with the song. To my ears it's a major work, full of power, grace, dignity, heart. A fascinating study in how song lyrics reach us. "No tame dog is gonna take my bone." That's perfectly clear, but the payoff line, the one that gives me shivers and a sense that I'm really hearing something that's important to me personally, is, "Cast the first stone." And I know what it means—it means that to keep your wildness and your creativity you have to take action on your own—even if it makes you look bad—you can't wait for the world to approve or tell you what to do. But I know this because I can feel it, and I feel it through the sound of the music, the voice, the totality of voice and instruments and musical structure. Mentally I recognize a contradiction here: the cultural context of the phrase is Christ saying, "Let he who is without sin cast the first stone," to halt the stoning of an adulteress—excellent story, wise and compassionate advice. But the grace of the song is that it's not afraid to contradict the meaning of the familiar phrase, causing all kinds of fruitful tension in the process, so that it isn't required to be about what it used to be about, and indeed even carries a subtext of, "Don't be afraid to reclaim the language." Anyway, monotone or whatever you want to call it, it's great rock-and-roll singing and a beautiful, moving, memorable performance. What a way to walk back into the shadows. Who were those masked persons? Now you see us, now you don't.

The band has left the stage. But they left this recording behind them, just to prove that they really existed.

And now for something completely different. **Zap Mama** is a group of five women of mixed European and African descent, singing a cappella (accompanied only by occasional percussion instruments) in a mixture of at least five languages that often blend or dissolve into pure sound or sounds. Their first album, awkwardly titled **Adventures in Afropea 1** (released in the U.S. on the Luaka Bop/Warner label), is fun to listen to, startling, and deeply rewarding, a successful realization of the unique musical vision of group leader Marie Daulne, who reports that she was inspired by "the double culture from which I come, Walloon and Bantu, Belgian and Zairean," and by her contact with the primarily vocal traditional music of the Pygmy peoples of Central Africa. (The term "Walloon" refers to the French-speaking inhabitants of southern Belgium, whose ancestors are a chiefly Celtic people living there and in nearby parts of France. Zaire is the equatorial African nation once known as the Belgian Congo, many of whose people belong to the Bantu group of tribes. The Pygmies are a separate people and culture, found in Zaire and elsewhere in Central Africa, whose ancient culture is threatened by the incursion of the "triumphant materialism of the modern world.") In a sense this album is an attempt by a modern woman to celebrate and reinvent "traditional African and European melodies" in the fashion of, and perhaps partly from the perspective of, the Pygmy musical sensibility.

It is a bold and very likable celebration, with a breadth and inventiveness that is staggering. (An excellent source of new ideas for the voracious scavengers/recyclers of Western pop, rock, and hip-hop.) If music is personality made audible, I would guess it's the strong personality of Ms. Daulne, and way the joint personality of the group members comes across, that allows this amazing mélange of rhythms and melodies and sources to be accessible and appealing to a relatively parochial American "rock" listener like myself. It is difficult for us (in this we are perhaps alone among all the peoples of the earth) to listen to and enjoy vocal music that is not in our own language. What helps me past this handicap most of the time (some days the album just annoys me, and I don't know why) is, I think, the presence of an engaging intellect with which I can identify, within and behind these voices. While sharing in the eclectic fun these Zaps are having (lots of giggles and playfulness before and after performances), and basking in the sounds of their complex and exotic-but-earthy vocal harmonies, I am also able to make a direct connection with a musical mind that has a very tangible story to tell me. "Listen," she seems to say, "this is from Tanzania, and this from Syria, and this from sixteenth-century Spain, and here are six vocalists imitating the sound of an internal combustion engine on a joyride. And here is a song about melody as an alternative to materialism, based on something I heard young Zairean girls sing while beating the rhythm in the river water. Isn't this planet a wondrous place?"

A quick track-by-track, just to give you a tiny idea of what you might be getting into: "Mupepe" offers four minutes of female chorus repeating steadily, "Ay yai ya ay ah ay / Ay yai ya ay ah oh," a canvas on which the lead singer first hums openmouthed (stretch those vocal cords, find the notes, invoke those melodic muses), then her sounds become words, rhythmic, repetitive, attractive word-sounds in what may be Pygmy or Zulu. Soon her voice is soaring, dancing, sudden slides and bright bursts ("wo tah!"), lots of melody but nothing I can hum easily, especially with the melodic chant counterpointing constantly, nor can I pick up the words, don't hear the title word, can't be sure of consonants or vowels on the words I do hear. Structure, but an elusive one. She gets gentle, whispers, then starts talking (not singing) in French; at one point I think she says (in French), "One waits one moment, and hears everything." Then a passage of heavy breathing, then notes, and then singing in the first language again, beautiful sounds, gentle and liquid and sparkling, chorus to the forefront then vanishing as the grunts return and singing voice and song trail off. The liner notes say, ". . . from a Central African Pygmy chant." Feelings are communicated. "Bottom" next, a round in English—"The boat goes to the bottom, to the bottom, and people don't care, standing in the middle of the . . ."—written by Jean-Louis Daulne. Female chorus sings the verse, solo voice scats wildly in response to and over them, chorus breaks up into parts at times, fascinating, effective, and somehow it seems much longer than a minute and a half. Third song—"Brrrlak!"—offers great onomatopoeia, and all kinds of singing voices interacting in complex segments that manage to sound loose and very free and at the same time brilliantly and carefully orchestrated (all arrangements by Marie Daulne). Don't know what the song is saying, or even what languages it's in, but I like it a lot.

"Abadou" is a Syrian song, strong Middle Eastern feeling, but against a Pygmy chant. Great percussive vocal sounds. All kinds of stuff in all these songs. And the arrangements work so well. Shifts and changes. Very demanding! Stretch your listening. And very basic and primal at the same time, something speaks directly to the molecular level. "Take Me Coco" was written by Celine 'T Hooft, another member of Zap Mama, and takes a new approach to the blending of chant and vocalizations. Words in African, English, and phonics. "All night I'm dreaming of you." "Te co co co co te te te, ayo ayo." Sometimes all these new sounds just overwhelm me; Zap Mama is definitely hit-and-miss as background music, occasionally perfect, often impossible. When I give my attention, however, I am rewarded and rewarded. Inventions, feelings, new stories, new journeys into the heart of human communication and music.

"Plekete" is the motorcar narrative, funny, brilliant. "Mizike" is the river-music song, lovely: "This is the story of those invaded by machinism . . . There's a friend, it's called melody. Hey! Mr. Music, come dance with me." Touch of Bob Marley, and yes, this music shares his fiercely local/universal vision. "Babanzele" is a long, almost pure Pygmy chant, recorded in the Belgian forest—a kind of centerpiece for the album, touchstone, but so is the one-minute Spanish church music that follows ("Din Din"), touching something deep in my European roots; both performances about the holiness of music, and the humanness of holiness. I like the organic body percussion on "Babanzele."

"Din Din" 's minute of great beauty and stillness flows into "I Ne Suhe" 's minute of earthy grunting humor, like something from the Beach Boys' *Smile* album. In your face. "Guzophela," one of the prettiest songs on the album, I wouldn't have guessed was "an anti-apartheid song" if the liner notes didn't say so. Life-affirming. Mostly Zulu, but the English part is charming. "I wanna dance, don't wanna cry." I like the way the languages as well as the voices dance together and play off each other.

"Nabombeli Yo." Hypnotic. Moving. Funny. How smoothly and brightly these Zaps switch gears; I mean within the songs, instant to instant. These performances (the last three are "Marie-Josee," "Ndje Mukanie," and "Son Cubano") are not about some faraway alien land or culture—they are about universal, everyday realities, accessed along paths that are ancient to some but radically new to us. Cross-culturalism is not quaint; it's cutting-edge. Welcome to the twenty-first century. Zap Mama's first album is a delight and a revelation.

Sometimes I think I have a complaint about **Prince**'s new three-CD compilation, *The Hits/The B-sides*, but then I listen to it some more and am surprised at my own desire to squirm away from the obvious: It's an embarrassment of riches. Is this guy a genius? Probably. Has he failed to live up to his own potential, much of the time? You certainly could say so. Is this compilation the perfect representation of his first fifteen years of recording? Nah. Should we bother with it anyway? Oh God, yes. It's an amazing collection of music. And it immediately becomes the new starting place for any consideration of Prince's body of work as a whole.

I'll go out on a limb and say, for the sake of argument, that three major artists emerged in rock in the 1980s and have survived into the 1990s: U2, R.E.M., and Prince. (Who else? Some are very good, but not strong enough to be central: Los Lobos, for example. Others are central but not good enough to make the list: Guns 'N Roses, Michael Jackson, Madonna.) Of these, R.E.M.'s body of work is actually the least messy—easiest to grasp, most consistent, though we may disagree sharply as to high points and low points. U2's body of work is somewhat tangled; with their shifts in image from sincere young turks to overblown (but imaginative) rock stars, it's hard to sort out one's feelings unless you're firmly in the "love 'em" or "hate 'em" camps, but still it's not hard to hold the set of all their albums in one's mind—*this* is their recording career so far.

Prince's body of work is far more complex, more difficult to form into any sort of mental picture. Leaving aside the stuff he wrote and produced for other artists, we're still confronted with a tangle of 12-inch singles, B-sides, unreleased albums, soundtracks, and a list of official releases (albums) that goes as follows: *For You, Prince, Dirty Mind, Controversy, 1999, Purple Rain, Around the World in a Day, Parade, Sign o' the Times, Lovesexy, Batman, Graffiti Bridge, Diamonds and Pearls*, and *Squiggle*. Which is my favorite? Well, it's either *Dirty Mind*—which first made me a Prince fan and still sounds terrific (even though it's only a half-hour long and several tracks are filler)—or else none of the above. Specifically, I think my favorite Prince album would be, if I could ever hook up the necessary wires to make myself a copy, the live *Sign o' the Times*, the soundtrack from the extraordinary film/videotape, never released as an audio recording. Oh well. I like *Parade* quite a bit, but it's not a great album. (A great artist should occasionally make a great album, don't you think?) *Diamonds and Pearls* was hard for me to get into, but Jonathan says it's a monster and I should give it another try. *Lovesexy*'s been waiting for years for me to give it another try—the all-one-track format of the CD is definitely a big stumbling block—but "Alphabet Street" and "Escape" on the compilation both sound so wonderful I may finally overcome my irritation. *Graffiti Bridge* is the only one I've actually sold as a used CD (but I like "Thieves in the Temple" and am glad it's on the compilation). I never bought *Batman* in the first place and am delighted it's almost completely excluded from the new collection. Anyway, to make a long confused rambling story short: If I had to settle for one Prince album, it would be *The Hits/The B-Sides*. And if I had to settle for just one disc, taken as a whole as a listening experience and not just as a container for favorite songs, it would be disc three, "The B-sides," which happens to be the only one of the three discs that you can't buy by itself (gotta shell out for the whole overpriced "box"). Another stumbling block. It's not a coincidence. Prince's whole strategy for survival, it seems to me, has been and continues to be playing hard-to-get.

I like this three-disc set *a lot.* I've been playing it plenty for months, and as I do I enjoy it more and more all the time, and my attention keeps moving to new songs or new groupings of songs. There's a lot here. And lots of things I want to talk about. Where to begin?

Prince needs to be listened to on his own terms. This is difficult to do, at least partly because he's done such an effective job of masquerading as a pop star for all these years, and that's not really what he is (and so one is constantly distracted, sometimes not hearing the grace and originality in the music because of annoyance at his poses or disappointment at unkept pop promises), and also partly because those terms are difficult to define. One of the great successes of *The Hits/The B-sides* is that by offering a temporal cross-section of this artist's work (for the first time), it goes a long way towards allowing us a larger and more appropriate sense of who he is, what contexts he works in, what it is he's doing. I hesitate to put words on it, but oh well, I think it's fair to say that "experimental composer" is a lot closer to the mark than "pop personality." Prince Rogers Nelson— known as "Prince" for the first decade and a half of his career (as semidocumented on this set, though six discs probably would not have been enough to give a true picture, especially since, like Picasso, Prince kept at least one major work for his private collection for every one he released to the public)—is a creative genius working as an experimental composer in the contemporary media available to him (live and programmed instruments and vocals plus mixing board in the home studio, with a significant sideline of orchestrated/spontaneous audio and visual live theatrical performance with vocalists and a band). The cognitive language of his work (lyrical, visual) is almost exclusively sexual, a rather formal language in its way, comparable to little else in contemporary music except perhaps James Brown's stubborn and brilliant, endlessly inventive formalism. Prince's noncognitive, musical, visceral language is very much connected to the dance floor, music as a free-form script for the motion of bodies, listener/participant bodies as opposed to performers. He doesn't compose for a dance troupe, except to some extent when staging a tour or film or video. He composes for ears and minds riding steady like gyroscopes atop bodies in motion, individual humans expressing sexuality and spirituality and consciousness of their existence by *dancing*. He stays close to his muse by dancing with her himself, not just in his work, but in the rooms where the DJs rule and lonely hearts seek to lose themselves or find each other or find God or get off or all of the above. He is in that sense part of a community of artists; he listens to and is influenced by what his contemporaries are doing (as the Beatles and the Stones did in their bright moment). His work exists in reference to a tapestry of dance music and popular music, primarily American, past and present. He listens (often to himself). He dreams. And he invents. The evidence is that, like Picasso, like Matisse, like Ellington or Davis or Dylan, he works constantly.

The results of his work are spectacular. And often frustrating. The hugeness of Prince's heart is apparent in an occasional masterwork like "When Doves Cry" or "When You Were Mine." But for the most part this relatively young artist (he's thirty-three) avoids real (personal) intimacy and vulnerability and gives us instead brilliantly crafted, imaginative, groundbreaking constructions in a language that refers to our common experiences of sexual desire and sexual sharing and sexual vulnerability without quite opening the Pandora's box of his own feelings at the moment that he's writing and singing. So this is my sometime complaint. I remember getting my hands on a similar compilation by another living, working artist, Neil Young's *Decade*, and being tremendously moved by the things I was hearing for the first time (as well as the rediscovery of old songs in a new context). "Winterlong," "Deep Forbidden Lake," "Like a Hurricane" (I had an advance copy of *Decade*, pre–*American Stars and Bars*), "Star of Bethlehem." Such richness, so much *feeling*. Prince is visceral in a very rewarding way, the grooves and beats he achieves and creates are tonics for our corporeality (yay, bodies!), but he is not yet a master of feelings. For me he came closest on *Parade* (though he might say *Lovesexy*, according to the almost autobiographical *Hits/B-sides* liner notes written by his friend and employee Alan Leeds), but he stopped short, held back (he was busy making a movie, but if it hadn't been that, he'd have been busy making more music), and then, characteristically, changed direction. So I'm acknowledging that a lot of the time I've wanted more from Prince than what I've actually gotten. But I also need to acknowledge that this was partly because I expected him to deliver it to me, as the Beatles did (they really were pop stars), as Neil Young has done in between periods of withdrawal and reluctance. Prince actually requires us to work a little harder, and I'm beginning to understand this better thanks to this retrospective, and I'm also perhaps learning new ways to listen to him that will make me a better receptor for all his tireless giving.

"Cream" is an astonishing performance. It is one of the few unmistakably classic singles of the 1990s—not in my singles book because, although it was a big hit, although I was a sometime Prince fan (going through a skeptical period), although I asked friends and strangers to recommend singles for my book, especially recent ones, I somehow remained unaware of it. This reflects poorly on me, I'm sure (hey, I never claim to be Mr. Up-to-date), but it also reflects the fragmentation of the contemporary American pop-music audience. At one time one could not have avoided awareness of a song like this. It would have been everywhere, saturating its moment. Those days weren't quite gone when "When Doves Cry" (one of the last truly universal hits of the rock era) came out in 1984, but they're gone at present. Oh well. Everything about this record is perfect. The beat, the (male) orgasm at the beginning, the beat, the tone of the vocal, the harmony vocals, the chorus, the lyrics ("cream . . . get on top"), the relentlessness, the innocence ("you're filthy cute and baby you know it"), the pure joy. The beat. The classic rock/pop/soul arrangement. "Sh-boogie bop." The echoes and the guitar on the last chorus. Oh, everything. I can play it over and over and over and just get deeper into the groove and the mood. It's fabulous.

I am also very fond at present of the sequence of songs near the end of disc two, starting with "Peach" (unreleased, probably recent), then "U Got the Look" (1987), "Sexy M.F." (1992), "Gett Off" (1991), "Cream" (1991), and "Pope" (unreleased, definitely recent). It occurs to me, looking at this list, that pop singles, like science fiction, require a "willing suspension of disbelief" on the part of the listener. This is a fantasy world, lyrically and aurally, and subtle shifts in how we feel towards the storyteller this time around determine to a surprising degree our ability to participate in and get pleasure from even the most well-crafted fantasy. I suffered from mixed feelings in relation to the Beatles throughout their career (sorry!), and so upon release and most of the time thereafter, "Lady Madonna" or "Yellow Submarine" could leave me cold whereas "Get Back" and "Eight Days a Week" charmed the socks off of me. Go figure. I can sympathize with someone, Prince fan or otherwise, being irritated by any of these songs (except "Cream"; you gotta like "Cream" the way you gotta like "Ticket to Ride" or "Hey Jude"), unwilling to grant the premise (lyrical/melodic/rhythmic/structural/attitudinal/sonic) on which it rests its tricks and triumphs and delights. But hey. I love this stuff. "Peach" for me is a gorgeous rocker on the classic theme of dance-floor lust (unusual for Prince in that this narrator totally cops to his own feelings of inadequacy), in the solid tradition of "Little Queenie" and "Brown Sugar" and "I Wish You Could Have Seen Her Dance." Great Chuck Berry tribute (rock and roll is not dead), and I personally find the grunt track stimulating and funny and tasteful. And that descending progression into (and out of) the chorus. So fine. Tracks like this and "Cream" achieve unself-conscious universality for me (song becomes your own, you can go wherever you want with it), but it does all come down to that suspension of disbelief (cool or uncool? friend or foe?) I suspect. "U Got the Look" seemed weak to me in its side two leadoff (I Am a Hit Single) position on *Sign o' the Times*, but now its pop posturing slides down real easy; I feel at home and in the groove with it and keep noticing new things to like.

"Sexy Motherfucker" is way ambitious, disguised as standard, more of the same I-want-you shock-the-squares funk riffing, but listen to what's happening here. Prince has flirted with uptempo horns before, but never so successfully—definitely a James Brown tribute par excellence—but whereas "Peach" is a kind of throwback, perfect in itself but happily going nowhere, "Sexy M.F." is totally contemporary, it opens doors; other performer/composers hear this and, consciously and subconsciously both, they respond. Same for "Gett Off," and the sequencing here (reverse chronology) is interesting and inspired. Prince, like any good DJ, approaches the creation and exploration of a beat with the seriousness of a particle physicist. Breakthroughs are subtle and arcane but their impact on us, the public, can be massive. And the beat is just the foundation. I love the melodic flute riff, and Prince's funny semi-rapping. Most remarkable here, and throughout this collection (listen to "1999" again), is the way Prince uses multiple lead vocals, either by recording 'em as joint leads and then twisting knobs to bring 'em up and down, as on "1999," or by giving people parts in advance so a live or partially live performance is achieved, which seems to be happening on "Gett Off." There are hallowed traditions for backup vocals and harmonies and split leads and echoing voices in rock and soul, most deriving originally from gospel; future toilers in these fields will trace their influences back to gospel, as always, fifties vocal groups, sixties pop and rock, seventies soul, and the complete works of Prince. His innovations are marvelous, legion, so natural as to seem obvious and, I predict, enduring. Meanwhile this is also, of course, another celebration of sexuality, and I feel called upon to note that Prince unlike so many others does not limit himself to female body imagery to invoke sexuality. His songs ("Gett Off" and "Cream" are obvious examples) are rich in imagery of the sexual male body, something genuinely rare in heterosexual literature/popular art, I think, especially in such a direct, unself-conscious (no snickering) fashion. His lyrics may seem pandering when listened to superficially, and I'm not suggesting there's great hidden significance here—rather I'm saying that, in sharp contrast to most of what floods the airwaves (and Prince could get some credit or blame for the taboo-breaking that made the current exploitation glut possible), the stuff Prince turns out seems to me intrinsically healthy. I mean, I'm not suggesting one-night stands, which "Get Off" explicitly refers to, are good for your spirit or your chances of maintaining your physical health. Rather, I'm saying Prince tends to portray male and female sexuality and sexual power and sexual neediness, etcetera, in a manner that gives equal value to both, especially when one listens to several of his songs together. There's a respect here for both sexes that is uncommon in songs dealing with this subject matter. You could grab lines out of context and dramatically prove the opposite, I suppose, but I'll stand by my assessment. Telling the truth about sex is in a certain sense just about impossible for any of us, but Prince, if you grant the fantasy context that he's consciously working in, his special language of desire and interaction, actually seems to me one of the more balanced and honest voices currently barking in the wilderness.

"Pope" is way, way cool. ("You can be the president; I'd rather be the Pope / You can be the side effect; I'd rather be the dope." Wow.) Not yet released as a single, this should be a huge hit, but nothing is certain these days. Kind of a cross between hardcore rap and a good Madonna single, with a handful of R.E.M. (à la "Ignoreland" or "It's the End of the World") thrown in, delicious beat and very intelligent. I don't know what most of it means, but in just the right way, the way that hints and fascinates and stimulates; whereas to the extent that I don't know what "7" means I get the strong feeling that I'd be disappointed if I found out. Oh. "Pope" 's not like that. It's tuned in to something, rich with the mysterious and unmistakable flavor of our moment, and the more I listen, the more pleasure it gives. More songs like this, please.

Disc three, "The B-sides," is frustrating at first if you're a Prince fan, because many if not most of these tracks were twice as long in their original version. Jonathan cites "La, La, La, He, He, Hee" as a favorite of his that's cut off here just before the good part starts, the payoff for all that buildup. I found myself missing the original "Erotic City," long a favorite of mine, until at least the seventh or eighth time I played the album, and then I began to feel at home with this four-minute version and aware of how well it works for this context. "Girl" is another one I have as a 12-inch, and first of all, I've listened to it far more since I got the compilation than I ever did in the eight years that I've owned the single, and second of all, the longer version is fun but the new short version is actually a better song. Let's just say that it would be very desirable and appropriate for Warner or whoever to someday release a collector's box of three or more CDs with all the full-length B-sides and other outtakes (and remixes—I've got a twenty-one-minute version of "America" here that's a trip); and in the meantime why not accept the artist's decision to create something new here, a seventy-six-minute album made up of twenty songs, B-sides recorded between 1980 and 1989, all of them clocking in between three and five minutes, thoughtfully sequenced (not chronological), an album as long and as varied and, surprisingly, as well-integrated (there's a unity of feeling to it) as anything Prince has done.

It's a wonderful album. Many of the songs are so intentionally outrageous ("Scarlet Pussy," "Feel You Up") that the first time I heard it, it sounded like a novelty record, a bunch of weird jokes that presumably would get old fast. But no. Another listen or two and the songs started growing on me, the melodies, the performances, the arrangements, the idiosyncracies that give each track a special and, for the most part, mysteriously attractive character. In their own way, these B-sides are just as hook-y as the A-sides (the hits). Great love and attention has gone into each one, and (ahem) spurting gobs of *imagination*. Perhaps one reason this record is so good is that the B-side is a perfect medium for Prince. It's a prankster's playground, an open public space of pure freedom, no censorship issues, it doesn't have the responsibility of selling itself (that's A's job), it's the bonus, the "extra" track—and at the same time it has that focus of being a track by itself, not part of a larger album. Prince loves to create one song at a time, all his attention on a single project, twenty-four hours

before a single canvas, sketching and erasing and redrawing and mixing the colors . . . I actually think he can *feel* his audience more
clearly when he's thinking B-side than when he's doing a song for an
album. The album's a general idea; the song a very specific one. Of
course not all these songs knew they were going to be B-sides when
they were being recorded, but . . . There's an unself-conscious magic
here, a power, that seems directly related to the particular combination of private and public space, hidden and open, that a B-side
embodies. "I Love U in Me" ("and she say, 'Oooh-oooh, I love U in
me' ") is a very graphic image, even for Prince, and from it he creates
such a tender and likable confection, really one of his better songs.
His slow dreamy falsetto stuff oftens goes over the top for me, but
this one is so sweet and simple and on purpose. There's a very female
quality in the performance, but not in a campy way; instead we feel
his receptive pleasure at her gently aggressive response to him. The
song is about, evokes the spirit of, interaction, particularly that te-
lepathy that occurs when two bodies are touching each other in so
many places and with such delicious attention and consciousness. I
become you, I feel you becoming me. That's a cliché, but this song
isn't; it's funny/absurd at times ("when she's making love it's like
surgery") but it never stumbles in its essential beauty, its extraordinary
musical texture. It's one of a kind. And so are all these songs on disc
three, from the bounciness and uncharacteristic directness of "Hello"
(Prince explains why his bodyguard grabbed that photographer, and
how he feels about being a public figure) to the bracingly comic
musical feast of "Shockadelica" ("the bed's on fire, your fate is
sealed . . .") to the fierce melodic beauty of "The Tears in Your Eyes,"
performed live in the studio with bandmates Wendy and Lisa. In
several cases (tracks two through five) the sound of an entire album
is neatly summed up in a song that didn't happen to get included on
the album in question. And each song flows into the next so com-
fortably, Prince's eclecticism often makes for awkward albums in
which certain tracks just bring everything to a halt, but not this time.
I might wish for "Another Lonely Christmas" to be a little shorter
but otherwise the seventy-six minutes zip by like an excited conversation with an old friend; if anything, I find myself wanting to go
back and listen more carefully to whichever song just played—I
missed some of the hooks that time, I want to experience them again.

I'm still not exactly sure what it is I like about this guy, why his
experiments are so much fun and so satisfying to listen to. Or why I
(and the public at large—this album doesn't seem to be selling well,

in any of its configurations) seem to periodically lose patience with him, shunning his new work only to discover later that I'd been cheating myself. He's different, that's all. He may sell lots of records some of the time, but he doesn't fit anybody's preconceptions. He's an original, a prodigious primal source of creative energy who can't be harnessed to any purpose other than his own enigmatic agenda. And he loves music. Probably even more than he loves sex although, happily, they're not mutually exclusive. Anyway, this set of CDs has given me a new start in my exploration of his musical universe, and I appreciate that a lot. New answers; new questions. I also recommend it for sheer listening pleasure. A feast. Take off your dress and your disbelief for a moment or two and dive on in.

And finally, here's an album that fascinates me and tweaks my sense of wonder even though it's not very well suited to my musical tastes (and doesn't ultimately have the power to expand or redefine my musical tastes, as most of the other artists mentioned in this essay have successfully done at one time or another). My friend Jean Trouillet in Frankfurt, the best world-music disc jockey I've ever encountered, turned me on to **Apache Indian** and his first album **No Reservations** a few months back, and the time I've spent with it since then has been a continuing education in the role and the power of music in this planetary community we can't help but live in.

Apache Indian (unaware of or unconcerned about the inappropriateness of his moniker to American ears—in fact you could say in a sense he's reclaiming the word from the Americans who have given it their own meaning and broadcast same via movies all over the world) is a young British resident of East Indian descent who evidently discovered dancehall reggae on the streets and in the clubs of Birmingham. Dancehall reggae is as related to rap music as it is to seventies-style reggae, although I guess if you place it (properly) in the "toasting" tradition you can leave hip-hop and New York City right out of the picture. Seems the style in Jamaica is (or was—I'm an idiot, don't take my word for any of this) for a DJ (meaning in this case the singer, not the record-spinner) to rap or croon over a prerecorded "riddim" track, in the studio or on the dancehall stage, electronic age on the one hand and totally a street-personality thing on the other. If you have a lot of talent *and* ego *and* balls (and luck) you may get your moment in the sun, and it probably won't last long. But you'll sing/talk with all the innocent brightness and soul of a fifties doo-wop group for as long as you can hold the brothers' and sisters' attention.

What's exciting about Apache is that he has simultaneously embraced Jamaican culture and his ethnic Indian identity and roots, and has made an impact. His first single, "Movie Over India," in 1990, apparently got a decent reception in Jamaica and was a hit in India ("number one in all the Bombay charts," he sings in a follow-up single, "Chok There"). This introduced modern reggae to India and made Apache a star in his native country, but what really intrigues me is the effect on his (many) contemporary bloods back in Birmingham and the other mean streets of the U.K. Suddenly (I imagine, I fantasize) in the minds of both the young Indian immigrants and their multicultural contemporaries (Jamaicans, native Brits, Pakistanis, et cetera, et cetera) you could be Indian and also be hip, or bad, or cool, or down . . . Music gives visibility, music gives identity. And melts old barriers. Apache isn't just a rapper or dancehall DJ who happens to be Indian; he makes being Indian the whole focus of his rhymes and his presentation. He creates his own patois—the songs are in English, but it's dancehall Jamaican English in style and crammed full of words and sentences and slang from India (Hindi?) and (presumably) from the local immigrant dialect. I don't know what "chok there" means, and I'm not sure anyone would (Indian or British or Jamaican) until they heard the song, and then it's crystal-clear. The language itself charms (rap and dancehall are in some ways a rediscovery of the power of the word, that is, of the *sound* of the word, direct mumbo-jumbo transcending side issues like content): "Me say ick, thor, thin / Me say char, ponj, shar / Fe all the Indian and all the Karlair / Nuff DJ them a have fe them own stylee / Some a wa-da da-da deng some a come folla me / And some a them a say O lord a mercy, p-numina ick p-numina thor 'n also in a three / But anytime me came me bring a bran stylee / And anything me say you have fe ball after me / Chok there . . ."

I like the rhythm of the language, the flow of word-sounds and the very personal consciousness this rhythm/flow/story communicates. The musical content (apart from the music of the language) is not as interesting. "Chok There," "Fix Up," "Feel It Fe Real," and "AIDS Warning" are the tracks I most enjoy listening to, with other moments here and there (the chorus of "Guru," "don a don a prophet a prophay," gets into my blood somehow; I don't consider "catchy" high praise but it's the right word for the more attractive tunes here). The lyrical content is interesting mostly because it runs counter to my expectations, opens me to a world full of attitudes more complex than or different from my prejudices. "Arranged Marriage" is a bold and appropriate subject for a song, and I can see the other kids from the subcontinent digging on having the subject acknowledged (how alien all these Western love songs must seem, that never consider such matters). But I'm surprised that this punky kid is all for it, and without irony . . . except for the one cute line, "When is the best time to tell me girlfriend?" (that his mum and dad have found him a wife). I appreciate the boldness of his anti-alcohol lecture, "Drink Problems," and am struck by the (presumably effective) appeal to racial pride on which he bases his argument. "AIDS Warning" is very catchy and most worthy (and not at all uncool; some of the sexual description is quite funny), though I wonder when he says "You have fe know about the AIDS upon the island," does this mean he is singing to Jamaicans only? To British youths, too, but not residents of India (certainly not an island)? Or is he taking on the *role* of a Jamaican DJ, with the idea that U.K. and subcontinental listeners will also think of themselves as metaphorical Jamaicans—I mean maybe "the island" is the planet? I'm intrigued. "Fix Up" seemed to me at first a great satire on the "Excuse me! You better fix up yourself" attitude of Indian immigrant parents and employers, the older generation, but a closer listen has Apache himself unironically giving his listeners this advice. (Or maybe there's subtle irony, not contradicting his message but acknowledging that he does sound like his parents but hey, that's cuz he actually believes they're right, "so listen, ragamuffin . . .") The point, anyway, is that Apache's innate conservatism is utterly consistent with his strong cultural identification, but at odds with my prejudices about what youthful music should or is likely to express. Us liberals, if that's the right word, tend to assume that the poor people of the world or at least the young people of the world (or the young poor people) (or the hip young people) will naturally share our values. What is rock and roll or youth-oriented pop music about if not rebellion against conformity? (Or anyway, the image of rebellion, conforming though that may actually be.) Well, watch out. Fascist (i.e., hatemongering) rock and roll is already an issue in parts of Germany and will be soon in other formerly "communist" countries. And the U.S. dance-music community is still trying to come to terms with a very popular Jamaican dancehall singer and his popular song ("Boom Bye Bye," Buju Banton) that celebrates getting rid of homosexuals in a very direct manner. Such a song is obviously undesirable in terms of what people like you and me believe is right, and since we like the singer, we hope he'll apologize and retract. But it ain't easy for us to understand that, as *Source* magazine points out, to the Jamaican dancehall community, "any apology by Buju to the gay lobby in the U.S. would be an act of treason, a capitulation to an imperialistic force bent on imposing an unwelcome lifestyle upon the fiercely-proud Jamaican people."

The world is not America writ large, nor is it a place full of quaint peoples who may someday mature into American values (liberal or conservative). We are ourselves insular, righteous, unaware of other ways of seeing things. As India and Jamaica (odd couple indeed) are linked by a kid in England paradoxically promoting cultural pride via an alien (but strangely appealing) music and style of talking, and as other ethnic kids in England discover some pride of their own thereby, we see Third World learning from Third World the language of pride (asserted identity) and its tremendous value in terms of survival. Survival in the face of alien values, in a world in which the tribes must increasingly intermingle and coexist. Of course we all know music promotes understanding. I think I'm saying that perhaps the misunderstandings it promotes and brings to the surface can be equally valuable, as steps towards a true communication and respectful (hard-fought) coexistence that has nothing to do with teaching the world to sing about Coca-Cola. There is a truth in "pop" music, in the simple fact that things become popular somewhat under their own steam. No one forced the fans in India to pick up on what Apache introduced; he just reached 'em, that's all. "An so me chatta mon fe everybody." A kind of truth that can possibly infiltrate and begin to crack open all kinds of ignorance, prejudice, righteousness . . . even our own. I mean, this is just dance music, right? It's dumb. It doesn't really have a message. Well, yes and no. (I mean, Apache's stuff is classically corny at times, but there's still that languaging . . .) I don't know. And that's all I'm trying to say, that I'm in touch with a new, slightly unfamiliar level of "I don't know" thanks to this strange (catchy) cross-cultural object, and I like that.

Stories. I guess I like to talk. Oh well. On behalf of myself, and Bob Dylan, and Prince, and Nirvana and the Velvets and the Zaps and Apache and all the rest of the posse, I'd like to thank you for listening. And for requiring me to listen (I need this sense of obligation, y'know, otherwise for me even listening to music I like gets put off to some never-arriving future moment).

Maybe the scariest thing about listening is that if I really hear something, I might feel the need to share it. And I might or might not find someone to share it with me. That's what *World Gone Wrong* (song and album) are about, I think. Life is risk. Disappointment is probable. "All the friends I ever had are gone." And yet . . .

Coyote goes to the mountaintop. Okay, all right, let's make another album.

5

WHAT THE VINTNERS BUY

The thoughts in this book are not mine. They came freely to me, and I give them freely away. I have no "intellectual property," and I think that all claimants to such property are thieves.

—Wendell Berry

I wonder often what the vintners buy
One half so precious as the stuff they sell.

—Fitzgerald, *Omar Khayyam*

The aesthetic news is encouraging. Something strong and pure and intelligent is coming through. If one reads or watches the news of the day, one would hardly believe it, because the news drug is a constant downer, with interludes of panic thrown in to stimulate the addiction. Something weak and impure and unintelligent blares from "the media" constantly, till we think it's our own thoughts we're hearing, our own perception of reality. It isn't. Turn that stuff off. There are many wondrous things going on even as we sit here.

I think we vote with our attention, and more often than every two years.

The seven artists (musicians, performers, songwriters) who've had my attention for the last few months are what I mean when I use the word "information." One of these albums is a reissue; the other six are all current, all by artists who are relatively young (twenties and thirties) and each of whom has a distinct musical character that unavoidably is received and felt as a "message." Or a set of messages.

There's a lot of wide-awake music coming out. And much of the best of it is coming from new faces, new voices. Songs have a mysterious ability to be both enduring and disposable. They allow a certain intensity of consumption (brief period of saturation, two weeks, six weeks) that is good for the soul. You lose yourself, you reappear. And on to a different song or album. For this good game we need a steady supply of energetic, inventive artists who also have something to share. No problem. Not this year, anyway . . .

Most encouraging. Am I making a mistake to look this gift horse in the mouth? I wanna know how the process works. I want to share with you all the moods and speculations that these songs—"Third Reel," "UFO Suite," "Fuck and Run," "Mr. Jones"—stir up in my mind and body. I feel very alive this month. I know there's an explanation here somewhere.

Let's start with "Mr. Jones," as it's the one more of you are likely to have heard already, assuming you ever listen to the radio (I don't, actually). "Mr. Jones," by **Counting Crows**, is a hit, in that funny modern way that a song becomes a hit without necessarily being released as a single, and it has propelled this unknown group's debut album, *August and Everything After*, solidly into the Top Ten (platinum status soon). I saw these guys open for Bob Dylan a couple of times, almost two years ago, and I liked them. So did Donna. Most of the other friends who saw the shows were indifferent. Heard a rumor some days later that they were signed to Geffen for what sounded like big money—$200,000—for an unknown act. Who knows how they decide these things? I liked the lead singer's presence, and some of the songs came through pretty well, considering the obstacles of loud unfamiliar ensemble rock in front of someone else's audience.

And then the record came out, even got good reviews, and still I didn't pick it up right away; you know how conservative we can all be when it's our money. Finally I was trading in a used CD with a glitch and saw a copy of this and figured, Okay, guess I'll give it a try. Maybe the artsy title and cover had slowed me down a little.

Not right away after I brought it home, but eventually, I gave it a few spins, was surprised and impressed but also uncomfortably caught up in the "Who do they remind me of so much?" game during the early listens. I'd seen a lot of Van Morrison comparisons, skimming the press, but that wasn't quite it for me—familiar but elusive. (That's how I felt when first listening to Buffalo Springfield: Gee, this is exactly like something I used to like a lot, but what?) Eventually I settled on early Bruce Springsteen, "For You" and "Sandy" live and I dunno, maybe "Lost in the Flood," and especially whoever it was *he* seemed to be trying to sound like then. The Band? Procol Harum? R.E.M. before they were invented? Ah, it's a hopeless game and disturbing somehow and I felt defensive liking this so-derivative album, but that passed and after a few more listens it no longer sounded like anybody but Counting Crows, most of the time.

And meanwhile people were telling me they'd heard this song that refers to Bob Dylan directly in a name-check and half-directly in the title, on the radio, or MTV, more than once, and suddenly this hundred-to-one long shot was coming in, like Geffen Records knew exactly what they were doing, buying this group with no buzz. They'd heard the songs.

I like the Crows' album a lot and I'm still nervous about it. When I first fell in love with it (that classic discovery experience, stray melodic hooks and bits of lyric stubbornly sticking in my brain, making me long to hear them again, gentle insistent desire for reunion and release), I was enthusiastic and at the same time wondering if I would get real tired of this after a few more listens. There's a slickness to it that sits uncomfortably with me at times, even while I'm enjoying what I'm hearing. And then song and album became a hit, and you know how hard it is to stay excited about something new when the rest of the world suddenly jumps into your little romantic moment. You wanna be considered a cool cat, it's safest to stay on the fringes. And yet I have this affection for the *universality* of this musical medium . . .

Still nervous, and still enjoying the hell out of this record. I have a friend who's decided that the single's great but the rest of the album doesn't measure up, but that's not how it feels to me. Oh yeah, "Mr. Jones" is special, gives me that "turn up the volume" rush, but I can get almost as excited and intrigued and sloppy affectionate about the other three openers (CD programming tip: Front-load the sucker. Most of the time most people hear the first two-thirds of what would have been side one at least twice as much as they hear the rest of the record): "Round Here," "Perfect Blue Buildings," and "Omaha"— good retro title; who doesn't dream of being the group that Moby Grape looked like they'd mature into? And I find lots to like in the rest of the album, too, even if maybe I'd be happier if they'd shortened the total experience a little. Jeez, albums are long these days. But don't cut the last song. "A Murder of One" has a dumb title and is overcooked, and the righteousness in the lyrics significantly exceeds any irony allowance, and yet it kicks in, catches me up, gets me off seriously almost every time. Music and words. Guitars, drums, keyboards, vocals. All these years and I'm still wondering how they do that.

Let's say it's an album about desire. Hey, would you believe me if I said that every album being reviewed in this essay is a thematic song cycle of some kind? Must be something that's going around. Or maybe it happens naturally when you focus your creative attention appropriately. Or it's all a projection of this listener's need to fabricate an illusion of meaning in the face of chaos. Uh, that latter bit could be a subtheme of *August and Everything After*. Physical desire and the hunger for meaningfulness. Great first-album stuff. (Okay these guys are at the end of their twenties doing a huge earnest-adolescent angst bit—that's what Geffen Records is all about, isn't it?—but hey, when it's done well it charms the hell out of me, and I'm forty-six.)

"Mr. Jones" anticipates and incorporates all these thoughts, even the ones in double parentheses. To "explain" (give a sense of what I mean) I'll probably quote lyrics, but first it's important to keep in mind that the words, even if they were written first, are actually the third layer of the song in terms of what the listener hears. First, we hear the track. In order to be a great single (and this is), you need a great track. This one has that perfect rubber-band tension at the outset and other memorable sounds (the guitar/organ drone) (the wonderful way-back chorus of background voices that comes in half-way through and builds insistently through the rest of the recording), plus a really tasty drum figure and, later, delicious percussive flavoring, plus effective invisible driving bass line sewing it all up and shuffling us happily along straight through this four-and-a-half-minute torrent of language. Fabulous, inventive music—listen to the song a few times in a row and you'll find you can drop out the foreground and just hear the track if you choose to.

The second layer is the vocal performance. Maybe we hear the track with our bodies (our constant feelings) and the vocals with our hearts (our immediate feelings). "Mr. Jones" is above all a virtuoso vocal performance, immediate, nonstop, and irresistible, a great example of how a singer's timing, the way he interacts with the track, is the source of the expressiveness we hear in his words. By his timing he makes us feel the presence of the created persona—this guy who almost doesn't dare stop talking—Mr. J's nameless companion, the narrator of the song. Adam Duritz (who also writes all the words, and some of the music) sings extraordinarily well on this song, and makes one curious to take a little trip to the future ten, twenty, thirty years) to see if he was able to grow into his talent beyond this career-making debut album.

The third layer we hear is the words, and these we think we hear with our minds. My point is that, more than we know, more than our minds know, what we hear in the words depends on what we've already heard (are already hearing) in the music and the singer's voice. The words become a container for all this, if they're supple enough to meet the challenge; they take on meaning to fit the felt truth, which is, of course, a little different for each listener. So when I quote words to argue for what a song says, I'm actually hearing musical and vocal performances as I quote them. They don't and can't exist as words—"lyrics"—alone. They're full of tone of voice, relationships with what's come before and since (dynamics), increments of melody and colors of chord changes and external rhythmic (non-vocal) punctuation, all kinds of highly emotional, very charged stuff.

So what is the narrative? Two guys watching girls in a bar, guy's friend talks to one (so she becomes real) who then starts dancing: "she's suddenly beautiful." This transformation has a profound effect on the narrator, who is suddenly jealous of his friend and blurts out this sequence of thoughts: "We all want something beautiful / Man, I wish I was beautiful." Does he want to be beautiful because then he could attract (be worthy of the attention of) someone beautiful? Or is he saying he wants to be her, the focus of attention? Probably he's not sure, and this uncertainty is what the song is about.

It's a song about every kid's desire (a variation on the characters in *Beavis and Butt-head* or *Wayne's World*) to be a star, and it comes off that way, a song full of irony that transcends irony in its flat statement of the way people feel. Pete Townshend can explain that the kid in "My Generation" is too stoned to talk straight, but for rock-and-roll generations, caricature and official spokesperson are the same thing. "Hope I die before I get old." "When everybody loves me, I will never be lonely." These are heartbreaking statements (and sweet, too), by which I mean they're too true to be merely ironic. They cut to the quick of our real (absurd, honest) yearnings and desires and fears.

Neil Young began his career with a song about fear of fame ("Mr. Soul"); it helped make him famous. Adam Duritz and Counting Crows have begun with a song about desire for fame. They have a video in which they sing/say, "When I look at the television I want to see me staring right back at me," and we understand clearly they're singing as us (the fans, the would-bes), not as themselves (now rock professionals). Weird. Amusing. But mostly it's just very powerful, because it cuts to the quick. With humor and pathos. "I want to be Bob Dylan." Because, Jonathan Richman explained succinctly, "He could walk down the street and girls could not resist his stare / Pablo Picasso never got called an asshole / Not in New York."

Ah, you can have fun with this song. Maybe the title suggests that for this generation, the person who "knows something is happening," but doesn't know what it is, is not some square outsider. It's my buddy. It's me.

I like the way he says "Ehh!" after "I want to be a lion." I like the way he says "Cut up, Maria!" and the words that flow from that phrase. I like the second climax of the song, in which he spits (after "I want to be someone"), "to-believe-to-believe-to-believe!" and the beat before the recurrent title phrase returns. Great stuff.

"Come dance this silence down through the morning." We all want to be romantic figures, too, in our own eyes, and why not? One of the pleasing things about this album is its unself-conscious (well, okay, self-consciously unself-conscious) romanticism, in lyrics and music both. Reminds me of (you're not gonna be ready for this) Jellyfish. They share a willingness to pick up what they like from past rock eras, fashionable or not, and make it their own, marching shamelessly and colorfully forward into a baroque new world.

Desire (and its contrapuntal theme, fear of love) makes its first appearance in the marvelously evocative "Round Here" (future heavy-rotation video, don't you think so?), which is mostly about sense of community, glorious subtle anthem based largely on the sound and the two-word title and chorus phrase. But its narrative concerns Maria from Nashville who "parks her car outside of my house and takes her clothes off," whose neuroses make her perhaps less approachable than that suggests: "The girl in the parking lot says, 'Man, you should try to take a shot [at making me]' "—meaning he hasn't, and no wonder, since her next remark (all nonstop talkers on this record) is about suicide. He ends up thinking about her too much and staying up very very late.

The song-cycle effect is nicely augmented by all kinds of not-too-subtle interactions between the lyrics of the various songs. We've already seen the recurrent Maria. The "very very late" of "Round Here" becomes the focus of "Perfect Blue Buildings," which seems to me a song about insomnia even though its conceit is the inverse ("help me stay awake"). He's singing to a woman who's "got an attitude of everything I ever wanted / I got an attitude of need," and while "Round Here" is a kind of boast, here he reports that "It's four-thirty A.M. on a Tuesday / It doesn't get much worse than this."

"Omaha" has a recurrent line about "Hey mister, if you're going to walk on water." The "mister" recurs in the wonderful "bones beneath my skin" verse of "Perfect Blue Buildings," and then in "Time and Time Again" all five of the songs that have come before are echoed in one verse: "I wanted the ocean to cover over me / I wanna sink slowly without getting wet / Maybe someday I won't be so lonely / And I'll walk on water every chance I get." (The fifth song, "Anna Begins," telescopes in on what happens to our protagonist when one of those beautiful desired objects gets real, gets close, tries to penetrate the proud scared male loneliness. "Oh Lord, I'm not ready for this sort of thing.")

Smart album. Clever—extremely—but also intelligent. And moving. And somehow true to life.

I like the riff of "Perfect Blue Buildings"—the interplay of vocal and drums—a lot. Lots of hooks in these songs. Seems like I notice new ones every time I listen. There are lyrics in "Perfect Blue Buildings" (including the title phrase) that don't do much for me, and other lyrics that I absolutely love, but it's the melodic hooks that pull me back again and again, singing the words in my head and making them meaningful even when I know they're silly. ("Lady Madonna . . .") And I'm tickled by the way "keep myself away" and "keep myself awake" come to mean the same thing.

Heather (the plant) in "Omaha" and "Rain King." The bird in "Rain King" and "A Murder of One." The color gray in "Mr. Jones" and "Anna." Falling and sinking and drowning in "Round Here" and "Perfect Blue Buildings" and "Time and Time Again" and "Rain King" and "Sullivan Street." The ticket in "Omaha" and "Ghost Train." Just enough overlap to remind us that these could be separate verses of a single song. "I walk in the air between the rain" in the first song and "I walk along these hillsides" in the last. And in between, trains and oceans and "I want" "I wish" "I need" and lots and lots of evocative, playful, satisfying, articulate music. The return of the rock keyboard. Hey, we left the light on for you.

There were three albums that I passionately loved and turned to constantly (for support and renewal) in the year 1966: *Pet Sounds*, *Blonde on Blonde*, and *Tim Hardin I*. Two of these are justly famous; the third is known only to the cognoscenti, one of whom you may become by picking up a copy of **Hang On to a Dream: The Verve Recordings**, a two-CD collection containing most of the earliest and best work of an astonishing and frustrating vocalist-songwriter named **Tim Hardin**.

The subtitle evokes past anthologies of great jazz artists, notably and appropriately Billie Holiday. Hardin had much of the talent (!), many of the personal problems, and none of the excuses of Lady Day. He is a minor figure compared to Billie or Hank Williams because of his lack of productivity (he was one of those charming, untrustworthy human beings keenly focused on doing as little hard work as possible during this incarnation), but the twenty-two performances contained on his first two albums have had and will continue to have a tremendous impact on all of the musicians and most of the other listeners who encounter them. They are treasures. They make up the first CD of this set. (The second CD is mainly for true fans, consisting of demos, cover songs, and warm-up tracks, many previously unreleased, from the same period as disc one, May 1964 to August 1966.)

I had the good fortune to be present at two extraordinary performances by Tim Hardin, and several good ones. Great good fortune, because apparently Hardin, a junkie, often played disappointing sets (i.e., falling asleep midsong) when he showed up at all. But when he was present with his music he was present in a manner that was unforgettable, untouchable. I saw him at an afternoon concert at the Newport Folk Festival in July 1966 (many of Dave Gahr's photos in the CD booklet are from that day), and I remember feeling awestruck—at the performance as a whole, and at a song called "If I Were a Carpenter" which wasn't included on the just-released first album. (It was a Top Ten hit for Bobby Darin in fall 1966, a vocal performance copied as precisely as possible from Hardin's demo recording; later, the same song was a hit single for Johnny Cash and June Carter, and for the Four Tops).

Then, late in 1967, I was at Paul Rothchild's home in the Hollywood Hills when Hardin and his wife dropped by—he had his guitar and he played and sang a few songs, and what I'd felt at Newport came back to me but even stronger. I've witnessed similarly intimate performances—living room, hotel room—by some fine performers, including (I'm boasting now) John Lennon, Bruce Springsteen, Joni Mitchell, Crosby Stills & Nash, Jimi Hendrix—but Hardin's impromptu sharing was, I think, the most exciting, the one that most made me feel like I'd just been present at the unveiling of the cosmic secret. Sweet essence of truth via music. Heart speaking directly (and so nakedly!) to heart.

You can get a pretty fair approximation of this experience from disc one of the new compilation, especially if you focus in on one song at a time. I still (after all these years) regard the first twelve tracks as an album, and like to listen to them that way, pausing the CD after track twelve to let it sink in. "How can we hang on to a dream?" indeed. The second album (tracks thirteen through twenty-two) doesn't work as well as a unit, it doesn't flow for me, although it contains some hypnotically powerful performances. The strange thing, in any case, is that Tim Hardin didn't assemble these albums. He seems to have been a compulsive nonfinisher. According to the notes on the box set, August 1966 is the latest date of any of the recordings in this set, and this set includes everything he did in the studio while at Verve, which covers at least the next two years, precisely the period in his life when the world was showing the greatest interest in his work. The producer and record company and Hardin's wife and friends tried to get him to write and record, and failed. Strings were added to many of the tracks without Hardin's cooperation (or active opposition; the impression one gets is that his mere participation was extremely difficult to obtain). His producer talks about giving him fifty dollars cash for every song he wrote that had two verses and a chorus. Few of the songs on this disc are any longer than that.

And yet these songs, many of them shorter than two minutes, are so powerful, so full of beauty, so endlessly rewarding. They're emotional epics. If you, like me, have had the melody and words and tempo of "Don't Make Promises" echoing in your head since whenever you first heard it, you may be surprised to look closely at how little narrative (lyrical or musical) it takes to say so much. Simplicity is mystery. "It seems the songs we're singing / Are all about tomorrow / Tunes of promises you can't keep." I've taken this song apart over the last few days and examined its rhythmic structure, its phrasing, the sounds of the instruments, the melodic transitions, and finally I've just had to put it together again, fascinated by my journey but none the wiser. Songs *are* about tomorrow. I understand that on a deeper level now. But I'm still not sure what it means.

It means that with music we can step outside of time. Music and love. But, according to this teacher (I mean Mr. Hardin), we can't stay there. And that makes him very angry. And he expresses this anger with an almost supernatural gentleness.

I don't want to romanticize the junkie, the dropout. But I am in awe at how skillfully (and, in his best songs, how subtly) he romanticizes himself. In doing so, he exposes the vulnerable beauty (tangled in pain, anger, sadness, fear, guilt, self-doubt) that sings in all of us. We feel it. We see our own beauty. This is quite an accomplishment.

The songs are gems. "Don't Make Promises" leaves an indelible impression. Words and music both are hauntingly beautiful, but most of all there's a pulse in it that, I don't know, opens the heart, induces a state of higher consciousness. Heard as a whole, separate, for example, from what the words might mean if they were just on paper, the song speaks with tremendous clarity. What it says is subjective, personal, different each time, but notice the sense of motion as the song moves from one section to another, a surge of confidence or optimism as the second verse enters ("We had a chance to find it / Our time was now or never"), followed not by disappointment, precisely, but a profound acceptance that includes as much sadness or bitterness as the listener's moment may require. There is a process at work here that is beyond comprehension, a way that voice and music communicate. "You're telling me lies in your sleep." He's certainly talking to a sexual partner. He could also be speaking to the universe.

Reimmersing myself in Tim Hardin's unique lush deliciously bittersweet musical universe has been a great pleasure, with interesting implications. I've enjoyed the opportunity to introduce Cindy and others to this little-known master, and have been more than gratified at their immediate, enthusiastic response. And my own process of rediscovery has affirmed something I also learned while working on *The 100 Best Singles*: The best stuff keeps its power. *Tim Hardin 1* is *still* a wonderful album worthy of comparison with *Blonde on Blonde* and *Pet Sounds*. It was just waiting for me to give it my time and attention again, anew, and now that I am doing so, it is repaying me a thousandfold.

"You looked to me like misty roses . . ." Something happens to me during the one minute and fifty-seven seconds of this song ("Misty Roses"), and in fact it has already happened in the first ten seconds, as soon as Hardin has spoken the title phrase. Time has stopped, and I have the opportunity to go inside the surface of things and look around, see all the clockwork of matter and energy flowing into and out of each other. It seems ridiculous to say the song only lasts for two minutes. It is infinite. And the mood of it, even as it expresses anguish, is almost impossibly calming and reassuring. What strange power did this man have? He was a paralyzed visionary, paralyzed perhaps by the vision itself (awareness is pain), but still managing to send out an occasional message in a bottle, each one stunning in its immediacy and beauty and self-honesty. It seems pointless to criticize such a career for not being longer, more productive, more energetic. Instead one is inclined to be thankful for each single bottle that managed to find its way to our shores.

"While You're on Your Way" has been haunting me recently. It's one of those songs (are there others?—there must be) where the title phrase is not heard until the last moments of the performance. Everything builds up to this phrase (in the listeners' memory and anticipation; the singer is cool as a cucumber, but we're on the edge of our chairs). Musically there's great strong familiar structure here—verse, bridge, verse, bridge—with a wonderful pulse driving through it that is not rock and not quite jazz, either, its own creature, *great* sound, contradicted by the lyrics that offer rhyme but no structural repetition, no release. And what a story these odd lyrics tell or hint at. When Hardin sings, meanings that other singer-songwriters would put into a line or a pair of lines are compacted into single words: the word "night," the word "feeling." Both *are* repeated, though not in the same position. The way the second appearance of each word echoes and changes direction from and builds on the first is fascinating; lyrics (and units of melody and phrasing) have relationships between each other as odd and deliberate and brilliant as those between objects or colors in a Matisse painting. "While you're on your way" is the only repeated phrase, repeated right after itself and just before the song's extraordinary punch line. Other simple words that are only spoken once also manage to take on astonishing resonance and significance: "words" "days" "things" "hope." The song invites endless relistenings. It's as brilliant and sui generis as "Reason to Believe," though hardly as universally accessible. "Reason to Believe" is built up in lovely repeating patterns of music and lyric, title phrase ending each verse, wonderful modest provocative phrases soaring in pairs in the bridge ("Someone like you . . .") and in the verse-openers ("If I . . .") and in the second line of each verse ("I'd find a way"). Familiar, comprehensible structure. But then the song takes off for the stratosphere before our very eyes and ears with the odd metrical structure of the chorus, weaving in and out so deceptively, and the peculiar emphasis on individual words ("find" becomes luminous), and also all through this short song the incredible combinations of words into phrases ("I'd find a way to leave the past behind"). Vocal intonations. Delicacy and richness of melody, melodic moments. And that pulse, no two alike, but all more like each other than anything you've ever heard anywhere else.

A feast. The leftovers (*Tim Hardin 2*) are almost as good as the original supper. They don't pulse, but they have many other virtues, notably an almost unbearable poignance; scary, because in a sense you know you're being conned by a master (masters and monsters are often one and the same) and at the same time it's the most fun you've ever had while being seduced, therefore de facto the real thing (or is that quod erat demonstrandum?). Anyway, you know how it is with a junkie lover: Now you see (hear, touch) him, now you don't.

There's a song about that. Maybe more than one. "Red Balloon" is about the junkie lover being distracted ("Took the lovelight from my eyes / Blue, blue surprise") by his jones. And "Tribute to Hank Williams" is about the singer who first takes the pain away from his fans with his singing, and then gives it back by taking away himself. ("Goodbye, Hank Williams, my friend / I didn't know you, but I've been places you've been." *Places*. A world in a word, and in its singer's phrasing.)

More favorites: "The Lady Came from Baltimore." (Charms us and her by calling himself a thief: "I was there to steal her money, take her rings and run / Then I fell in love with the lady, got away with none." Poets will complain that the deft use of melody and intonation makes for unfair competition, but they're just jealous that no couplet of theirs has stuck so firmly in my mind.)

"Never Too Far." I wanted to write this whole essay about the beat and the language of "Never Too Far." Bossa nova. New boss. What is his obsession with lies? Poor man. Because he tells them, he thinks he hears them everywhere. Again the word "tomorrow," rhyming with "Don't Make Promises," stopping time for the moment it's spoken, and never quite starting it again. And he's aware of this power, and can comment on it: "In my wandering sense of time / I'll try to see enough to rhyme / Your changing line." Breathtaking and heartbreaking. I get lost in this music, even as I cling to it to lead me out of here. Sometimes I doubt he knows what love is, yet no modern singer has spoken of love more powerfully. Haunting. Again.

I am also in awe of both versions of "It'll Never Happen Again." And then there are at least two previously unheard takes on disc two that are major additions to the oeuvre: "If I Knew" and "First Love Song." Demos. Awkward. Unfinished. Unforgettable.

How many hours of actual work went into the creation of all this magnificent intellectual property? Who should properly own it, exploit it, control it? The manager/producer with his timely fifty dollars? The long-suffering widow/victim? Some record company that bought the masters? Who decides who gets to ever see the painting that the genius/painter sells to buy groceries or heroin? Where did the power in that painting truly come from?

And to whom among us does it truly belong?

Here is another fellow. I listened to his album because someone told me it was as good as Neil Young's *Ragged Glory* or the Waterboys' *Fisherman's Blues*. It doesn't achieve that standard (those are best-of-the-decade albums, like Leonard Cohen's *I'm Your Man* or *Violent Femmes* or R.E.M.'s *Fables of the Reconstruction* or maybe—Cindy's nomination—*Loveless* by My Bloody Valentine), but I certainly have no regrets about having been introduced to **Joe Henry**, no complaints about the enriching hours I've spent with his recent tour de force, **Kindness of the World**. I've tested it more than once by going straight from Tim Hardin intoxication and endazzlement to my favorite song on Henry's album (other listeners and reviewers have different favorites, always a good sign), "Third Reel." It stands up unflinchingly. Indeed, it not only sounds thrilling even in the face of fierce competition, it creates a hunger in me such that I am compelled, when its five minutes are over, to punch the button and hear it again.

"Third Reel" is, once again, extraordinary pop poetry created through word-writing, melody-grafting, and heartfelt performance. An essay-poem, mysterious, evocative, phrases as charming as Emerson's or Thoreau's. In the setting of "Fireman's Wedding" and "I Flew Over Our House" (other songs on the album, providers of context), it's a jewel of Americana, a love song to some specific local place and individual person (she has a name—"Louise"—the town does not, and as the title suggests, it could even be a town in a movie, or maybe they're filming our lives), big (subtle) vision, big language (understated), big heart. A waltz. "Our song." An instant classic. A waltz.

An invaluable slice of intellectual property, but too "out there" for any country station, and probably too country for anyone else. So don't try to pay the rent with it yet.

And how'm I going to tell you why I love it so much without quoting every word of it, and getting myself tossed in jail for the heinous crime (theme of this album) of pauper's affection and, ah, unfair use?

Impossible. Every phrase demands the next one; I want to point with awe at them all. Little ingots in Fort Knox. I want to give them away. I want to come over to your house and play you the record, but even then you might not be caught by the magic on first listen (it took me some time before the song burst out of its shell) and so I'll have to sit you down and recite (close the blinds, I may not have bought a license for this just by purchasing or taking possession of the CD):

> "Well they've torn up the streets
> And burned off the fields
> And turned all the dogs to the woods
> They took up the cross
> But they lost the third reel
> And the picture was just getting good
> Evening is crawling
> Summer is lost
> They're dragging the pond for it now
> They've painted the windows all shut
> And the frost
> Has warmed everything up somehow."

That's just the first verse, without even the payoff chorus (extraordinary pledge of affection), and the next two are better. I recite them to myself (music playing in my mind) and am flooded with pleasure, emotional baggage, spiritual excitement, tears in the corners of my eyes. Makes me sad. Ecstatically happy-sad.

I need you to listen to this song. Someone else feels the same way about the title track, or the bonus song that goes unlisted but is known among fans as "Ghost."

Who is this Joe Henry? Well, this is his fifth album in eight years, with no "success" so far except some very good reviews. He's got roots in North Carolina, Detroit, and Los Angeles (how's that for triangulating the country?), lives in the latter, and has been married for some time though this album certainly makes one imagine the singer as a sophisticated (good with words) small town (American heartland) handsome alcoholic with a broken marriage and a heart bursting with contradictory but deeply-felt regret: "If only this time I was wrong / If only you were here / If I was only half as strong / If just tonight a mile was only half as long / Then I could walk from here" ("Buckdancer's Choice"). "We all have stories, I suppose / But in mine she always goes" ("She Always Goes"). The album's on Mammoth, a gutsy and likable North Carolina indie record label, and was recorded more or less live in a studio in New Orleans, in eight days, with a superb band that includes Gary Louris and Marc Perlman of the Jay-hawks. Victoria Williams sings backup vocals on two songs and comes across as ethereally attractive as Emmy Lou Harris behind Gram Parsons.

Who is he? A very good songwriter with a gift for communicating what it feels like to be a man, as life, usually in the form of love relationships lost, faltering, or wished-for; confronts us with our failures, needs, and values. On this album it feels bleak and hopeful both at once, with a gleeful (perverse) pride in the elegance of all this suffering. No. Not of the suffering. Of the human world in which it takes place, whose beauty we notice because our distress has momentarily opened our hearts and eyes.

He's a guy who can communicate feelings. If John Hiatt's and Jackson Browne's new albums sound to you like people who've gotten used to doing whatever it is they do, but you can always give another listen to *Bring the Family* or *Late for the Sky*, you will probably find *Kindness of the World* well worth checking out—assuming you're open to an album that may not be a masterpiece like the aforementioned, but which does succeed in exploring related musical and emotional territory in a fresh, energetic, intriguing, and genuine manner.

You can see I'm a little cautious about recommending that you rush out and buy this album. It's extremely well realized, and you won't find this particular vision (self-deprecating, self-absorbed, self-revelatory) or this particular dry slow raggedly ornate and opulent sound anywhere else. But there's no way of knowing how well this particularity may sit with you. I like all the songs and am thrilled by a few of them, but I usually can't listen to the album straight through—too slow, too inward, maybe too much of a good thing. It's a mood piece. When I'm in the mood for its unusual pace and perspective, nothing else can ring my bell. Other times, I have to admit, I'm hesitant to answer the phone.

It's certainly an album with a message, and it's extremely successful at the important task of keeping us from being too sure we know what that message is. For me, the best evidence of Henry's genius may be his selection, execution, and placement of the album's one cover song, a clever, familiar-on-the-first-listen country weeper by Tom T. Hall from 1973 which fits the situation and voice of this album's fictionalized narrator so perfectly it's eerie. The song is called "I Flew Over Our House Last Night." I doubt that Hall's version has any supernatural implications—i.e., images of flying perhaps without a jet—but in this context the song works on all sorts of levels, our hearts and minds full of language like "I saw Davy climb a tree / To be nearer to his Lord" ("Kindness") and "You can jump for your life from your place in the trees" ("Third Reel") and "Tonight I feel I'm floating" ("Kindness" again). But that's all undertones. The overt imagery also resonates extraordinarily with the rest of the album: stewardess wanting to comfort the narrator; his strong evocation of sense of place even (or especially) miles above it all and flying off in another direction; the delicacy of his wondering, "Did you toss and turn [in your sleep] as I flew out of sight?"; his defensive, sarcastic, and yet understanding (and wounded) self-portrait ("the man your friends all say has only brought you down") . . . it all resonates with each of the other songs here so perfectly you'd think Hall wrote it for Henry, and then you realize it's the other way around, eleven songs and performances perfectly crafted to fit the spirit and imagery of this one. "Ghost" in particular is given flesh and specificity by being on the same album as "I Flew Over Our House." The woman sleeps, holding a ribbon in her hand and "a picture from back then." You can never quite capture the story in these songs, which is the key to their power, but it's not hard to imagine that the ghost the narrator's confronting is the same guy who flew away in Hall's song, with so much regret, so many years before.

Specific ambiguity. It's a talent. "One day when the weather is warm / I'll wake up on a hill / And hold the morning like it was a plow." (Lovely song, lovely melody, almost overpowered by the rawness and loudness-in-the-mix of the singer's voice, an intentional effect, unsettling, a challenge to each listener: Accept me warts-and-all when I'm in your face; I won't let you just grab the romantic parts and run.) I read a piece from a small L.A. paper about Henry's career struggle (not alluded to in any way on the album itself, which I appreciate, though the narrator does at times sound like a man with no occupation other than loving and failing to love). "I'd like to play beautiful theaters and make enough money for my wife to quit her job, but I think it's pretty foolish for me at this point to sit around expecting that . . . I don't want to spend my life selling ten thousand records and having to beg my way into making another one. I just want to be successful enough so that I can make another record, and until someone tells me differently, I won't expect anything else." Or as he puts it in the song, "I'll cut myself a row / And follow it until / I know better by God than I know now."

I can identify. An album about failure, self-examination, renewal, and perseverance. And sense of place. Information worth processing. Sometimes I think he sings, ". . . cut myself a rose." I see him sniffing it, and then handing it to a woman, or maybe to me, with a smile. Thorns and all.

The only trouble with **Exile in Guyville** by **Liz Phair** is that it makes you think too much when you're not listening to it. You could even talk yourself out of liking it while caught up in the storm of mental weather it induces. No possible danger of not liking this album while it's actually on the phonograph, however. Nineteen ninety-three's most likely nominee for classic status. Those damn critics got it right again.

Exile in Guyville is a jukebox jammed with hits (great B-sides, too), the kind of selection that's especially satisfying because you find surprises and new favorites all the time. For a while I thought the album's claim to greatness rested squarely on the extraordinary trio of relationship songs in the middle of the CD, "Fuck and Run" "Girls! Girls! Girls!" (more easily identified as "I take full advantage . . .") and "Divorce Song." Three killers, no question about it, but this week and this evening my attention is riveted just as intently on "Mesmerizing" "Stratford-on-Guy" (the airplane song) and "Strange Loop." I want to put a nickel or fifty cents or whatever it takes these days into the machine and hear the song blared out into a room full of friends and strangers so loud they have to stop their conversations and just feel it.

Listen (these are not just words; you're hearing rhythms, riffs, genuine vulnerable human presence, the beat, spirit):

> *once I really listened the noise / just went away*
> *you tossed the egg up & I found my hands in place, boy*
> *baby I'm tired / of fighting / I always wanted you / I only wanted*
> *more than I knew*

The genius of this album is that the words and subject matter are so sharp and involving, and Liz Phair's vocal presence and personality so immediate, you hardly even notice the music sneaking up behind you with a tire iron. Like its namesake, Exile is most of all a musical album, full of hooks and inventions and enticing sounds, simplicities that work together in subtle and unexpected ways to satisfy very complex longings on the part of the listener. The power of the lyrics both contributes to and is an extension of the power of the music.

About that namesake. Phair named her album after the Rolling Stones' sloppy immortal 1972 double LP *Exile on Main Street* (a tip of the hat, like Lenin borrowing from Chernyshevski). She goes further: There are eighteen tracks on her album, as on theirs; there's a clear and very laudable Rolling Stones influence in her music (although she takes it in fresh directions, unlike most Stones-influenced guy bands—she's able to learn from the Stones' structural innovations without being limited by them; and she has said in interviews that she wrote each of these songs in direct response to the counterpart song on the Stones' album. Whether or not this comment was designed to seduce critics and anal-retentive rock-and-roll fans, it has certainly done so. What a concept!

The problem is, there really is no correlation, or very damned little, once you get past the delightful opening song "6'1"," which has several lines that could certainly be directed straight at Mick Jagger's 1972 public image (hey, I imagine Phair has read *I'm with the Band* like all the rest of us). I stood next to Liz Phair in the bar at the Casbah after her recent San Diego show and listened while she told my friend Jon Kanis that she had in fact written each song by projecting the singer/narrator of the corresponding Stones *Exile* song as a love object and going from there. She admitted the process was too arcane for anyone else to see the connections, maybe, but yes, that had been her process. I believed her as she spoke—she has a very direct, honest manner. But sitting here listening to both records, for what it's worth, I have to say I believe she exaggerated a good tale, like Bob Dylan and Woody Guthrie before her, and now loyally stands by that exaggeration. If she asserted that "Never Said" was inspired by the Violent Femmes' "Never Tell," I'd buy it in an instant; but I can't see "Never Said" as a response to any aspect of "Tumbling Dice," no matter how arcane. Nevertheless, anything that gets me and other people (some of them maybe even Stones virgins) to drag out our copies of *Exile on Main Street* is absolutely a good thing and not to be complained about, koff koff.

And *Guyville* does indeed resemble *Main Street*, as I suggested before, in its unusual musical density. Both albums can be tremendously difficult to get a handle on. They won't settle into a recognizable form. And both have a way of sticking around long after you might have thought you were done with them. Sink those hooks . . .

What I want to talk about (we'll get around to gender provocations—"I take full advantage of every man I meet / I get away / Almost every day / With what the girls call, the girls call, the girls call murder!" Doesn't that just make you crazy? I've lost some sleep over it . . . Isn't it brilliant?—later, I promise) is song structure. "Johnny Sunshine" is a fine example. The song is three minutes twenty-five seconds long, and is a set of three chants in five contrapuntal combinations, each about forty seconds long. I mean, she starts off with a rock beat and growling (restrained) chainsaw guitar, as she chants a little litany of accusations ("You took the car / It was my favorite one") in an angry-but-affectless housewife poet chant. At around the forty-second point this chant is joined by another voice, also Phair, reciting long sweet mournful (but affectless) lines against the chanted staccato ones: "I think I've been taken / For everything I own . . ." The first chant repeats while the second one unfolds. Then at 1:17 both are interrupted by a third chant, this time an impersonal chorus (Phair's voice doubled) that sings/accuses, "You left me nothing / Johnn-y Sun-shine / You left me nothing," accompanied by jangly guitar. This middle section, like the first, is a single chant; the fourth section (starts at 2:02) brings back the chanting voice from section two ("I think I've been taken") and plays it against "You left me nothing." In the fifth section the choir is alone again (still chanting "Johnny Sunshine / You left me nothing"), free to soar in ecstatic detachment with a force that has somehow built up throughout the composition/construction. Layers of irony interweave the layers of music, and you are free to hear whatever you need to. For example, is there something in the way she says his voice that suggests that she—the narrator—is still a fool for this Peter Pan/Neal Cassady rip-off artist? You fill in the blanks. But the musical experiment is brilliant, soulful, loose, and gritty and, I think, very successful. Like listening to the Beatles, you really only hear the finished product. "Interesting sound." Indeed.

A related experiment with more of an edge on it is "Flower." There are only two chanting voices in this one: first a high girlish one with a summer-camp singsong—"Every time I see your face / I get all wet between my legs" (I watched her sing the whole song a cappella onstage at the Casbah, unflinching; she definitely has brass balls, or the equivalent—joined after thirty seconds and for the rest of the two minutes by a lower womanly-voice counterpointing a similar singsong, different tempo, different words: "I want to fuck you like a dog / I'll take you home and make you like it." She could be singing to a Jaggerlike sex object (the kind you contemplate from a distance) in this one, certainly—and/or playing the role of a phone-sex employee, in which case shall we assume bitter sarcasm beneath the humor? If you're a boy, is it appropriate or highly inappropriate to be turned on by this performance? Phair is smart, and I think just as willing to push female buttons as male ones (in terms of whom she pisses off): "You act like you're fourteen years old / Everything you say is so / Obnoxious funny true and mean / I want to be your blowjob queen." The sound of the song is sweet. Alternative. Likable. Different. Outrageous.

"Mesmerizing" is the first of four astonishing songs in the nine through twelve positions (in the future books and records won't have beginnings and ends, just sectors). The way the rather ordinary rock-and-roll instrumentation on this album is employed is not ordinary at all. Some songs are just voice and electric guitar, others add a bass or drums, not necessarily both, and when there is a full rhythm section they're not necessarily playing at the same time. It's very much the album of someone with a cheap four-track recorder in her house that she plays around on, whether that was actually the case or not. Put A over B and see what it sounds like. "Mesmerizing" is self-descriptive—it sounds fantastic, especially that lead guitar, the hand claps, the organ fills. Basically a song about a healthy (and slightly demonic) acceptance of female power: "I want to be mesmerizing, too." The opening is wonderful (Phair's guitar, I think, plus co-producer Brad Wood's maracas). Authoritative, impressive, mysterious vocal. ("Don't you know I'm very happy?" What is she feeling as she says that?) Casey Rice plays the lead guitar riff after "mesmerizing, too" but in fairness what makes it great is the melody of the riff, and the arrangement, both probably Phair's creation. This is a songmaker with a vision. What a great piece of rock and roll. It has a freshness I associate with some of Buddy Holly's inventions.

"Fuck and Run" is a high point, would have been the smash hit single if there were any radio stations that could even announce such a title. ("*Dar*ling, here's what we'll do, just change *one* word, '*Kiss* and Run,' just for the airplay version, for the kids like you growing up in Aberdeen who would never have a chance at hearing your lifesaving message unless they see a cardboard mobile of you in K-mart . . ."

(Okay, I can see I need to interrupt this essay to say something about the death of Kurt Cobain. *Exile in Guyville* is one of the most successful indie albums (meaning not distributed by one of the six "major" record labels) of the last few years—it's sold about 200,000 copies in the U.S. What jumped in my brain is how small that is compared to what a hit album sells through the majors—200,000 being the number of estimated *extra* sales (before the suicide, which will probably boost unit sales substantially) Geffen Records expected to get when they convinced Nirvana to change their album cover and the title of one song after the fact to beat the arbitrary (publicity-seeking, hypocritical) ban on the *In Utero* album that the Wal-Mart and K-Mart chains of retailers had imposed. Geffen and Nirvana (through their management) announced this humiliating bit of ass-kissing in March, and one of the band's managers (quoted in *ICE*) revealed for spin-control purposes the rationalization used to help the guys knuckle under: "One of the reasons they signed to a major label was so that kids could buy their records at a K-mart, where Nirvana, growing up, bought *their* records. They really want to make their music available to kids who don't have the oportunity to go to 'mom and pop' stores. They feel really strongly about it, strong enough to make some alterations . . ."

(In hindsight, Geffen Records and Nirvana's management, Gold Mountain, must have forced the band to make a decision on this during a time when they as insiders knew—based on some of the stories that have been coming out—that Cobain was increasingly stressed-out, confused, suicidal. We also know that they allowed him to experience the pressure of having to decide whether to headline Lollapalooza next summer, do the spring tour of Europe, et cetera, et cetera. Twenty-twenty hindsight is easy and unfair and in this case extremely unkind on my part, and very possibly nothing could have saved Cobain from his selfish, self-important act of self-loathing, but it's not unreasonable to suggest that someone could have seen that turning down the external pressure always helps. I mean Geffen Records/MCA, like any corporate record company or book publisher, is structured so that all decisions *must* maximize the quick buck—hey, if it kills the goose that lays the golden eggs, remember that the goose has been *proven* to be replaceable—so whaddaya expect? But isn't it possible to imagine a manager saying, "No way, we're not even going to let you *talk* to our clients about that, they've got more than enough on their minds already"?

(The music business is a monster. So what else is new? Here, kid, let us manage your intellectual property for you. Our credo is, Let nothing get in the way of the free flow of information . . .)

"Fuck and Run" indeed. Anyway, it's a very straightforward song about being single, which is remarkable for its economy and accuracy, and most of all for the way the narration works with the song structure, the "hooks" that characterize a great pop or rock single. What I'm trying to say is that the song starts out very strong, musically and lyrically, and then ratchets up the intensity not once but at least three times, and those moments of satisfaction and adrenaline rush are what we the listeners experience as "hooks," those fulfilling moments in songs that make us want to hear them again and again. And in a really good, really exciting song the hooks further the narrative, so that I get involved, I live the story (in this case, a story of sudden, uncomfortable self-awareness, expressed as complaint), I sing along with, "Whatever happened to a boyfriend?" and I scream along (after the deliciously rising tension, perfectly expressed by the music, of "I'm gonna spend another year alone") with "Fuck and run! Fuck and run!" This is the essence of punk, this scream that the song pulls out of me, and the essence of rock and roll before that. It lives. It rules. Phair's guitar-playing and the tone of her voice are inspired from the first moment, and why not? She has a vision, she has something to say here. A searing (and universally familiar, I believe) portrait of an encounter (the simple three-line verses), surrounded by a portrait of this woman character's thoughts and feelings as she responds to the moment she finds herself in. "Almost immediately I felt sorry, 'cause I didn't think this would happen again . . ." Felicitous phrase. Rock and roll is a form of poetry that is specifically concerned with the creation of a few good phrases.

These phrases, I repeat repeat repeat, are not given us by a pencil but by a human voice. Tim Hardin is not immortal as a page poet. Liz Phair writes well but the impact of those seven ordinary words "I didn't think this would happen again" has everything to do with the speaking of the words, the singing of the words, the location of the words within a flow, a rhythmic sequence, of music. This musical sequence is the narrative of the song, as much as the story the lyrics tell and imply. We experience a synergy of music and words (and instruments and voice, and rhythm and melody) that gathers most of its power from what are called synergistic effects. A + B. It is the music of the song, together with the impact of the images the lyrics conjure, that leaves us ready (and, after first listen, eager) to be devastated by the song's climactic couplet:

"*I can feel it in my bones*
I'm gonna spend my whole life alone."

After which we just naturally yell "Fuck and run!" as loud as possible to try to release some of the feelings that that couplet and every magnificent moment of this song have brought forth in us.

(The closing phrase "ever since I was twelve" can be taken as an intentional bit of attention-getting via shock value or, similarly, an autobiographical tease, and Phair definitely likes to pinch our tits musically or verbally at the ends of her songs; but it is also, I think, an appropriate and consciousness-expanding acknowledgment of the fact that for a woman the sexual life very often does begin at twelve, if not younger, in the form of attention given (and then, very often, abruptly and coldly withdrawn), whether this attention includes actual fucking or not. What the character is saying is, "This is familiar to me. This is familiar to me for a long, long time; longer probably than I care to confront or admit.")

"Girls! Girls! Girls!" is a duet between Phair's voice and her guitar, and the richness of the interplay is wonderful. Again I think it could be called counterpoint, two related but separate melodies augmenting and contradicting each other. She does not sound like any kind of folkie—indeed, these songs without bass or drums are just as rhythmic and inherently noisy (chaos in order, order in chaos) as the ones with added accompaniment. They all sound like a Liz Phair sound, once you begin to get used to that idea, related to but different from a Jonathan Richman sound, say. Crude/sophisticated, and always idiosyncratic. I find the "I take full advantage" chorus very catchy, which I suspect is one reason the song bothers a lot of us males. It gets under the skin. And, in the nature of things, most of us do have painful experiences of being manipulated by females, probably since about the time we learned that Mom was a separate entity, with the power to deny us our wishes.

"Divorce Song" transcends gender, however—it could be a gay couple; it just doesn't matter. How few songs really address these little and big squabbles that make up such a significant part of most of our lives! Very straightforward musically; this one almost *is* folky, with a blues-rock ending (hello from Chicago). Phair is brilliantly, painfully articulate: "But if I'd known / How that [asking for separate motel rooms] would sound to you / I would have stayed in your bed / For the rest of my life / Just to prove I was right—" Brilliant, but I've cut it off in midsentence, right in the clever transition to a whole new verse/thought/revelation: "—That it's harder to be friends than lovers / And you shouldn't try to mix the two / 'Cause if you do it and you're still unhappy / Then you know that the problem is you." Her tongue is sharp (we wouldn't believe this narrative if it wasn't!) throughout the tune, but her generosity towards her (the character's) ex is atypical of such songs: "You've never been no waste of my time / You've never been a drag." Such statements matter. Liz Phair's songs manage to be very basic, often about very central and obvious issues that aren't addressed often enough, and yet they can be subtle and thoughtful and emotionally complex at the same time. Bravo.

Others songs are just hard to figure out. For one thing, she mumbles. And references can be elusive. I mean, I've seen those "Sea Monkeys" ads in the backs of comic books, but if you haven't, it could be hard(er) to gain entrance to "Gunshy," which I think is about a housewife feeling trapped by her housewifely state of mind. "Seems like the small things are the only things I affect." I'm guessing wildly on that last word, but the pillow-soft inaudibility of the lady's voice is part of the song's uniqueness and power. Maybe (as with the Stones at times) what you don't hear is what you get.

"Stratford-on-Guy" has one of those rock-and-roll choruses that's so great (very Stone-ish), you just have to make it mean something Significant, and so you do. The way she digs into the word "hour" is irresistible. And I love the description of coming into Chicago from the perspective of seat 27-D. (On the other hand, not knowing what she's getting at with the references to Galaxie 500 and Brigitte Bardot is a distraction. Oh well.)

"Strange Loop" (weird title) ends the album with a bang, another excellent relationship song with a hooky pop-guitar figure (turn it up louder!) and a sing-along chorus ("I always wanted you . . .") and one phenomenal bit of phrasing ("Baby, I'm *tired*") and the climactic couplet at the beginning of the song this time: "The fire you like so much in me / Is the mark of someone adamantly free." That about sums it up. A cheer for Brad Wood and Miss Phair's tasteful and bright and bang-on co-production, with help from Casey Rice; they all done real good. Did I promise to say more about gender provocations? That line about being "just a cunt in spring" is rather striking (though the song "Dance of the Seven Veils" is one of the few that doesn't really work for me). The prophetic quality of "Help Me Mary" ("turn my disgust into fame") is impressive, or maybe just a demonstration that prayer combined with fierce willpower can change lives. "Shatter" is fascinating in its structure and mysterious implications. I like it that she's not (yet) predictable. The San Diego show was fun but not great (she hasn't yet found herself as a live performer)—and the new songs sound musically very promising (couldn't hear no words). New album already recorded, due in the fall. Last thing I want to say is some kind of nod to Chrissie Hynde, who pioneered ("Brass in Pocket,"

"Tattooed Love Boys") much of this territory, in her own inimitable fashion. Is rock and roll a sound, or a set of values? I think it has to be both at once, and that's just for starters. Rhythm and vision.

A sound and a set of values is the whole story of **Uncle Tupelo**'s new album *Anodyne*, and it's a story well worth hearing. If Phair's album's a jukebox, Uncle T's is a fantasy alternative country radio station playing great punky stuff in the background that seeps into consciousness a chord here and a phrase or a riff there, till you're shouting along something totally weird like, "There's only circumstances, but it's the difference that gets in the way!" and you have no idea what song this is or what decade it might come from, but gee, they've been playing it a lot lately and it's getting into your blood.

Wonderful album. Rock and roll or whatever you wanna call it is all about assimilation, always has been, I mean from the very first day or before, and here we still are at seventeen, twenty-seven, thirty-seven, forty-seven, or whatever years old, with our electric guitars and some kind of 8-track or CD-ROM reissue of Hank Williams, Robert Johnson, Billie Holiday, Howlin' Wolf, Buddy Holly, Little Richard, Jimmie Rodgers, the Jam, Louis Jordan, Roky Erickson, Om Khalsoum . . . you know what I'm talking about. We're hearing things. Obvious things, too, meaning for our moment the Beatles Neil Young Brian Wilson Prince the Who Bob Dylan R.E.M. Van Morrison Otis Redding Patti Smith Velvet Underground Hendrix Zeppelin Aretha Miles and of course our contemporaries, from Sonic Youth to Pearl Jam to XTC to Dr. Dre to Bonnie Raitt . . . Any individual music-maker is only listening to a few of these things at the present moment, probably, but he or she is hearing them intensely, in new ways, getting excited about certain emphases or possibilities, and meanwhile there's all this other input in the memory banks, conscious and unconscious, all this music we've already heard, from *Sesame Street* to Stravinsky, Gershwin, Bach, Stockhausen, the Kingston Trio, Rodgers and Hammerstein, Elton John—no generation or culture has ever listened to or been exposed to such a variety of music. The invention of the marketable recording unit brought this to pass (I consider radio a secondary factor, at least from 1967 forward), and so here we are, and the new musics of our age—jazz, rap, rock, and the fascinating boundary-less pop hybrids that are springing up around the globe—are musics made by musicians who are also this new kind of listener.

And the music they make is about personal expression, and innovation, but it's also, hugely, about assimilation. We can't help it. As artists we may hear many different languages but we only speak one language, at least at any given moment; one that is shaped by our unique natures and also by all the sources that have taught us what language can be and have given us the desire to speak it.

So we assimilate these sources, consciously and unconsciously, and include them within a musical language of our own. Sometimes, as in the case of Counting Crows (or Jim Morrison when I first heard him) (or Elvis Presley when he burst on the scene), the sources seem undigested, and we suspect we are being offered warmed-over copies of existing archetypes. But then if you listen, you may find that this artist is achieving something new and worthwhile through these quotations, is in fact (in the best cases) keeping the earlier music alive by incorporating it into the ongoing conversation.

Other artists, like Björk or the Breeders or Pavement or Cindy Lee Berryhill or R.E.M., are slightly less obvious in their borrowings, so that our first impression may be of the differentness and wholeness of the sound, and then as we listen we hear more and more quotations, become more aware of some of the sources and influences that have been brought together in this new amalgam.

Uncle Tupelo on their new album (it was apparently preceded by three others, two described as loud and thrashy and one as soft and folky) create a sound that is fresh and familiar and idiosyncratic all at once. I haven't heard all the cowpunk bands—maybe there were some that sounded like this—but if any of them turned out an album that came together this well, I'd think someone would have told me about it. To a much greater degree than the works already discussed in this essay, it is an album where the music sticks to the listener much more than the words do, and where the impact of the album listened to as a whole is far beyond that of any particular song. So I can't really do my lyric-quoting thing this time and hope to get something across to you. And I don't know how to quote on paper the friendly mournfulness of the guitar-and-fiddle riff that opens the album ("Slate") or the pounding insistence of "Chickamauga" 's guitar/vocal/drums combination, or the teasing melodic riff (dobro, guitar) in "Fifteen Keys" and the way it taunts and tantalizes the singer. The hooks on this album are odd ones; you can't always point to them or hold them in your brain, can't whistle 'em to yourself (for the most part) between listens, but then that feeling when you hear them again is so reliably bittersweet and satisfying and (if you're so inclined) meaningful, that, well, it's the kind of disc that gets a lot of spins once a person connects with it. If radio stations played sectors of albums instead of individual songs, this one could have broken big time.

Actually, I have a career suggestion for Uncle Tupelo. If they're as good a live band as this album suggests (like Joe Henry's, it was recorded live in two weeks, and, interestingly, it was recorded by the same engineer-producer, Brian Paulson, though in Austin instead of New Orleans), and if they have incredible stamina and willingness and an ability to hang in for the long haul, they might want to follow the Grateful Dead model. Tour forever, play the same songs over and over but different each time, have fun doing it, and let the word get out. Kids would like this stuff, if other kids told them about it, and maybe just as much so in 2001 or 2020 as now. Hard work but steady work . . .

I guess I offer this thought partly in the awareness that even though I've met quite a few people who are enthusiastic about this album (I was originally turned on to it by a record store clerk/owner who testified so convincingly he got the sale), it still is quite likely that the potential audience (or reachable audience, which is what really matters in financial terms) is not large enough to keep these guys on a major label very long, even if their next album is equally appealing (always a challenge). And on the other hand it's extraordinarily difficult to sell enough albums through an indie label (for reasons of distribution and promotion—reaching those potential listeners) to keep a band on the road and in the recording studio and also allow the band members to keep their families in shoes and shredded wheat, as my grandpa used to say.

You either get rich in this business, or you have to quit after a few years and get yourself a day job. There's very little middle ground. Weird. But I have to admit that this rather Darwinian environment does function fairly well to produce a constant supply of interesting new music by ambitious (hopeful) newcomers. I do strongly regret that Ron Elliott and Sal Valentino of the Beau Brummels, for example, weren't somehow empowered to go on making superb albums together year after year, decade after decade, but on balance this stinking system works okay for us listeners. For the musicians . . . well, throughout history it's always been feast or famine for music-makers; mostly the latter, but just enough of the former to continually entice the hardy and the talented. (It's possible, though, that no one told Kurt Cobain that you need a strong stomach to be in this line of work.) (Sorry, black humor. Today I guess I'm irked that he had the bad taste to quote Neil Young's hymn to Johnny Rotten in his suicide note. Somehow it reminds me of Charlie Manson saying he got the idea from reading *Stranger in a Strange Land*.)

Um, Uncle Tupelo. They're playing in the background as I write this. Mostly I don't like to have music in the background—I actually prefer silence much of the time, and like to give albums my full attention when I listen to them—but *Anodyne* works well as ambient music, even for me. The differences in the voices of the two singers (they're also the guitarists and songwriters, Jay Farrar and Jeff Tweedy) contribute effectively to the total tapestry; the songs all sound like they're cut from the same cloth but there's just enough variation to make the overall effect intriguing and attractive rather than tiresome. This is done through varying the instrumental combinations, as well—guitar-driven bands can easily fall into a loud thrashing ringing rut of sameness, but again the balance point between too much differentness and too much sameness seems particularly well realized here. The signature country instruments—lap steel, pedal steel, fiddle, banjo, mandolin—help create a sound that is full of echoes of familiar musical language without losing its freshness and modernity. Years ago Sandy Pearlman borrowed the term "readymades" from Marcel Duchamp and pointed out the centrality of the practice in rock and roll. This music is necessarily a very tight and careful mix of the new and the familiar; too much of one or the other and you lose the dynamics that allow the music to speak to us. The quest is always to zero in on that personal balance point, where the singer/musicians can speak their hearts as of this present moment and we the audience can feel equally tuned in and on time (personally and collectively) as we listen. A grand illusion, like all communication—and it works.

I'll stick to my position that this is an album of moments more than of songs, and that you'll delight in it as a complete canvas or not at all, but there is one song that runs somewhat counter to that flow for me and creates a pleasing wholeness of its own. It's called "No Sense in Lovin'," and musically it's distinguished by the interesting way the singer, Tweedy this time, times his words. (There's a lot of unusual breaking-up of verses and normal patterns of singing lyrics on this album—the songs on paper would seem to have familiar and straightforward structures, but the line-breaks, the pauses and breaths and continuities, as sung, are peculiar and delightful.) "I don't know" pause "what" pause pause pause "you've been through." The pacing of the word-thoughts, and the interpolations of instrumental commentary, and the shifting moments of transition and resolution within each verse/chorus, add tremendously to the impact of the song, which is about the difficulty of loving someone "who hates themself." I was identifying fiercely, having suffered through a similarly abusive relationship once upon a time (Tweedy captures the subtlety of the torture extremely well), when suddenly, after many listenings, I realized that the brilliant climactic hook of the song (best pause of all, the one all the others have been building up to) can actually be heard as a kind of turnaround, leading into a last verse that echoes the first ("You don't know what I've been through") and thus suggests, uh-oh, that the addressee may not be the only one who has this problem. Excellent song. "It's all a part of our bad inheritance" neatly sums up and makes unnecessary many millions of words that have been written on the subject in recent years. We count on songs to perform this service for us.

I could go on and on—you know I could. But that's enough for now. Thanks and a tip of the hat to Hoyt at the Last Record Store in Santa Rosa. The hell with Kmart.

I've worked really hard at liking **Pavement**'s second album, *Crooked Rain, Crooked Rain*. How a record gets into your house is one question—I bought this CD the day it was released because I'm so fond of their 1992 album *Slanted and Enchanted* (I was further revved up by an early rave review in *Rolling Stone*, front of the section, hot shit)—but how you decide whether you like it or not once it is in your house is another question. Do you give it two chances? ten? twenty? I think the answer for all of us is that it depends, first, on the strength of the expectations we bring to it (which might make us throw it aside in disgust after one listen because it's not what we thought we wanted, or might make us hang on for ten hearings because he/she/they've never let us down before) . . . and it depends, second, on what rewards and promises of rewards we do get each time we listen. (*Crooked Rain*)[2] is full of wonders, snatches of melody, bizarre and intriguing vocal transitions (executed with passion), charming and/or exasperating attitudes, brief barbed messages telegraphed from within larger bursts of ad-lib nonsense, a unique musical personality and intelligence, an independence and iconoclasm whose depth is surprising and encouraging, a lot of neat moments, very few songs whose titles can be remembered on demand, relatively few songs that fully take on an identity as songs. This is intentional. But challenging, at least for me. *Crooked Rain, Crooked Rain* will have a considerable influence on other musicians and will certainly strengthen and probably increase the Pavement cult, and I recommend it strongly for anyone who is curious to know what the collective musical (and in a sense, generational) mind is thinking.

And yet, when I talk about the messages I hear in the music I listen to, ideas (musical or intellectual) are not what I'm mostly talking about. First and foremost I'm talking about the pleasure and/or satisfaction of release (of anger fear pain enthusiasm loneliness joy aliveness) I get from listening to the music in question. I am drawn by little pleasures and intrigues that hold my attention, and I find value in the depths of emotional release that I experience as I spend time with albums I like. Thinking, in other words, is not enough, even very smart thinking or very hip thinking, even if it's musically smart and hip as well or instead. I stick with a record when I get release and pleasure from its musical and verbal narrative, and from the narrative of the performance. It's not enough for me just to be impressed. I need to identify myself with or into the music in some way, I need to make a visceral connection.

And I keep thinking that's about to happen with *Crooked Rain, Crooked Rain*, and it does for a moment, and then it doesn't again. Slippery. Falls away from me.

It's supposed to fall away. I know. And I've wanted to love it for that quality, but I haven't quite been able to. I suspect the (understandable) difference between *Slanted and Enchanted* and *Crooked Rain, Crooked Rain* is that the former is self-consciously self-conscious and the latter (following public recognition) is Self-consciously self-conscious. $(CR)^2$ is a collection of songs most of which purposely deconstruct (fall apart) before their three minutes or six minutes are over. Phil Dick used to write novels like that. I liked that effect better.

This is very much a matter of taste. I've had trouble with Sonic Youth, too. There's a lot that appeals to me keenly on their album *Dirty*, for example, but there's a lot that frustrates me in the same songs, and I've listened and listened, expecting to suddenly relax and find the place in me that just loves the album, and it hasn't happened. This is probably my deaf spot (one of my many deaf spots), or we can chalk it up to de gustibus non est disputandum. I think it's kind of a comic absurdity (excesses of twentieth-century humans) that I listen to and imagine I appreciate as much different music as I do. And one of the things that's appealing about Pavement, especially to rock critics (and to indie-rock record fans, many of whom, I'm sure, are compulsive record buyers and collectors, always on the lookout for something suitably obscure to connect with), is that they (specifically Stephen Malkmus, who has apparently emerged from anonymity as the primary creative force behind the group's unique sound and sensibility, though co-founder Scott Kannberg, aka Spiral Stairs, seems to have played at least a Brian Jones role in the sensibility department) . . . Oh God, my digression got too long . . . What's appealing about Pavement is that they speak from the gentle edge of information overload. They know they (and we) have heard too much music, have too many calls waiting, for there to be any reason to try to answer another one. Sometimes they even put this in words ("Music scene is crazy, bands start up / Each and every day") ("Say good night to the last psychedelic band") ("Good night"—different song—"to the rock-and-roll era / 'Cause they don't need you any more") . . . but most of all it's in the music, coming up with a great catchy tune with wild changes like "Unfair" and even attaching to it wonderfully geographical lyrics full of California-driver energy and then instead of pulling it together with a musical bridge and maybe a payoff message or image, there's a kind of musically and mentally collapsed image in the final minute-plus, flailing around screaming about "I'm your neighbor and I need favors," a comment maybe arising from the earlier description of the California aqueduct, a famous huge one-way neighborly borrowing . . . but it doesn't work as a song, as a narrative, unless you just dig exploding narratives, which could be a matter of taste, or it could be as phony as claiming to enjoy exploding cigars, I don't know.

My personal opinion is these kids are taking acid too often and in too small doses, but what do I know?

My favorite song is "Range Life," which I realize now I've been unconsciously hearing as "Ridge Life," an image I like better—if I lived in Stockton, my fantasies would be aimed at the high foothills, not the dreary dusty range. Pavement is one of the first California bands to sound as regional as someone from Austin or Athens, and you need to know a rather specialized geography to decipher their lyrics: ". . . from Sacto northern Cal." Hey I know what he's saying. We got the original Valley Boy here, but that's a geographical in-joke, too. The other unifying thread in these not-quite-lyrics—many of them do truly seem to be improvised in the studio, with occasional nice touches like, "And they're coming to the chorus now"—is references to the music biz and the meaning of the attention one attracts. *Slanted and Enchanted*, you see, was a truly left-field success, selling very well through reviews and, mostly, word of mouth (remember when Suicidal Tendencies' first album took off that way?) and catapulting the band into a kind of hero status when they actually refused to be impressed by or interested in the money the major labels started waving at them. *Significant* money, as in the old "we've established what you are; now we're haggling over the price" gag. Pavement shrugged. (Asphalt shrugged?) Indie-rock fans (and maybe many of the rest of us) had been praying for someone to have the chutzpah to do that, to turn down the (probably apocryphal) million dollars, not for political reasons but for aesthetic ones. "I could really give a fuck." We have a strong collective desire for such freedom.

And yet, ironically, "Range Life," with its broken falsetto and haunting melody over a deceptively straightforward song structure and mostly audible and comprehensible words (cryptic, but likably so, accessibly so), falls apart in the last verse, not musically this time (the lack of a last chorus is actually quite effective), but by the intrusiveness of Malkmus's sarcastic putdowns of two "competing" bands, Smashing Pumpkins and Stone Temple Pilots. A careful listen suggests that the real subject is "meaning," and that the singer makes no claim that his work means anything, either; indeed he seems proud that it doesn't . . . but it doesn't matter, the scorn is authentic and ultimately comes off as childish and distracting. "I'm cooler than you are." Probably he is. Or he was, until he made that claim. Anyway, it just makes it hard to love and delight in the song as a whole as much as I would like to.

Cindy says they use unusual chords, in a new musical lineage related to My Bloody Valentine, Sonic Youth, and the Breeders (and the Fall, according to reviews I've read)—not the basic major chords like G, C, D that underlie most of the music we listen to, but something inventive and "modal" and truly alternative. I don't have an ear for that, but I do recognize the differentness, in the melodies and the changes within the melodies, in the (very distinctive) sound of the singer's voice, and in certain basic assumptions about what a song or recording or performance is, how you approach it, what it's for. New compositional values. New colors, new types of relationships between colors. The future of painting will be affected by these canvases. The only thing is, I'd be exaggerating if I claimed to be receiving the information encoded here. It intrigues and attracts me. But whenever my attention does manage to hitch a ride for a while, it always ends up being abruptly abandoned somewhere on the side of the interstate, far away from any recognizable exit. Darn. Brush myself off, stick out my thumb, start over. I did sort of enjoy the ride . . .

New values? Or just another assertion that the old values are bankrupt? I don't know, and I'm confused because I have my listening techniques and they work well for me with a wide variety of musics, and then I come up against stuff I respect but can't quite gain access to. I'm fairly certain Pavement could have made an album just as innovative and off-the-wall as this one that would also have given me great emotional (and intellectual) satisfaction and would have allowed me to promise you you'll find something transcendent here if you just stay with it. But, uh, they didn't. And every indication is, they didn't want to. They're rejecting me as a listener the same way they rejected those record companies (sort of—this new album, like the last, is on Matador, a New York indie that also put out the Liz Phair album; but the new Pavement album is partly distributed by Atlantic/Warner under a probably noble experiment to see if an indie label can get within fifty yards of a major and not be transformed instantly into Geffen Junior).

Confused and rejected. I'd rather be slanted and enchanted, any day. But there's an aesthetic here, unexpected and consistent and original. I want to make it give me something that I'm used to getting from songs and records I like, and it won't cooperate. Oh well. Maybe we'll connect again next time. Or maybe someday I'll be able to look back and give Pavement credit for teaching me that there are other ways to do this dance.

If **Cindy Lee Berryhill** were not my girlfriend, it's possible I would find myself listening to her new album *Garage Orchestra* even more frequently. It is, I think (though you know I can never be "objective"), that most precious of marketable recording units: a record that becomes a good friend. There's not enough music like this in the world. I've stood by for the last year or two watching this album come into existence, and I still don't understand how it happened.

I also don't know what will happen now, and I have to admit that's distracting. Part of the drama of rock and roll is that each artist and each new work inescapably exists and is perceived within a context of (commercial) success or failure. You can be Pavement, ostensibly not concerned in the least about success (or actively trying to dodge it), and that very fact becomes your public context and even part of the reason for your popularity. Counting Crows, now that their first single and album are huge hits, are naturally perceived and judged (and resented) in terms of the drama of their elevation from nobodies to somebodies. That's just the way we do things around here, and they knew it and sang about it before it even happened. "When everybody loves me, I will never be lonely." This promise has an empty ring to it. And yet "big stars" is what we become anyway, because someone needs us to play that role.

Success can be embarrassing, mind-deadening, and may even lead to fatal self-destructiveness, but of course the Cindy Lee Berryhills and Joe Henrys and Uncle Tupelos of the world are more concerned with the consequences of lack of success, since it makes it very hard for your beloved creation to find its intended listeners, and also tends to reduce the likelihood that you'll get the financing necessary to record and promote your next work of art.

Success or failure. Suddenly the important thing is not the beauty and humor and glorious musicality of this set of recordings, but whether or not it falls between the cracks of possible airplay formats. Nevertheless, as I said before, what's amazing about the music business at present is how well it does function, despite its obvious corruptions and blind spots and structural inefficiencies, to keep bringing forth a terrific variety of new (and old) artists and new sorts of music. So let me put aside my very personal considerations about whether I'm going to have to run to keep up with my friend's skyrocket or help her climb out of debt and discouragement, and just tell you what it is I like so much about this record.

It's joyful. I don't remember that ever being the conscious intention or objective, but as soon as the CD came out and was on the turntable, that was unmistakably the key to the album's personality— it makes a joyful noise. I got a letter from Brian Cullman that expresses it well: "Pleasure is one of the hardest things to convey in music, in song. Yearning, sorrow, longing—that's a cinch, but real pleasure, upfulness, the spark and the light, is one of the hardest feelings to capture without sounding smug or contrived. Cindy Lee's record seems very much to be a celebration, very welcoming and openhearted. Pure pleasure."

Playfulness. The other thing this album seems to be to be about is sense of wonder. That's addressed directly in "I Wonder Why" ("I love those great big things that make you wonder and feel all funny inside") and shows up fairly obviously in songs like "Radio Astronomy" ("Then I checked again / To see if I was right / This had never been / Detected by light") and "UFO Suite"; but more than that, there is a constant quality all through the album of wonder at the magical properties of sounds and music. What happens if you put this and this together? The bizarre instrumentation of the album (the key players are Randy Hoffman on orchestral percussion, including timpani and vibes, Renata Bratt on cello, Giovanni Verdi on stand-up bass, and Chris Davies on electric bass, plus Cindy on electric—never acoustic—guitar; you'll also hear viola, banjo, violin, jaw harp, flute, autoharp, clarinet, and vocal harmonies) comes from a childhood ambition to be Professor Harold Hill from *The Music Man*, and an adult fascination with the sounds constructed live in a recording studio by the two greatest amateur orchestra leaders of our era, Phil Spector and Brian Wilson. These guys are considered geniuses, but, elevation to sainthood aside, what they were doing was bringing in musicians not ordinarily associated with a rock or soul band and listening to their instruments and then applying those sounds, often in unexpected combinations, to the music they heard in their heads. A funny little gift—maybe not as rare as perfect pitch, maybe rarer— this ability to hear and organize musical parts in your mind. That's one reason this album bears up so well under repeated listenings: There are all kinds of interesting parts going on all the time, pleasing and intriguing bits of musical business, sometimes different than anything you've heard before and other times happily familiar but always surprisingly suited to the musical, lyrical, structural, and/or emotional spirit of the song. And all these parts just naturally contain and express the conductor/composer's delight at the wonderful sounds that instruments make and the magical power of placing one sound or melody on top of another sound or melody. It's not an ego trip (that comes when Mr. Spector is talking to the press later). It's more like a religious experience.

It's fun. This is not an "art" album. It's a music album, a low-budget chunky-electric-guitar-driven pop album, girlish-voiced singer-songwriter "chirping, howling and moaning" (the phrase is Andy Langer's, from the *Austin Chronicle*; actually, there's a fair amount of just plain singing in there, too), a portfolio of her songs— well-crafted, wacky, most of them story-songs of one sort or another ("UFO Suite" is a Technicolor movie), all of them first person but not all of them featuring the same protagonist necessarily, unless she's a shape-changer, which may be what the first song ("Father of the Seventh Son") implies.

"Father of the Seventh Son" skrees at first to see if you can be scared off, and if you can't then you're cool and are invited in to see the show. Berryhill has written liner notes (a throwback, or maybe Dylan has restarted something) illuminating each song, like a headphone tour in a museum. "This song i suppose is a history of a particular genealogical lineage beginning with the great molecular batter that brought forth the earth, and ending up at the surf shop in hermosa beach." The punctuation is weird to show that she's her own kind of creature. The lyrics are like that, too, swooping from charming clarity to inaudible absurdity and back again: now you're following the narrative, now the train's gone into a tunnel, now you're following it again but everything looks different. *Lots* of neat musical stunts on this one (still talking about "Seventh Son"), plus a fine groove when the rhythm section kicks in, but most of all I like the sound of her voice (an acquired taste, like Joe Henry's, Jay Farrar's, Liz Phair's, Lou Reed's, Bob Dylan's), especially in the chorus. And the way she says "hither thither." The opening words of the album— "Stole an angel's wing and started to fly"—resonate nicely with Counting Crows and Joe Henry and all the other romantics I've been listening to. Even Pavement are romantics. ("Silent kid, no one to remind you . . .") It comes with the territory.

"I Wonder Why" 's a particular favorite. Nailed it for posterity; I was afraid maybe she wouldn't (Great songs get away all the time; ask any songwriter's companion.) Wonderful performance, especially the plucked strings and the vocal harmonies and the solo rhythm-guitar turnarounds. And the timpani. This song is a perfect place to start if you want to get a sense of the richness and delightful crudeness of the *Garage Orchestra* arrangements. Like the name implies. The co-producers (Berryhill and Michael Harris) are both big Beach Boys and Velvet Underground fans. Ragged glory. Someone else would have made it too pretty, with this melody the temptation's tremendous. The mix on this track (and throughout the album) is a miracle.

Lots of weirdly pretty melodies. This week I'm entranced by "Etude for Ph. Machine."

The arrangements are all Cindy Lee's, by the way. I notice Liz Phair also made a point of giving herself a credit line for arrangements. And rightly so. Another trend. Women arranging their own stuff (Björk, Tanya Donnelly, PJ Harvey on her demos at least, Kim Deal, Marie Daulne) is a significant part of why there's been so much good music around lately.

What's great about the mix is you can easily listen to the vocal and/or any aspect of the track. And get great pleasure from both.

And you know, that might be all I have to say. I like all these songs, and many of the most spectacular ("Gary Handeman," "UFO Suite" "I Want Stuff" "Song for Brian") I haven't talked about yet, but it's embarrassing, zeroing in on favorite vocal and musical moments in these performances that seem to be talking to me the way a good record seems to be talking to whoever is listening to it, except in this case maybe sometimes it really is me . . . Part of my rationale for including this album in this discussion, in spite of the obvious difficulties in "reviewing" something I'm so close to, was that it could provide a different and fruitful angle on the linked questions that are tickling me this month: where the songs come from (what the vintners buy) and who owns them (are music and art and writing and speech to be conceived of first and foremost as property?).

What I'd like to argue (and I think it's the position I've usually taken about my own writing) is that, to a significant degree, the songs come from and belong to their listeners.

I'll take it as an article of faith that almost all of the music (or any kind of art) that really moves me is inspired creation. That is, the person or persons who created it were not following a set of guidelines so much as they were trying to realize (make real) an inspiration that seized them at some point very early in the creative process and continued to be the primary or ultimate guidance they turned to throughout the work. One telltale sign of inspiration is that it often goes contrary to what is reasonable, logical, expected, normally done. An artist who *tries* to be innovative often ends up producing a bunch of limp ideas—limp because there's no life and consciousness in them. An artist following her inspiration, on the other hand (and keep in mind that while we may foolishly think we can describe our inspiration in words, to ourselves or others, we almost never can; we can only feel it, and constantly grope in that direction, and be forced to go on working by nothing more than the vague sense that we still aren't *there* yet), ends up being innovative only because she keeps being given problems (or creating problems) that she can't manage to solve by any of the techniques she's already familiar with. And innovation is just the beginning. The real payoff with inspiration is passion, sincerity, purpose, universality, the sound of a person speaking and singing new language in a voice that is uniquely her own . . . which somehow turns out to be, when the wind is right, exactly what you or I as listeners needed and wanted to hear. This voice speaks from and for the artist, but it would not have come into existence unless there were someone there (or at least the illusion, or sensation, of someone there) to speak to.

We create through our listening. This is magic, if only because it contradicts the normal flow of time. When I write, I feel you reading my words, and constantly make choices based on that feeling, even though you are definitely up the timeline (a month, a year, a decade in the future) from this moment in which I work. Without that listening, the artist is unemployed. I don't just mean unpaid; I mean he or she has no work to do, no ability to make herself work in any meaningful or satisfying fashion. The audience creates the art through the artist. Haven't you ever had an excited conversation in which you heard yourself saying things you didn't know you knew? The person you were talking with brought those things forth from you, with his or her need. You could feel that at the time. Their need and sincerity gave you authenticity, energy, inspiration.

What the vintners buy, ultimately, according to my peculiar argument, is not grapes or sulfites or wooden barrels, but the moment of our imbibing. That gives them purpose. That gives them work. That allows them to make choices, and to create something precious thereby.

This does not fit the property model. And property, which still dominates our culture, our civilization, our worldview, has a simple way of dealing with things that don't fit its model: it acts as if they don't exist. I own this land, this song, this magazine, this piece of software. Pay up. "What if I don't/can't/won't?" you ask. Then I'm afraid I'll have to call the cops. They work for me, you know. They owe their souls to the company store.

"Intellectual property" is the buzzword for "Meet the new cop." GATT and NAFTA are an opportunity for third-world or fourth-world people to pay a royalty on every "improved" seed they put in the ground, and on every byte of information that flows to and through their boondocks, including the weather report. In terms of music, the rules of the game are that you can smash as many pumpkins as you want as long as you do it for Polydor International or one of her five sisters. Cindy's on Cargo but they're hoping to make a distribution deal with RCA. For her sake and theirs (and ours, the listeners) they want her to be able to sell more than ten thousand albums. And there are, I believe, more than ten thousand customers who would gain pleasure and other intangibles from hearing her music.

And I'm not saying the system doesn't work, and I'm not saying it's evil, and I'm not even saying it should be changed. But in fact it's always changing, and our awareness has an impact on this process. So I'm on my soapbox today to say, these seven albums I've singled out and many others besides, have Power. They tell me more of what I need to know today than all the newspapers on the planet. And they are also much more useful when I want to share this knowledge with other people. This is an encoding of information—words and music, songs, albums, performance—that touches our hearts and minds in ways that matter and that have (ahem) authentic value-based content. Human feelings. Vision. Rhythm. Spirit. Insight.

Please do not fall for the deception that this Power belongs to "big stars" or "big record companies" or "geniuses" or "lucky stiffs" or anyone at all who is someone other than you.

What I've learned from living with a songwriter/performer (like from living with myself, but it's more visible this way) is that the process by which the good stuff comes into existence is, and probably always will be, truly mysterious. But I know where it starts. If something strong and pure and intelligent is coming through, it starts here in our attention. "I met you, Brian, and I fell in love / Last night." The song's about a dream. And what the dreamer is dreaming about is communication. "I knew your skin would feel this right." "I just kept thinking about the choruses."

Copyright © 1994 by whoever has ears to hear. Please, keep us working. Thank you.

6

THE PRESENCE OF YOUR ABSENCE

Loneliness is universal truth. Music, popular or otherwise, is one of humankind's three great efforts to fill this gap (the other two are sex and religion). (I omit companionship because it's not an effort. It just is. Different category.) Music reaches out for something. Deliberately, intelligently, passionately, yet mostly unconsciously. This is an essay about Smokey Robinson.

And his listeners.

Where do songs come from? I'm itching to get to the songs themselves, but first I need to dredge up again an extraordinary quote from 1967, which I used as an (unexplained) epigraph to my 1968 essay "How Rock Communicates." Smokey told *Hit Parader* magazine: "I have never consciously written a song through a personal experience or an inspiration. I never write about things that happen to me. A lot of writers will say they did a song because they were in a certain mood but that's never happened to me. I can write happy when I'm sad or sad when I'm happy. I just get an idea and work on it."

This comment was repeated to Michael Lydon in 1968. Lydon (in a *Rolling Stone* essay included in his fine book *Rock Folk*) quotes Smokey's "theory of songwriting": "Make a tune that has a complete idea and tells a story in the time allotted for a record. It has to be something that means something, not just a bunch of words on music. But I can write about anything. Some people say they write from experience. Not me. I can never remember having something happen and writing a song about it. I write songs no matter what mood I'm in; it's my work, dig?"

I don't dig, actually, but I'm willing to take his word for it. I'm also willing to accept that Robinson may have changed his approach, or rather his perception of it, sometime after 1968, for David Ritz, co-author of Smokey's hard-to-find 1989 autobiography, writes in the notes to the new box set (**Smokey Robinson and the Miracles, _The 35th Anniversary Collection_**): "As a writer, Smokey's sensitivity allowed him to work autobiographically. After the premature birth and death of twin girls, he tried to console Claudette—and himself—by turning the tragedy into a pledge of lifetime love, 'More Love.'"

Ritz then quotes some lyrics from the song that completely fail to make his point. "I'll always belong only to you" is a great line as performed, but not exactly intimate or revealing. There isn't even a hint in the quoted verse, or in the song, that this pledge of eternal love is in response to a mutual loss. Presumably Ritz is sharing with us something his collaborator shared with him about the circumstances of this song's composition, but the effect on consideration is to _strengthen_ the claims Smokey made to his interviewers back in the era when he was actually writing his string of masterpieces ("More Love" was released in May 1967). "Happy when I'm sad" indeed.

My favorite song in the whole world tonight (okay, it got left out of _The 100 Best Singles_; so sue me) is "The Hunter Gets Captured by the Game," by the Marvelettes, released December 1966; lead vocal Wanda Young, written and produced by William ("Smokey") Robinson. Not everything Smokey's written is poetry, by a long shot, but the first verse of "Hunter" stands up to the best of Bob Dylan, Chuck Berry, or Robert Johnson. And what an astonishing vocal performance! This is an auteur record, surely, like it's not taking anything away from Ronnie Spector to speak of her extraordinary singing on "Be My Baby" as evidence of her future husband's vision and genius. Going behind the scenes for a moment, we flash back to the origin of the Miracles, pulled together by fourteen-year-old Smokey as the Five Chimes in 1954. By 1955, Ronnie White, Pete Moore, and Bobby Rogers were all already there, as they would be for the next seventeen years, along with Smokey and, much of the time, Smokey's wife (and Bobby's cousin) Claudette.

Flash forward to Smokey telling Lydon (1968): "I don't think I'd still be in this business if it wasn't for the Miracles. We've stayed together because we legitimately love each other." Back again to 1964–66, when Smokey as producer and writer saw Wanda Young, who had been mostly a backup singer to Gladys Horton's lead, as the "sleeping giant" of the Marvelettes. "She had this little voice that was sexy to me," and ultimately he succeeded in creating two great songs for and with that voice, "Don't Mess with Bill" and "The Hunter Gets Captured by the Game."

And the point of this story is that although Smokey seems to have been generous with every Motown artist he worked with, I believe he truly did love his fellow Miracles with all his heart . . . and by recognizing and realizing the greatness in Wanda, he was also expressing his affection for Wanda's new husband—Miracle Bobby Rogers. Like Brian Wilson knew and beatified his brothers' voices (yeah, and his cousin's, too).

"Every day brings change, and the world puts on a new face / Certain things rearrange . . ." As sung, as recorded, with that eerie harmonica/organ intro and amazing vocal–and–snare drum groove, this couplet is pure evocation of Mystery, open-ended in its implications and so specific in its mood and texture that it's the precise equivalent of a Philip K. Dick novel, except, being a three-minute song, it starts right off in the mood of the climatic scene. Things are seldom what they seem. Reality is a mimic. You can't trust it not to turn into its opposite. But the way to stay on top is to turn upside down with it.

These thoughts are unspoken, but palpable as a globed fruit. Meanwhile there is, as promised, a story being told. The intriguing song title/chorus phrase is, of course, a metaphor for a romantic relationship. But from the first notes of the record, we know that this metaphor is also something bigger, a meta-metaphor, something about the world and every day that we're in it. A scene is set, as in *Heart of Darkness*, that almost breaks our minds with its poignance and intensity and scary ambiguity, but meanwhile there's this narrative to cling to, bringing us into the maelstrom and, it is promised, out again. Except we leave some important part of our consciousness—listen to the changes as the rhythm guitar steps forward on the second couplet the spin of the melodic build, and that phrasing: "trailing" "fox" "preys" "rabbit"—and our souls behind.

And then—still working on the first verse here—"Ooo ooo ooo ooo, you were . . ." What was that?!! Who sang that? What is she doing to me? Song comes apart into its component elements, and we confront the abyss and bliss out at the sound of Wanda's voice, both at once. "I looked up and I was in your arms." Exactly. "What's this old world coming to? / Things just ain't the same." Young Jonathan Richman couldn't have summarized it more succinctly. Into the chorus now, hook after gratifying (and subtle, tasteful, *different*) hook, climaxing with the return of that opening riff/hypnotic, transmuted now into an instrumental break dividing and linking the two verses, rewiring our perspective from journey in to journey out.

An absolute masterpiece. (Patti Smith covered the song in one of her first appearances with her full band.) I haven't even mentioned Wanda's "Oh yeah"s. Who is this woman? They hold the song and universe together like pegs or rivets; and suggest the existence of an explanation for all this, or maybe just make it evident that the explanation you've already arrived at is woefully inadequate. Which is how it should be. Continuous resolution and no resolution. Pure pop pleasure, with an intelligence so paralyzing it couldn't possibly be conscious or intentional. Or accidental.

Within a month Smokey and the Miracles recorded "The Love I Saw in You Was Just a Mirage" (another Phil Dick story, another utterly gorgeous lyrical/musical/vocal masterpiece). Something was going on.

Or was it? Smokey is an elusive talent. Now you see me, now you don't. The occasion for this essay is the release of a new four-CD Smokey Robinson and the Miracles anthology (not really a box set so much as a gatefold album), *The 35th Anniversary Collection*, along with a companion volume, a superb one-disc compilation of rare and unreleased tracks called **Smokey Robinson and the Miracles, Whatever Makes You Happy: More of the Best (1961–1971)** (Rhino). Carey Mansfield and Claudette Robinson produced the four-CD set; David McLees, Bill Inglot, and Carey Mansfield produced the Rhino disc; and both collections were remastered by Bill Inglot and Dan Hersch. My pal Jonathan Lethem, a fellow Smokey fanatic, makes an interesting point: there's no evidence anywhere in the credits of any participation by Smokey in these projects. Claudette writes a stirring, personal foreword to the *35th Anniversary* booklet, but there's not even a one-sentence message from Smokey. "Smokey's not here," says Jonathan. We look at each other. There is some kind of *deep truth* in this observation ("Elvis has left the building"). I'm not sure I can articulate it. Digging around in the used-cassette bins at the local record store, I find a Temptations tape with a Smokey song I've never heard before. The title is "The Further You Look the Less You See."

This essay, like all my essays, is not precisely about Smokey Robinson but about the experience of listening to him. Keep that in mind as I go nutso analytical on you now. The question only seems to be, what makes this mysterious fellow tick? The real question is one I'm asking of myself: Why do I love his songs so much when I hear them; what is it they set ticking in me?

Smokey Robinson, in a modest way, is a very Shakespearean writer; by which I refer not to his storytelling particularly, but to his love for language, and his use of wordplay, simile, metaphor, contradiction, homilies, puns, all manner of language tricks, to catch and hold the attention of his audiences: the court/music biz on the one hand, and the workaday public, the paying customers, on the other. Jugglers, jongleurs, fools, magicians. Artists. This sort of artistry is not passionate in the emotional sense; Smokey does not and has never tried to regularly bare his soul in the manner that Otis Redding or Aretha Franklin seem to in all their good performances. There's deep emotion in his work, but it is contained, wrapped in a package. Shakespeare was not particularly autobiographical, either, though the soliloquies often give at least the impression of an author directly shouting out his own deep feelings. But the two Bills are as passionate as Beethoven when it comes to sticking their hands into the clay of their art form, which in their case is language (verbal and visual and performed for Shakespeare; verbal and musical and performed for Smokey). Smokey loves the lyrical (and, to an only slightly lesser extent, melodic and rhythmic and structural) language of song. He is indeed an analytical philosopher of song, a Wittgenstein, interested in the meaning of meaning. To what extent does saying a thing make it so? Taking the role, usually, of a lover, Smokey's format is the convoluted assertion, the statement that draws its strength from the pleasant effort the recipient goes through to decipher it, capture it, receive it, figure it out.

An extreme and thoroughly delightful example is the title song of *Whatever Makes You Happy*, one of two songs included in both collections. The character who sings "Whatever Makes You Happy" is a hopeless masochist, but Smokey pushes him beyond all imaginable limits until he becomes in fact the blissful devotee he asserts himself to be. This is achieved through the unself-conscious (even joyous) sincerity of the vocal performance, and through the magnificent directness and clarity of the lyrics' assault on normal emotional logic. "If my sadness brought you gladness, I'd be glad to be sad." How can one be glad while sad? By making sincere sadness a gift of love, of devotion, so that it is contained within a "larger" feeling. But logic is about to be stretched further: "If my feeling bad made you feel good, I would always feel bad." This is elegant and also—please don't miss the point—very funny. The rhymes, the meter, the timing, all contribute to an irresistible deadpan humor. The chorus broadens our smile by musically and lyrically expanding the expansiveness: "And I wouldn't think twice about the sacrifice, anything that I'd have to do . . ." Punch line: " 'Cause whatever makes you happy, makes me happy too!"

Are we supposed to believe these assertions? The speaker convinces me that he believes them, but still the answer is: no. We (as the listener, the beloved) are simply meant to be charmed. And disarmed. The purpose of romantic poetry is not that it be believed forever or even at the moment it's spoken. Its purpose, rather, is to delight the listener and create in her or him a receptivity. This is addressed more directly in "I'll Try Something New": "I will build you a castle with a tower so high, it reaches the moon . . ." No, perhaps he won't, quite. But haven't we always wanted someone to make such promises?

The charm of the narrator of "I'll Try Something New" is that of the unrepentant romantic; but the charm of the speaker in "Whatever Makes You Happy" is more giddy, obsessive, scary. One simply seeks to repeal the laws of nature. The other, however, seeks to repeal the laws of emotional transactions, and since an emotional transaction is what is actually taking place, this has a skitterish edge to it. All bright musical cheerfulness, the bridge repeats the point and, by being more specific, expands the speaker's promises even further: "Even if you wanted / Someone else to take my place / Although I love you so much, I'd still give you up / Just to keep a smile on your face." The verse returns with more wordplay in the now formal (established) manner: "If my x your y, then I'd y my x." ("If my sorrow brought you joy, I'd enjoy my sorrow.") And off into the sunset trilling, "Whatever makes you happy, ooo ooo ooo." This person clearly needs to be institutionalized. And yet we can see ourselves in him.

And, oddly enough, this song, written in 1962 (recorded at the same session as a much better known masterpiece, "You've Really Got a Hold on Me"), seems to mirror its author's careerlong stance regarding his artistic identity: "The market, man, the market is people. It is the kids who are buying the records. This is the people you're trying to reach. I think that satisfying people, on the whole, if you're in business, is more important than self-satisfaction" (to Michael Lydon, 1968). This is clearly not false modesty, not an attempt to be fashionably unpretentious. It is what the man believes, and how he directed his own work during his most productive and inspired years. Smokey Robinson is perhaps the only great performer of his era who was also a major producer (of other people's records, not just his own) and a successful and active music-business executive. Strange combination. But Wallace Stevens was an insurance-company executive when he wasn't writing poetry. And Henry David Thoreau was a bum. All of us are a little off in some fashion.

(Does it make him happy to make us happy? Does it make him happy to know he has the power to make us happy, or to feel himself exercising that power? Does it make him happy to collect and spend the money we fork over to our happiness providers? Did he semiretire from his job as "young America" 's poet laureate in the early 1970s because it wasn't making him happy anymore? Do we need to know the answers? The guy in the recording—and his background accompanists—will forever speak to us, personally and reliably, and in the present tense.)

Inspiration. Smokey claims in those interviews I quoted that he doesn't write from inspiration, but on this I beg to differ. There are, as one might expect, great songs and not-so-great songs on these five compact discs (and on the other discs and tapes and albums I've dragged out to extend my current Smokey studies into the realms of his productions and his solo work). And the only way that I know of to explain to myself the difference between the two is to speak in terms of one song/recording as a product of pure inspiration, and the other as something no more or less than a good day's work.

I claim, in other words, to be able to hear inspiration even if or when the author claims it's not there. "The Words from My Heart Get Caught Up in My Throat" is nothing if not a workmanlike bit of pop songcrafting, and yet there's something that happens on this recording that thrills me. What is it? It's not the craft (I assert), although the craft is certainly a vehicle that makes possible its arrival. It is *enthousiasmos*. The song's subject matter is routine and clichéd. But the song soars. I assert, without analyzing its charms, that something comes to life here. God, or Elvis, has entered the building. Spirit is walking through the bass player's fingers. And the singers' voice.

More than one singer (include all those house musicians, too). One voice.

And when that life breathes itself in, song or painting or whatever it is transcends its subject matter, at least from the perspective of the listener, and is suddenly able to speak metaphorically, in the sense that we start hearing things beyond the simplest literal interpretation. At this point the song is speaking directly to its particular listener, often about the immediate circumstances he or she find him/ herself in. This is magic, but it happens all the time. One aspect of this, but only one, is that every work of art can be heard as being about itself, about this act and moment of creation. In this case, Smokey could be speaking (consciously or unconsciously) of obstacles that come up during his creative process: "My heart is getting discouraged with giving me line after line after line / But my lips can't relate what my heart has to say; they stutter and stammer each time." Paradoxically, however, these words are being written and performed at a time when lips and heart *are* able to get themselves into alignment, making expression possible. And every one of us listening, regardless of what the song is about for us, can feel the joyous sense of release that results.

(Of course, I'm a writer, and was frustrated in this fashion not many hours ago. So I listen and come up with this interpretation. You see how it works.)

As must often be the case with these chronological retrospectives, the middle two discs (of *35th Anniversary*) are the most rewarding. Familiar story: author searches for voice, finds voice, speaks eloquently for a glorious while, loses voice again. Remember, the artists we're speaking of (rock and soul recording artists) are working in a pop marketplace. It's an exhausting medium. It exhausts you, then it drops you (or props up your empty carcass, to see if you can still draw flies, I mean, paying customers). Or, if you have the rare good sense Smokey seems to have been blessed with, *you* drop *it*, before you completely exhaust yourself. You go on and do your work in other forms, that may not be appropriate to being shrinkwrapped and sold at a discount at Price Club. (Of course, your shrinkwrapped manifestation will give the impression that you must have lost your juice back in 1971 or so, but you learn to live with that. You're not allowed to leave a winner. You have to successfully pretend to be some kind of a failure in order to get permission to quit the game.)

Smokey's other form, to the extent that it's visible (no reason I should know what else he might be up to in his life), seems to be live performance. Since leaving the Miracles in 1972 (he decided to leave in 1970, when his second child was born, and would have escaped sooner had it not been for an accidental number one record late in 1970, "Tears of a Clown," recorded in 1966), he quit the road for a couple of years, then began touring as a solo act (Claudette insisted; his restlessness and dissatisfaction were not serving him or the family). He has also recorded solo albums, lots and lots of them, most of which I haven't heard, but the ones I have checked out— and what I've been able to gather from other WR (William Robinson) fans corroborates this—are ciphers, perfunctory jazzy easy-listening constructs with only a fading footprint here and there to suggest that the creative force we know as Smokey ever even visited these sessions. But reliable sources assure me (alas, I have never seen him live, and he's not the sort of artist whose concerts turn up in the bootleg CD stacks at record swap meets, wrong demographics) that he can be joyously and righteously and inspiringly *present* as a performer of music for a live audience, that marvelous ephemeral form that allows one to be an active engaged artist every working day of your life without the disadvantages that come from leaving a trail of Product behind you. I'm addicted to product myself, but I do understand how, unlike performance, it chains one to the wheel of maya. C'mon, baby, one more Top Ten hit. Do it for your lawyers this time.

So how shall I tell you the story that *I* create (unconsciously, spontaneously, as listener) from these not-exactly-raw materials? I'm afraid of being too chronological (although I get frustrated with *35th Anniversary* for its chronological sloppiness, one 1962 track with a whole different vocal sound tossed into a sequence of 1961 tracks for no apparent reason, and so forth), because it makes it sound like this is an old story and even a brief one, whereas in fact it's a story still unfolding for me long years after I first adopted Smokey (and the Miracles) as a personal favorite; y'know, one of those artists who helps define to me who I am ("I'm the one who loves you").

Education is about pulling at a thread and unraveling a whole ball of yarn. A different ball for each seeker. Curiosity and the power of attraction draw us to the thread; continued attraction and a good narrative (one thing leading to another) hold us to it, so that we keep pulling while the universe unravels. I like artists like Smokey Robinson, and Ray Davies of the Kinks, because they live in universes unique to themselves that I find mysteriously familiar and accessible and inviting. They are not great singers in any abstract sense but they can be truly great singers of themselves, of a song that no one but Ray Davies or Smokey Robinson would write, saying things no one else would say that I needed and need to hear said. What people mean when they say they love music is what I feel when I listen to certain songs (recordings) by these and other handpicked artists. This sound makes me feel good. This chorus-phrase speaks for me. I want to hear this track again, I want to revisit this place, I want to go further into something that I can feel very clearly is here for me. Want to unravel, and be unraveled. Smokey doesn't do this to me with every song, but that's okay. I became a fan when I realized the same person/group had done it to me more than once. I became a true fan when he had connected with me like *that* some number of times more than five that might as well be infinite.

The artist's story is not my story. I like the stories of how Claudette joined the group, how Smokey met Berry Gordy, how Smokey's first successes with Mary Wells established him as a hitmaker (and gave him the power to take charge of his own sound), how Smokey and the Miracles parted friends and so forth. But my story is all about when I first heard "You've Really Got a Hold on Me," and "The Tracks of My Tears," and what happened last week while I was listening to "From Head to Toe" or "A Fork in the Road." Why I got so excited. Why I am *still* excited.

Smokey may see himself as a white-collar toiler in the (well-paid, and you can retire early) fields of songcraft, and I acknowledge his perspective, but I am required to see him as a visionary artist, because that vision is tangible to me, it is what speaks to me so enticingly from his work. This luminous quality is not present in all his songs, but when it is there it is both inexplicable ("Going to A Go-Go") and inescapable.

So let's look at the origins of vision

We don't think it up. Nor does it fall from the sky arbitrarily, a gift from a random god. When Smokey wrote "You've Really Got a Hold on Me," after two years of struggling (often quite awkwardly) to come up with another hit for the Miracles after "Shop Around," and also after a rather thrilling six months in which the first two singles he wrote and produced for Mary Wells became Top Ten hits, he was doing what he'd always done; he'd had an idea and he was working on it. Lyrical idea first, probably, and then a musical idea, and you can see how interwoven those can be: idea—it's possible to love someone but not like them. "I love you, baby, even though I can't like you." Nah. "I don't like you but I love you." That could work, maybe, if the "but" was strong enough. Now (already) the musical ideas start. Got to balance the two halves of the phrase, so the second half mirrors the first, so the listener notices this key bit of wordplay. Picking out some notes on the piano. What rhymes with "love you"? Thinking of you. "I just can't stop thinking of you." Okay, so it's a song about obsessive love, being hung up on somebody, that's why don't like but do love. So the verse melody could rise in steps like this, and then— What's a good payoff phrase for an obsessive love situation? "Babe, you've got me so hung on you." Mm, not strong enough. Besides, can't end in "you" again. "You've really got your hooks in me." I just used "really" in that Mary Wells hit. But Berry says not to be afraid of copying yourself. Okay, let's see . . .

Just working on an idea. But sometimes it takes on a life of its own, something in the words or the chords or the concept or all three excites the songwriter so much, he's operating on some higher level of creativity, things just seem to fall in place, the adrenaline is flowing and it's like this is the song he's been waiting all his life to write, so he's not afraid to use up some of those favorite ideas he's been saving, the floodgates are open, when he realizes he can turn "got a hold on me" into "hold me!" (and back again) it's more than a simple pun, it's like a deep insight into the way the universe works that he's never been able to articulate before, and then during the sessions he comes up with that little mood-piece intro, a variation on the Duprees' "You Belong to Me," that somehow resonates with and gives depth to all of the changes in the song even though it's never actually repeated . . . This state of creative excitement (it goes beyond cleverness; let's say it includes a kind of respect, and awe, and surrender) is called inspiration, and it doesn't have to happen before you start writing. It can strike right in the midst of the process, and suddenly without half knowing it you're playing for much higher stakes here. And the listener—after the song is written, and sung, and recorded and mixed and released—can tell, can feel it, there's George Harrison overcoming shyness to say to John, "I know you can't figure what I hear in this group, but anyway, *you've gotta hear this song!*"

Something happens. A sound. A mood. A concept that just clicks. Doors are thrown open in the songwriter/artist and what comes through those doors—if anything—is his personal vision or a piece of it. Private truth, personal style. It cuts through the ceaseless attempts to mirror public truth and contemporary style. That doesn't work. Or it might, if this was really about giving people what they want. But that's not enough. Smokey speaks of "satisfying" people, and to satisfy them you have to give them more than what they know they want. You have to give them what they didn't know they wanted until they heard it. And the place that comes from is inside you. Whenever you find a way to throw those doors open—

Most of Smokey's best songs originate in and center around some kind of wordplay. He likes contradiction and contrast, especially contrasting pairs ("You treat me badly / I love you madly"). He can get great mileage from moving an object to the front of a sentence ("Mistakes, I know I've made a few"). He loves any kind of metaphor, but especially an extended one ("I've got sunshine on a cloudy day / When it's cold outside, I've got the month of May") (Note the combination of contrast and metaphor, note that these opening lines constitute a riddle, which is then acknowledged directly: "I guess you'll say, 'What—?' " The listener is challenged to guess the riddle's answer before the singer reveals it at the end of the verse.) He enjoys expanding on a cliché ("From Head to Toe"), or turning it around ("Choosey Beggar") and *then* expanding on it. He likes "if" clauses ("If Romeo and you had ever met / There never would have been a Juliet") (notice the riddle, notice the lovely metrical pattern and internal rhyme, and keep in mind that none of this needs to be pointed out, every listener hears and feels it). He likes logic, or more precisely he likes the syntax of logic ("If you can want, you can need / If you can need . . ."). He respects and treasures the metaphorical and therefore evocative power of a single word or phrase ("Swept for You Baby"), and he doesn't mind a little innuendo ("It's Growing") except that somehow the gracefulness of his rhymes and verses and melodies makes it difficult to hear any of his endless songs of seduction (romantic poet through and through) as anything but gentlemanly and innocent. Possibly it was frustration with this self-created image that led him to speak of sex so directly on many of his solo recordings.

The point is not precisely that Smokey uses the above-mentioned techniques. The point is that there is a certain pleasure he gets from using them, especially when it works out well, that he communicates to us very clearly and that is central to what I call "his vision," the primary content of his work. In the same way there is a primary content to Brian Wilson's work, whether we're talking about his composing, his production, or his singing, that cannot be summarized in words but is unique to Brian and his personality. We are attracted to a Brian Wilson or a Neil Young or a Patti Smith by their music but also by their presence within that music. Philip K. Dick has a presence that permeates all his fiction and nonfiction, regardless of subject matter. It is because these artists are true to themselves (not necessarily by choice; often they can't think of any other way to do things), I think, that their work has in this sense such consistency. "Bad" or "good," it always sounds like Brian Wilson, like Smokey Robinson. Yes, it's a sound. But it's more than a sound, or a "style." It's a personality (not a persona, which is a much smaller thing), a presence. Bob Marley. Jimi Hendrix. Billie Holiday. Each of these people has a unique musical presence that can be evoked by discussing that artist's bag of tricks but which is certainly not equivalent to that "bag of tricks." We are not our tricks and habits. Rather, our tricks and habits, Neil Young's minor chords, Smokey Robinson's intricate wordplay, are expressions and extensions of us. "Before you can pry any secrets from me, you must first find the real me." Easily done. I knew the real you the first time I met you in song.

My thesis, which is unprovable and anyway a half-truth at best, is that we meet the artists who are important to us in those works of theirs in which they meet (connect with) themselves, that the electricity (called inspiration) of *that* meeting creates an aliveness, a presence, that we in turn feel when we look at the painting or hear the record. "Starry Starry Night" sizzles with intensity and is full of private meanings for every sympathetic viewer; but it is nothing more or less than Van Gogh's picture of the way the sky looked and felt to him (or even to an imagined person) on a particular evening. He could claim that there's nothing autobiographical about it: it's a painting of the sky, of a workman, of a bowl of fruit. He could claim that we're overlaying biographical information onto it, and he'd be right about that. But he couldn't claim that it isn't visionary, or personal. That's in the eye of the beholder. I may not know anything *about* Smokey Robinson from listening to his music, but I do know Smokey Robinson, I think. And there's nothing he can do about it. That's the price you pay for putting yourself out there.

The first CD of *35th Anniversary* is historically fascinating but not always fun to listen to. Certainly it's a treat to be able to go back to 1957 and hear the Miracles' first recording; or to be able to compare the original "Shop Around" (1960) with the speeded-up version that became a hit (this tells us more about Berry Gordy's genius than Smokey's, but that in itself is illuminating—and I notice that Gordy was not able to get Smokey to write more songs "of this type"); or to hear "Way Over There" before the strings were added. I think the version with the strings is probably a better pop song, but the version that's here shows more clearly what a great gospel/R&B song it could have been, in the hands of a different producer (Gordy had his eye firmly on the suburbs) and with a different lead singer (Smokey may have learned a few things from Clyde McPhatter, but he was real clear that who he wanted to be was Sarah Vaughan). But I only count one great performance among these twenty-six, "I'll Try Something New" (December 1961), and regarding that song, which I included in my book *The 100 Best Singles*, I have to make a special announcement. Attention, please. The version of "I'll Try Something New" which I rave about in my book, and which continues to be one of my all-time favorite Smokey creations, is not the one included in *35th Anniversary*. This box set quite properly uses the single mix (and edit) on all songs that were released as singles. I didn't know until now that the version of "I'll Try Something New" that I'm familiar with is a different mix (and a vastly, vastly superior one). The only place I know for sure that you can find it is on the vinyl version of the 1973 SR & the Miracles compilation, *Anthology*. I imagine that it's the album mix from the 1962 album called *I'll Try Something New*, and I'd like to think that it represents Smokey going back and mixing the track the way he'd always intended it to sound. But in any case, it's worth searching for. And kind of shocking (but oh so true) that the mix can make the difference between a fairly good record and a holy treasure.

"Bad Girl" (1959) is intriguing because, although its straight-down-the-middle doo-wop vocal made it a sonic throwback even then, its use of language reveals the mature Smokey Robinson ready and eager to burst out of the nineteen-year-old boy, if only anyone would notice. If anything, though, his intelligence and his innate respect for women probably hampered him in his effort to get a hit single (things haven't changed much in thirty-five years). A lewder vocal approach would have jumped out of the radio and made the slyness in the lyrics more accessible, but it also would have contradicted the ultimate message of the song, Smokey's eternal message: I love her/you, I worship you, your only flaw in my eyes is your rejection of me. I suppose another problem for a black vocal group was that if your likable record was too risqué it wouldn't get played until the white copy version came out. Smokey and the Miracles recorded "Bad Girl" just as the Playmates' "What Is Love?" was breaking big—the hook in that song was "sways with a wiggle when she walks," but you gotta have white-bread voices *and* faces to get away with that sort of thing. "Bad Girl" is about a guy who gets laid ("She's not a bad girl because / She made me see / How love could be") and left, and who wants to make the point, in spite of what his friends say, that to him the only thing "bad" about her is that "she wants to be free" (of him). It's very cleverly constructed (and possibly right over the heads of its listeners), full of Smokeyisms like "She's not a bad girl / To look at . . ." and "Make this bad bad girl be good!" with diction and meter and melody and phrasing and rhyme all working together to get the emphasis just right. "Be good!" also triggers a delightful musical moment: Smokey and the Miracles have been going up the melodic ladder and just as they seem to climax, Smokey's solo comes in one step higher up with a triumphant "She—," kicking off the last verse.

In this, and particularly in the chords and changes and bits of harmonic business in another 1959 Miracles single, "I Need a Change" (included on *Whatever Makes You Happy*), I hear a kind of missing link between what rock and roll sounded like in the fifties in all its myriad forms, and what rock and roll started sounding like the day the Beatles released the *Please Please Me* album in March 1963. I'm sure there are a great many such missing links and that the roots of the Beatles' melodic and harmonic ideas must be evident to many listeners, but for me that aspect of their sound (as opposed to the Buddy Holly, Muddy Waters, Chuck Berry, Everly Brothers, Little Richard aspects, which I could grasp immediately) seemed to come out of nowhere. "I Need a Change" is strange and wonderful. The lyrics are dumb and dull except for the lovely odd universality of the title phrase, but the music has a texture that is unique and even revelatory, with the result that the repeated phrase "I need a change" takes on dramatic resonance—that is, the song seems to speak to and for this listener—in a way that is never achieved in "Bad Girl" despite all its cleverness and elegance. It's a track of more than historical interest. It will brighten your afternoons. (It also contradicts the *1961–1971* subtitle of *Whatever Makes You Happy*, but so it goes.)

There are ninety-seven tracks on *35th Anniversary*, and another eighteen on *Whatever Makes You Happy*, plus sixteen cuts produced and written by Smokey in the recent Mary Wells two-CD collection and thirteen by Smokey in the similar Marvelettes package. I find all of these to be of considerable interest—that's what happens when an artist has a consistent vision and gift and you happen to connect with it: every newfound story or song is like a piece from some larger puzzle—but at the same time I have to repeat that for sheer listening pleasure it's disc three of *35th Anniversary* plus tracks sixteen through twenty-five of disc two (and tracks three through fourteen of *Whatever*, an excellent place to start if you're not ready to spring for the box set). Too often in the early years, flashes of greatness—a verse here, a bridge there, a turn of phrase somewhere else—are buried in an expanse of monotonous backing tracks and predictable song ideas. The Miracles' golden era began in January 1965 with "Ooo Baby Baby." (The preceding year was taken up with a couple of singsong numbers that have never appealed to me, "I Like It Like That" and "That's What Love Is Made Of," and then a charming transitional single that unfortunately was left off of *35th Anniversary*, "C'mon Do the Jerk," silly subject but an inspired performance.) Nineteen sixty-five, 1966, 1967 were the great years, followed by a few more years of good songs that just aren't wound as tight, performances that are enjoyable but not immortal, until finally Smokey parted from the Miracles in '72. About half of disc four is made up of post-Smokey Miracles tracks (good 1970s Motown fodder, but not my cup of meat) and post-Miracles Smokey tracks ("Cruisin'" and "Being with You" are terrific, "Sweet Harmony" is likable, and the others unfortunately sound like teasers for a solo album retrospective that could be called *20 Years of Blandness*).

Smokey's outside productions start in 1962 with Mary Wells. In 1963 he took on the Temptations, producing most of their records through early 1966. He started with the Marvelettes in 1964 and did a string of Marvin Gaye singles in 1965, and also found time in those two years to write and produce "My Smile Is Just a Frown" by Carolyn Crawford, "When I'm Gone" by Brenda Holloway, and the Contours' "First I Look at the Purse." In mid-'66 he pretty much stopped doing production for anyone except the Miracles and the Marvelettes. He was touring a lot. And he had a day job, vice president of the rapidly growing Motown corporation.

Smokey's presence on "Ooo Baby Baby" is awesome. Some kind of line has been crossed. He has arrived at that moment of artistic self-confidence which means total control and total freedom. He no longer wonders what this voice he's been given is supposed to sound like. Suddenly, he *knows*.

The man in the song is asking his woman for forgiveness. For reasons of my own I'm going to suggest that he could be talking to the Muse. "I did you wrong, my heart went out to play / But in the game I lost you / What a price to pay!" He is repentant, and this time it's not enough to say it and have it be so. He has to act it out.

"I'm crying: ooo ooo ooo, baby baby . . ." This is the act of penitence, and he performs it out loud, in front of God and us and everybody. In front of himself. The "ooo"s are church, the "ooo"s are

Africa, they are a baring of the breast, they are the voice that is beyond language. The man of words finds himself with something more important to say.

Don Waller tells a funny and appropriate story in the liner notes to *Whatever Makes You Happy* about a guy who eats psychedelic mushrooms and hears this song, the line about mistakes, "but I'm only human," and is overcome. "Oh man. Smokey understands," he says, and insists on hearing "Ooo Baby Baby" over and over for an hour. Smokey is that kind of artist, is Waller's point. When he's in his groove, he lets you know that he knows. Yes. And "Ooo Baby Baby" is that kind of song.

Music is comfort. Like the breast to a newborn. It's a very comforting song.

I say "song," but, as Linda Ronstadt has proven (by giving us the contentless version), I mean "performance." It is not Smokey the writer who understands, in this case. Or maybe it is—but not the word-writer. It is the guy the last stanza of whose song (except for three "baby baby"s thrown in for punctuation) consists entirely of "ooo"s.

What do you hear in that voice?

"Ooo Baby Baby" got to number 16 on the pop charts, the first Top 20 Miracles hit since "Mickey's Monkey" (written and produced by Smokey's friendly rivals, Holland-Dozier-Holland) almost three years earlier. The next single was "The Tracks of My Tears" (recorded, it turns out, one day before "Ooo Baby Baby"). It, too, got to number 16. It also single-handedly established Smokey Robinson as a literary figure—"the greatest living American poet," Bob Dylan is widely quoted as having said at the time. There can be little doubt that he was thinking of "The Tracks of My Tears." And also that what he was trying to say is that poetry is not in books but in the air.

Is Smokey Robinson a literary figure? I don't think so, not unless Billie Holiday is, not unless you include song and musical performance as categories of literature (okay with me; but I'd like it remembered that poetry could just as well be considered a subset of song). But there's both an elegance and an indirectness about "The Tracks of My Tears" that make it *feel* poetic. The elegance is in the language and imagery of the four-line chorus ("Take a good look at my face / You'll see my smile looks out of place / If you look closer it's easy to trace / The tracks of my tears"); but splendid as this is, it needs its music, its riff, and the vocal performance in order to exist as poetry. On the page, unless you read it with the music/performance in your mind, it's flat, unappealing. But hear it as music, as a record, and suddenly it touches you with every bit of the warmth, aliveness, intelligence, and subtle beauty of a favorite poem.

The speaker turns himself into something inanimate for a moment, a picture or representation of a person, which on close examination seems false ("smile looks out of place"), an android, inauthentic. This invites even closer examination, which reveals not tears but (marvelous, subtle image) the tracks the singer's tears have left on his face . . . proving the falseness of his smile but also revealing him as authentically human. Which is exactly the intention: He's singing the song to prove to someone that he has feelings, even if he doesn't let them show; that he needs her and wants her back in his life.

It's a song about deception. And since deception is presented as the norm—probably a fair description of human life (or at least social life) in this century or any other—I find the word "easy" particularly intriguing. ". . . it's *easy* to trace the tracks of my tears." Yes, my nature is to hide my feelings. But what I'm telling you in this song is that in truth I feel naked before the world. One close look and my deception will have been worthless. You will easily see the truth about me. (And I want you to.)

There's a marvelous bridge in the back half of the song, starting with a burst of stop-time (later used in the Four Tops' "Reach Out I'll Be There") and then a quick recapitulation with visual aids (like an aspirin commercial): "*Outside*, I'm masquerading / *Inside*, my hope is fading." He mentions being a clown and then climaxes with a classic bit of Smokey rhyming (pre–hip-hop rap): "My smile is my makeup I wear since my breakup with you." This is not in the least "poetic" but it's utterly delightful, especially the way he puts the emphasis on every syllable, and it builds perfectly (old Smokey trick) into the last verse, which turns out to be chorus (twice through and fade).

Everything communicated by the lyrics of a song must be supported and indeed given meaning by the music (instrumental, vocal, melodic, rhythmic) that accompanies or coexists with or is the vehicle for those words. To give an extreme example, "ooo ooo ooo ooo" means nothing on a page by itself. Smokey's poetry is a musical poetry, and it's noteworthy that "The Tracks of My Tears" is one of the songs he co-wrote with the Miracles' guitar player, Marv Tarplin. "When I collaborated with Marv Tarplin," Smokey told David Ritz, "the songs always began with Marv's guitar. His riffs or rhythmic lines gave me the first inspiration. In all other instances [with other col-laborators] I usually began the tune myself and urged them to con-tribute." So that haunting guitar riff (heard by itself as the intro to the song, and in the background or the fabric of the sound thereafter) existed first, and the lyrics followed. Small wonder that what is ul-timately achieved is a sound; a sound that draws forth poetic imagery from lyricist, singer, and listener alike. He writes inspired language, they sing (and make instrumental music) with great feeling and af-fection, and we listen with unusual openness, primed to hear some-thing profound.

Riff first; feelings follow. This is not as self-evident with "The Tracks of My Tears" as it is with, say, "The Last Time" by the Rolling Stones, also recorded in January 1965. But true nonetheless. Dylan that month was recording "It's Alright, Ma." Spirit was walking. And a good riff can be like a spirit-catcher, focusing performers and lis-teners on the truth that's available at this moment.

The tracks of "The Tracks of My Tears" can be followed back to "Laughing Boy" ("I believe you've been crying"), which Smokey wrote for Mary Wells at the end of 1962, and "My Smile Is Just a Frown (Turned Upside Down)" which he wrote for Carolyn Crawford in the summer of 1964, at about the same time that John Lennon wrote a song called "I'm a Loser," which includes the lines "I'm not what I appear to be" and "Although I laugh and I act like a clown / Beneath this mask I am wearing a frown." Smokey may have heard this song before writing "The Tracks of My Tears," but he certainly didn't need to. The story line seems to have been one that insistently presented itself to him whenever he was beating his brains trying to come up with some (non-autobiographical) song idea. It happened again in 1966 when Stevie Wonder and Henry Cosby gave him an instrumental track they'd written. It had a calliope on it, so Smokey thought "clown," so: "If there's a smile on my face / It's only there trying to fool the public . . . Like a clown I pretend to be glad." This is a song, "Tears of a Clown," which I've never cared for (that in-strumental track is overbearing) and which has an odd history very much tied up with the repetitiveness of its theme. Motown U.K. rereleased "The Tracks of My Tears" in 1969 and it became a Top Ten hit, the Miracles' first chart success in England. The head of the record company was looking for a follow-up single and discovered that there was another "Tears" song in the Miracles catalogue. He pulled the song off the 1967 album it had been buried on and it became a number one hit in both the U.K. and the U.S.A. (Smokey and the Miracles' first number one record). So maybe Smokey's muse knew what it was doing when it kept coming up with this same trite idea.

The clown who doesn't want to show that his heart is breaking is an archetype also found in an 1892 opera called *I Pagliacci*. In the very pretty "My Smile Is Just a Frown," Smokey gives his fifteen-year-old vocalist the unlikely line, "Just like Pagliacci did / I'll keep my sadness hid." This same line returns in "The Tears of a Clown" but with a little less conviction: "I'll try to keep my sadness hid." For me "Tears of a Clown" is a case of Smokey consciously or unconsciously poking fun at both himself and Stevie Wonder, but anyway the public had the last laugh. Which makes me remember the words of Kurt Vonnegut, in an introduction to his novel *Mother Night*: "You are what you pretend to be" (I'm approximating) "so watch out!"

I am very glad to have all of the material on *35th Anniversary* and *Whatever Makes You Happy* available to me and in such a convenient form, but what makes this a vital aesthetic event as well as an archival one is the sudden availability of so many previously unheard or hard-to-find tracks from the golden era of 1965–1967. It is as if *Greatest Hits Volume 2*, one of the finest rock/soul albums ever made, has just been doubled in length with very little loss of quality. There are some tracks from this period that don't quite work, notably the ballads "You Must Be Love," "My Love for You," and "Oh Be My Love." But there are at least a dozen other "new" tracks that are thrilling (and I have to acknowledge that two of my favorites are B-sides of singles I own, that I just hadn't listened to until now). Many of these—like almost anything new that's worthwhile—need to be listened to a few times before they start to yield up their treasures. It's a wise investment. "A Fork in the Road," the B-side of "The Tracks of My Tears," is a ballad that works, a lighter-than-air vocal confection with a real edge to it, standard Smokey tale of a lover bemoaning his loss, whose only wish is to encourage other lovers not to make the same mistake. The protagonist sounds like no one so much as the Ancient Mariner, buttonholing a traveler to tell his cautionary tale: "I know I may be just a stranger / Let me warn you there's a danger . . ." The strength of the performance is its energetic commitment to the difficult extended metaphor (lovers as great romantic travelers, constantly facing the threat of forking paths that may cause them to part), a commitment that somehow works its way into the song's frail melody and imbues it with tension and beauty, a haunting, memorable grace.

But if I am captured by the otherworldiness of "A Fork in the Road," I am equally entranced by the sheer gleeful mundanity of another 1965 relic, "From Head to Toe." Talk about mysterious luminosity! Whence cometh the bouncy musical presence that can occupy a bit of fluff like this ("I'm gonna ask you to go steady"), or like "Everyday" by Buddy Holly, and make 'em unforgettable? Confidence and sincerity play a part, I think (check out the sincerity of Buddy Holly's love songs, and the sort of playful rhyming he liked to wrap his voice around, and see if he doesn't remind you of Smokey, not in style but in his essential nature), and then there's this love of music which, since music is this person's whole universe right now, reaches us as love of life. Love between man and woman here and I suppose in all of Smokey's best songs, actually becomes an allegory for something larger—whatever that might be. A vision of how to be in the world. "I got a little heart inside me beating / And with each beat it keeps repeating / Your name . . ." This song's about joy. Benny Benjamin (drums) and James Jamerson (bass) (truly legendary rhythm section) create a metronomic dance beat you just can't shake free of, and Smokey leans his vocal against that groove like an ancient zen hip-hop master, bright sensual innocent celebration of beauty and physicality, with a call-and-response chorus so zestful atop the suddenly naked (no melodic instruments) percussion that the listener has no choice but to join in the surrender. "Yours yours from head to toe / All the way down . . ." Indeed.

It's interesting, I think, to ask what it is that attracts a listener (like me) to a particular artist's work when the form and content of that work vary significantly from piece to piece. I like Smokey Robinson for his wordplay and the unique and oddly consistent vision of the universe his wordplay somehow conjures up for me (no one else could tell a girl he adores her by describing in detail the process by which you soak wallpaper to peel it off a wall!), but I am equally attracted to a song like "Going to A Go-Go" or the Temptations' (Smokey-produced) "Get Ready," in which the riff, the beat, the kineticism of the music, is the obvious attraction and the words seem ordinary or even dumb. I love the sound of Smokey's voice in "Ooo Baby Baby" and "Whole Lot of Shakin' in My Heart" (an uptempo 1966 Miracles track that he neither wrote nor produced) and his 1969 cover of the Supremes' "My World Is Empty Without You" (Jonathan points out that Smokey immediately and eerily conjures up a mood of emptiness that was completely lacking in the original version) . . .

and indeed his voice is a strong part of my attraction to all of the Miracles' music, and yet it's not for me a particularly strong or identifiable voice (certainly not as innately appealing as Marvin Gaye's or Otis Redding's or Sam Cooke's) and I'm not even sure what I like about it . . . except somehow it's the way the words sound when he sings them, the way the rhythms of the music and the language reach me, the magic of the song structure, rhymes and timing and great transitions, little curlicues of one sort or another; I love those things in his songs, and his voice is the unique vehicle for all that business. But I also hear his voice in songs he writes and produces and doesn't sing, and sometimes in songs he sings but didn't write or produce. It's hard to find the consistent thread here. I've been listening to Smokey long enough, and to enough other artists who are like him in some fashion but are not him, to be very sure of the particularity of the hold he's got on me. But I'm not so sure what the name of this something is.

Going back to Ray Davies (Buddy Holly) (Philip K. Dick), I am forced by the unyielding data of my own preferences, the things that truly speak to me as a listener or reader or whatever, again and again to the conclusion that there is such a thing as a vision or voice that belongs to an individual artist, and *that* somehow resonates in that person's work (or a period of that person's work) in a very compelling way for each receptive listener. The Kinks' music jumped out at me from the beginning, and continued to appeal to me on deep, mysterious levels album after album, single after single, from 1965 to 1969. Some of their songs that were popular I found tiresome ("A Well Respected Man"), and others that I adored ("See My Friends," "Dead End Street") weren't popular at all. If I tried to list the qualities that I believe appealed to me in their work, I'm sure you could come up with another band or artist whose work contains the same qualities and yet might leave me cold. In other words, analysis ultimately fails, and I find myself heading back to vague words like "personality" and "vision." Presence. The presence of Ray Davies or Smokey Robinson is not manufacturable or quantifiable. And ultimately, therefore, not measurable; and any attempt to characterize it will be misleading to exactly the extent that the person being spoken to imagines they know something of the nature of the artist without actually meeting the artist in his or her work.

Presence is finally a private matter. I/thou, like the structure of most of Smokey's love songs. It exists only between the artist(s) and the individual listener. I mean, certainly we can speak in general terms about Elvis Presley's or Edith Piaf's presence as a singer. But if we try to give technical reasons for that presence, we bump up against the limits of music criticism. We are talking actually about a relationship, the relationship of one person (the singer) with a multitude (the audience), who can be described as a multitude (they gave Elvis seventeen number one records) but who actually exist only as individuals, one set of ears at a time. You exist, Smokey asserts to the lover or love object he's addressing, because I say that it's so. "I've Made Love to You a Thousand Times," he sings in a song off his solo album *Touch the Sky*, "even if it's only in my mind." What is upsetting about the song, a mistake I don't think he ever made in his days with the Miracles, is that in the course of its story he blurs *for the listener* the question of whether this is idealized love, or a desire that needs to be acted out, perhaps inappropriately. His character crosses the line from romantic fool to dangerous obsessive, stalker, even creep. Oops. Well, the times changed, of course; that's part of the problem. But also I think somewhere along the way Smokey may have lost his (unique, masterful) hold on nonreality. And so he ends up (in the very title of the song) violating his listeners' privacy, something this quintessentially moral man was simply incapable of doing in any of the thousand songs he sang and created and made love to us in during the Miracles era.

I exist (this is the listener talking now) because you say it's so. You respect me enough to share your basic doubts about the solidity and sanity of the universe, like in that song you and Marv Tarplin wrote for Marvin Gaye: "You tell me lies that should be obvious to me / But I'm so much in love with you baby that I don't want to see . . . If truth makes love last longer / Why do lies make my love stronger? / Ain't that peculiar, baby?" How can I explain what I feel when I hear this song? It's that percussion thing between the verses, the way it gets in my blood, and then Marvin riffing against it when he sings "Uh uh uh (uh uh uh) / Hey hey . . ." and I don't know, there's this great bass line and guitar and it all just builds to this point of intensity that isn't even on the record; it's like it's in my mind, but I hear it or feel it every time, and suddenly the words "AIN'T THAT PECULIAR!" sum up everything I want to say about my life or the way the universe is, and I feel good 'cause I'm letting it out and 'cause I know somebody understands— It's not that I'm in love with a lying woman or anything like that, it's just *the feeling I get from the song* . . .

So I have high expectations. When I hear "Baby Please Don't

Go" by Them I want a great involuntary Scream to come out of me somewhere in the middle of the record, because that has happened, more than once, and so I'm disappointed if I play the record and it doesn't even make my blood race. When I play "Going to A Go-Go" I want to feel the walls of the empire tremble. (It helps to turn up the treble. I know it's got a great bass line, but that's how you have to listen to Motown sometimes, twist the treble to distort and just *trust* that the bass is present, tying all the noise together.) When I listen to "The Love I Saw in You Was Just a Mirage" I want to be knocked on my ass from the first moment, the sheer perfection of it, "There you were, beautiful . . ." I want breathlessness, I want to fall in love with Smokey all over again at that moment, like I did before, and before. When I get a two-CD collection of Marvelettes tracks with lots of songs by Smokey, I want to discover another "Hunter Gets Captured by the Game," for the sheer joy of the experience and so I can be the hippest guy in town and tell all my friends. Hasn't happened. Yet. Maybe I'm listening wrong. Sometimes these things sneak up on you.

I want to always be impressed by the word dances in "Choosey Beggar," ready to quote them at a moment's notice, like I can quote the bridge (except for that great rhythmic underpinning) in "Yester-love": " 'Yester-' is / The prefix / That we fix / To things that / Have gone by / Forever they say," and then the inevitable WR poignant snapshot of a lovelorn everyman: "But even though my yesterlove / Has slipped through my fingers / I find it still lingers / Here in my heart today." The rhymes. The rhythms. The melodic dips and swirls. The rest of the song doesn't quite live up to the bridge; a tendency towards too much syrup in the arrangements was already starting to show itself. I admit it: I'm looking for the artist to give one hundred percent in every song, every performance, every recording. But only because I live for the moments when he does. I *want* him to build me a tower so high it touches the moon. I want to know that he, or whatever unknowable Presence is speaking through him, still loves me.

So many songs I haven't talked about. "More, More, More of Your Love." "You Only Build Me Up to Tear Me Down" (great vocal). "If You Can Want" ("and it's my philosophy . . ."). "Don't Think It's Me" ("I" am not my heart, my eyes, my lips, my ears, my arms. Uh huh). And then there's the Temptations singing William Robinson, which should take up two CDs of the forthcoming five-CD Temptations box, but surely won't. Maybe someday . . .

Music reaches out for something. The consistency of that part of Smokey's vision that can be articulated, mostly because it's the word part, the "story" part, is remarkable: (a) I'm the man (woman, if Wanda or Mary is singing) for you. (b) He doesn't appreciate you, but I'm right here waiting. (c) You treat me badly, I love you madly. (d) You're not here anymore, and my loss is my closest friend. (e) (incorporates all of the foregoing) I'll do anything for you. Okay, these are the stories he believes people want to hear, and that's why he tells them. The character he plays is called True Love. And every time he sings he's reaching out for that feeling his listeners give him when he sings this story in their ears.

Listen closely. You can hear the hunger in his voice.

And then after a while maybe you can't anymore, but that's all right. How long is a man required to stand naked before the world?

The most recent message from the Smokey we once knew, on the evidence of these collections (and happily, such evidence is never complete), is his surprise 1981 masterpiece "Being with You." It sags just a bit in the middle with that damn bridge from "Baker Street," but never mind, it's pure Smokey through and through. Listen to his voice; if you were meeting this man for the first time you'd know him instantly. "Where've you been?" No, that's not an appropriate question; listen to what the man's saying:

> "I don't care what they think about me, and I don't care what
>   they say . . .
> I don't care about anything else but being with you."

This is love, is madness, is a consistent and complete philosophy of life that may or may not be "correct" but that can and has held its own with any other philosophy. It is particularly popular among artists. And those who appreciate artists.

Vision. Is closely related to another v-word, value. One way to understand philosophy is to think of it as asking the question, What is of value? (Philip K. Dick broke this down into two parts: What is real? and What is human?) The Smokey who only cares about being with us has an answer.

> "One thing I know for sure is really really real:
> I never felt before the way you make me feel."

Same to you, buddy. And thanks.

7

BACK TO THE MIRACLE FACTORY

"We have been trying to construct a language and a history." That's what I wrote in my journal a few months ago, in the first flush of excitement, first week of listening to **Neil Young**'s new album **Sleeps with Angels**. Now it occurs to me that what we are (mostly unconsciously) trying to accomplish as we listen to the never-ending flow of new "rock-and-roll" records is also or more particularly to erase and forget a language and history that aren't true enough any longer, more restrictive than helpful, not close enough to home. Trying to forget and remember. Reprogram the beast.

The beast is me. This is not a boast or confession. It's just a piece of information—I, the creature listening, am a part of, extension of, this undefined larger thing within which I live and with whom I love and struggle. Just a reminder. Safety-pinned to my shirt by my mother in case I wandered off.

Books will be written and TV programs filmed about the origins and true significance of the safety pin.

Artifacts. "Jim, I want you to take this entire sector and digitize it." "Yeah, and what about all the people who inhabit it?" "So now they'll live forever. Anyway, we need the space."

"Embracing you with this / Must be the one you love / Must be the one whose magic touch / Can change your mind." Neil Young goes deep. How does he do that?

He does it not by calculation but by intention. The extraordinary power of *Sleeps with Angels* and the very different *Ragged Glory* (the Neil fans I've met who don't yet appreciate *Sleeps* seem to be having trouble with their expectations of what a Neil + Crazy Horse album ought to sound like) versus the mysterious wimpiness of *Harvest Moon* and *Unplugged* can be explained, I think, by supposing that, consciously or unconsciously, Young didn't intend for the last-mentioned albums to make strong statements. Maybe they're even intended for that part of him and of his audience that doesn't want to kick up the shit. This doesn't have to be cynical. It can be (and, looking at his oeuvre as a whole, is) part of a conscious process of exploration. And Young's success as an artist, I suggest, is partly due to his willingness to explore things and carry them to completion even at the risk of coming up dry. Holding back his own judgmental side may result in albums as empty as *Long May You Run* or most of the Geffen offerings, but I believe it is also what allows an *Everybody Knows This Is Nowhere* or *Tonight's the Night* or *Sleeps with Angels* to come into existence.

Breaking rules. Not just for the sake of breaking them. But because you have this tiny intuition, which you follow in the face of all the inevitable doubts, that this could be the path that will allow you to express or give form to your feelings. Very often it's about what you're not doing more than what you're doing (not requiring yourself to stay within acceptable distortion levels and other universal standards of musical professionalism) (not caring that these two different songs have virtually the same backing track . . . maybe even getting excited about the idea). Freedom. Is not a concept. It's a way of doing the work. And not license, either. Because that intention is a cruel taskmaster, and it's on you all the time. Insisting that you do things its way and, unreasonably, even insisting that you learn to love each new assignment. Rejecting hard-fought victories because there's not enough love in them yet, whatever that's supposed to mean. Shit. Back to the drawing board. Back to the salt mines.

Back to the miracle factory. The fucker's done it again.

"Safeway Cart" is a masterpiece. Riding around Germany on the DeutschBahn this past October, I'd hear the squeal of metal on metal as the train lurched out of the station and immediately think of the signature guitar sound that opens (and, in a subtle way, recurs throughout) "Safeway Cart"—what is that? not a melody, not a rhythm (the rhythm riff comes in around it), but not just a sound, either; it's musical, got a bend in it, two notes so it sort of is a melodic hook of the crudest variety, crude but brilliant in its sophistication, a wail, ancient lament, and then the ticking of that bass line, "like a Safeway cart rolling through the street." I wonder if Neil's overseas listeners know that Safeway is a supermarket and that homeless people adopt these carts, but maybe it's as unnecessary as explaining

McDonald's (Trans Ams, of course, are another story) . . . The six and a half minutes go by in an ecstatic instant and I want to play it again and again. Music as natural and as powerful as breathing.

Neil Young remembered the assignment. Rock and roll has always (since Elvis) been a topical music. It's about our physical (and emotional, situational) environment and the way it feels to live in it. I went to hear Drive Like Jehu in a local club and I couldn't tell you anything about the words (did they use words?) or the structures of the songs, but they remembered the assignment, too; everything they did spoke eloquently of how it feels to be in this body this year reading this newspaper dealing with the reality or illusion of being exactly this many years old and just filled with the trembling repressed chaotic uncertainty and power/powerlessness of it all. "Driveby . . ." "He sleeps with angels tonight." Kurt Cobain matters not because of himself anymore but because we actually are connected through our contemplation of him. "He's always on someone's mind." This is a fact. "The king is gone but he's not forgotten." It's not about sentimentality. It's about the immortality of our collective need. "It's a random kind of thing." Neil Young has recorded an album about murder and suicide (and the power of love) that is not at all exploitative (almost impossible to achieve in the grunge or rap context, but remember, old Neil ain't gonna sell that many albums anyway, western hero though he may unquestionably be). A cry from the heart. An album for 1994.

I'm not done with "Safeway Cart" yet. It's a masterpiece exactly in the sense of being a mature, fully realized work by a master, as measured by (the only acceptable yardstick) the extent to which it touches the listener. Real as the day is long. What is the nature of this mastery? Not great singing. Not great lyrics. Not even great guitar-playing—though that's certainly the element most easily singled out, western hero equals guitar hero, which as with Hendrix is our shorthand for saying master of sonic space. The song's power, its essence, lies in its overall and moment-to-moment sonic picture, the space and feelings (including sense of motion) that its sound creates. In this the sound of the instruments (and their amps and the room, et cetera) is very important, like Matisse's colors, but just as important (as with Matisse's canvases) is the placement of the colors and forms/ images in relation to each other and in relation to their actual or conceptual container, the edges of the canvas, the space and time of the musical performance.

At 00 seconds the train squeal begins, eventually fading at 07.

But its primary impact is in the first two seconds, firmly embedding itself in our brains (I realize that in addition to having just railwayed all over Germany, I've been living since early this year in a place where the trains go by, and blow their whistles, several times each hour; the sound is inside me) before bass and drums come in at 02, true start of the song, transition from random loud ambience (you are Here) to motion, order, purpose. Almost simultaneous with the beginning of the rhythmic pulse is the launching of the dominant (contrapuntal) riff, a wonderful groaning sound, bass slide, two continuous descending notes (though sometimes the second is only implied), or, if you will, attack/release.

At about 29 the first bit of guitar punctuation (similar to but sonically and melodically distinct from the bass-guitar groan; since both are punctuations we never actually hear them both at once, though the time-space between them is forever changing, a dance) comes in, and then at 36 the start of the vocal. "Like a Safeway cart . . ." and we immediately know, intuitively if not consciously, that the phrase refers to the *sound* we're hearing; that insistent thump thump thump thump of the pulsing rhythm line (bass and/or basslike keyboard plus understated drum), this *feeling* the sound expresses; now it gets a visual image (shopping cart rolling by itself—if there's a homeless man attached he's entirely invisible—through the city at dawn, in the ghetto, darkness on the edge of town, desolation row). Lyrically this is a "Like a" song, like "Like an Inca" or "Just Like Tom Thumb's Blues" or "Like a Hurricane" or "Like a Rolling Stone." Simile. *Something* is like a Safeway cart and/or "a sandal mark on the Savior's feet." What? It. What the song is about. Get the concept? Let it pulse through you—

The lyrics serve purely to locate and evoke. They do not attempt to tell a story, nor should they, although the song itself is so eloquent (particularly the two nonverbal verses of squalling melodic guitar) that a story possibly emerges anyway, the protagonist of which is not the cart at all (maybe it's seen or imagined out a window) but a female named "baby" who's been watching much too much TV; I think she's the whole damn United States of America but I'm not saying Neil intends that, although of course as a listener (this is what I mean by topicality) I *feel* that he does.

Everything opens out in those marvelous feedback guitar solos, articulate (full of poetry) verses in themselves, the first at 1:42 between vocal verses two and three, the second at 4:18, climax of the song, followed by a long vamp, a final vocal verse (repeat of the first), and still longer vamping (this pulse, not the great punctuation, we're being told, is the real content of the song, feel it, feel it) with a fade starting at 6:08 and a lovely surprise organ part as a kiss and farewell almost at the end of the fade, so atmospheric, what a marvelous series of subtle and deliberate sound effects/melodic fragments this song is! The emotional high points are the guitar solos, screaming, crying, calling out to God, but every part of the song (even or especially the long repetitive vamps) is paradoxically rich in musical and sonic embellishment even as it constantly gives the impression of stark, spare simplicity. Cindy says the driverless cart gives her a feeling of spooky inanimateness, no people here, while Christ's sandal mark is a contrary image of the divine and distant becoming human. I also note the gentleness and poignance of a sandal mark where one is expecting stigmata. The song veers into self-parody (but consciously and effectively, the author breaking his own spell only to impose a greater one) when the two images are combined so that the cart rolls "past the Handy Mart to the Savior's feet," conjuring an image, perhaps, of a big plastic Jesus out among the strip malls and fast-food joints . . . hey, maybe it's Bob's Big Boy. The main thing anyway is how amazingly graceful the entire sound sculpture is, portrait of the urban moment or whatever you want or feel it to be. Graceful and durable. I always liked "T-Bone" on Re●ac●tor but this seems to me a huge step forward in a similar direction. How great that these musicians are so willing and able to cooperate in the creative process (i.e., the modesty and skillfulness of the drummer; rock and roll's not usually about understatement). I like the "Chopsticks" pianolike bass line following each vocal phrase, reminding me of "?" and the Mysterians' "96 Tears" and many other fragments of our collective musical past.

"Trans Am," "Driveby," "Sleeps with Angels," and "Change Your Mind" are almost equally powerful—major works to place alongside "Cowgirl in the Sand" and "Rockin' in the Free World" and "Love to Burn" and "Tonight's the Night" and "Don't Be Denied" and oh, don't get me started. A really good Neil Young album always sends me back into his catalogue, an astonishing place I could wander around in for months. Sleeps with Angels as an album stands up gorgeously when confronted with all this brilliant history—its five potential classics are bolstered by seven other very likeable and intriguing tracks, and the entire sixty-three minutes goes by like a one-hour reunion with a close friend who has all these stories to share about what's going on in his life right now.

The unself-conscious musicality of this album is stunning. It creates an environment in which it is possible to imagine ourselves as living within a greater human community linked by shared values, even as so much external evidence (the elections, the "news") seems to say otherwise. What music communicates above all else is immediacy of feeling. Barriers and defenses dissolve. When this happens we feel our commonality. Every emotion is actually a constellation of feelings, and so it's not so easy to put what we feel into words. But words and music, in the motion-structure of a song, a performance, do the job very well. They allow for ambiguity. And they also speak eloquently the specifics of the emotional moment the music arises from.

Listen to "My Heart," the opening track. It has a childlike innocence about it, a sound and a deliberateness that for some reason make me think of the *Nutcracker Suite* or a Shirley Temple film. It's an unusual sound, lilting and magically still, both at once, created by the harpsichord (if that's what it is) and the way it's played and also by the vocal phrasing and the delicate, deliberate stops and starts of the melody, the arrangement. It works very consciously as an introduction, an invocation, an announcement that we are departing on a journey together. The final track of the album, "A Dream That Can Last," brings back the instrumentation and the mood, twin performance, benediction and completion, this time punctuated by a slow, powerful drumbeat that somehow incorporates much of the musical territory that has been covered since the record began. Now the lead instrument sounds like hammer dulcimer. Whatever. The resonances between the two tracks, and the more subtle resonances within the album as a whole, are wonderfully effective. The album hangs together as mysteriously and memorably (all one distinct flavor, even with all this splendid variety) as *After the Gold Rush*. In addition to the strong sonic links between these bookend songs, notice the thematic bridgings. "When dreams come crashing down like trees" becomes "I know I won't awaken, it's a dream that can last," spooky image and a spooky sound but still in context, somehow affirmative. "A young girl who didn't die" and the angels on the corner provide echoes of the defining songs of the album, "Driveby" and the title track. A story has been told. And continues to unfold, as we listen and listen again.

And again. Crazy Horse is a fabulous band. Songs that seemed unremarkable at first, like "Prime of Life," just grow on me and grow on me, and the groove has everything to do with it. Wow. That rhythm section. The rumor I heard was that this album was recorded as a kind of continuous rehearsal or jam, just get together day after day and play and play, no takes, just live recording, and maybe listen to the tapes later to see if you got anything. Long stretches in the studio, interrupted because of Kurt Cobain's death, finally back in the mood and then another interruption when someone close to the band was killed in a driveby shooting. Anyway, if you go through Neil Young's catalogue, you'll find how much of it is really Crazy Horse's catalogue as well. What freedom they've attained together! The band formed twenty-five years ago during the sessions for *Everybody Knows This Is Nowhere*, also produced by David Briggs and Neil Young. Go find another set of co-workers in rock as consistent or as loyal to each other. Ralph Molina on drums; Billy Talbot on bass; and Frank Sampedro joined in 1975, rhythm guitar, replacing Danny Whitten, whose death along with Bruce Berry's was exorcised on *Tonight's the Night* (not listed as a Crazy Horse album, but in fact it's Young, Talbot, and Molina with Nils Lofgren and Ben Keith sitting in). Going back to "Prime of Life," the lyrics are nothing special but the performance just shimmers, driving the vocals so they say more than these words seem capable of. Love that "Cinnamon Girl" taste on the borrowed chorus. And the whistling sound. *All* these sounds. Hats off to the horse. And faithful rider.

And in the midst of life comes "Driveby." A simple, beautiful, heartbreaking song. Listen to that fuzzed guitar tone, after the last "shooting star" in the bridge, after and coexistent with all those noble piano chords, music that will live inside every one of us at least as long as "Helpless" has, if we survive that long. A twenty-two-year-old friend of mine vanished suddenly this month, accidental drowning not driveby but just as random and senseless. What can be said? The drums again are the very heart of the track. And the mood, the buzz of the bass, the colors in the vocals, the whole sad perfect fierce *mood* of the thing. "You feel invincible." And then you don't. "Driveby . . ."

"Driveby' "s an elegy. "Sleeps with Angels" is just as powerful, and totally different. Single of the Year on my personal radio station. A song like this can't be invented. It has the kick of pure inspiration. The freshness of the riff is exactly what rock and roll at its best has always been about. The boldness of the sound sculpture is breathtaking, and the risk pays off beyond any possible expectations. For those of us who thought the digital age might mean the end of such perfect imperfections, wrong again. How about the tone of that guitar after "town to town"? This is the whole movie in less than three minutes.

A different sort of heartbreaker. Sympathy for our own devils. The song also captures the intensity of the news. With compassion for "she" who is the survivor, who is the other confused one, who is us, living at this tempo, who is everyman.

It was pointed out to me, after I'd been listening to this album for a little while, that "Western Hero" (fifth song) has exactly the same backing track (different vocals, of course, and different guitar overdubs in spots) as "Train of Love" (song nine). As soon as it's pointed to, it's obvious, but I don't know how long it might have taken me to notice on my own. Despite all the similarities, the songs don't sound the same, and even now I can't easily impose "Train" lyrics on "Hero," or vice versa. This is fascinating. It's like a little essay on what gives a song its identity. The low vibrating guitar in "Western Hero" does give it a different mood than the lyrical, slightly generic "Train of Love," but I think what really keeps the songs from sounding alike is the difference in where the title phrase falls in the melodic line—"western hero" at the end of the line ("sure enough, he was a western hero") and "train of love" at the beginning ("train of love, racing from heart to heart"), so that when we think of or hear each tune, the notes/beat/whatever that we first think of are different, unrelated. Another song pairing within the album, and a delightful mindfuck. This many years into the rock-and-roll era, how can there still be dumb little ballsy tricks like this that no one (in my admittedly limited memory) has ever played on us before? And where does Neil find the nerve to be so simplistically outrageous? It's his power, his nature, and he's never lost it. "Western Hero" comes closer to being a Neil Young cliché than anything else on the album ("Train of Love" 's not far behind), but it's saved, I think, by its lack of irony. The message is refreshingly unclear. The Marlboro Man image (and self-image) of America has changed, the "black-and-white" clarity (or seeming clarity) of the frontier or World War Two is gone, and how should we feel about this? The singer's not sure. The listener's not sure. The hero himself is unsure, which is what keeps him from being a hero still, perhaps. Shall we open fire on him? Wouldn't that be cowardly on our part, now that his six-gun and iron hand are gone . . .

More pairings reveal themselves. "This time we're never going back" / "This train is never going back." (The one moment where the two songs merge together.) And the reexamination of absurdly familiar language—"he fought for you, he fought for me," "to love and honor, till death do us part"—to see what truth might be hidden its mind-numbing ordinariness. "To love and honor" actually becomes the emotional high point of "Train of Love," full of pain and risk and commitment, whereas the most haunting moment in "Western Hero" is "He's different now . . ." One possible message in the pairing of the songs is that the clichés that apply to personal life can be more easily redeemed, rediscovered, made new, than the clichés of public life. Putting it another way: To be heroes to ourselves and our loved ones is still possible and indeed necessary, however difficult, as we grow older and wiser; but public heroism and the values that underlie it are a much more tangled and less available realm.

This resonates with the obviously personal (but somehow public as well, if only because it comes at the start of the album) assertion in "My Heart": "This time I will take the lead somehow." *Sleeps with Angels*, like so many of Young's albums, is about marriage—his marriage to his wife and family, and his marriage to the world, through his work. When "shadows climb up the garden wall" and "the first leaf falls" in "Prime of Life," these signs of autumn can be felt as cultural (what's going on out there in the world that he releases albums into) as well as personal (he and his wife are getting older). And the message of the song (the mirror shows both ways) seems to me to have to do with the I Ching's advice on how to lead in such a circumstance (even though "a sage might feel sad in view of the decline that must follow"): "Be not sad / Be like the sun at midday." Not surprisingly, the theme of nostalgia (personal *and* cultural) that runs throughout Young's oeuvre ("Sugar Mountain," "Mansion on the Hill") shows up here as well: "When I first saw your face, it took my breath away." But the way Young locates this statement within the song (he speaks of the past but specifically as a gift in the present, from the king to his queen—and to his people, too, perhaps) makes it, too, an act of conscious leadership (do as I do) (tell her you love her) and generosity, an act of nonsadness, of renewal. (You have to be careful of your gestures these days, since Kurt presumably died partly of guilt at only pretending to be a hero. Neil, indirectly, offers us a different model.)

When I say the album is about marriage, I'm thinking, of course, of "Change Your Mind." When you take this fourteen-minute, forty-second song, and add to it its six-minute, twenty-second coda, "Blue Eden," you get a twenty-one-minute epic pretty much smack in the middle of this (surprisingly listenable) sixty-three-minute extravaganza, and it certainly asserts its presence by sheer size (well balanced, however, by the other major songs, which assert their presence through their beauty or their subject matter or both) (and then at least four of the lesser songs gain strength by their location within the record and the way they make pairs with each other—an extraordinarily well structured album). So the unambiguous message of "Change Your Mind"—one of Neil Young's earnest, exhortative works, like "Don't Be Denied" or "Don't Let It Bring You Down" or "Last Dance" ("you could live your own life") or "Tired Eyes" ("please take my advice") or "Love to Burn"—is powerfully felt throughout this CD, and necessarily colors how we listen and respond to every song. In "Sleeps with Angels" the impact of the suicide is described not in terms of a generation or the music biz but in the context of a marriage, a relationship. This is disturbing, surprising. It makes these people more real. "Train of Love" is overtly a song about marriage, while the line "I know in time we'll meet again," and the repetition of "lonely" and "lonesome," set up a contrary tension. The two songs that start the album ("My love I will give to you it's true / Although I'm not sure what love can do") ("When I first saw your face . . .") also support a hearing of the album up through "Train of Love" as a story of courtship and renewal of vows (a recurring story on post-Geffen Young albums, methinks). The last three songs, however, offer no suggestion that the first-person narrator is or is not in a relationship with someone. They're about other aspects of the individual's adventures in the universe.

The "unambiguous" message of the epic is, You need love. It is the only thing that will protect you from the world (verses two and three) and from your restless ego (verse one). You need to make love. You need the "magic touch" of your partner, the person you make love with. *Don't let another day go by!* Tonight's the night. Or this morning. You need to be touched. And what that touch does (this is the interesting, the slightly unexpected, the hypnotic part) is change your mind.

I'm telling you (he's telling me), Change your mind.

A song with a message. He tells us what to do. And he is also very specific about *how* to do it (by regular lovemaking). Okay. I'll give that some serious thought.

Meanwhile, the musical spell the song creates, during the singing of these words and during the long musical passages between words, is mesmerizing. There are several ten-minute songs on *Ragged Glory*, and they're wonderful, and they're also obviously, invigoratingly, long; but "Change Your Mind," unless I'm listening very closely, goes by so quickly that often I find myself wanting to hear it again. Some kind of latter-day evolution of "Cowgirl in the Sand," it doesn't have the same extraordinary climaxes and yet in its own way it's almost as satisfying, another masterful piece of sound sculpture. Driven by a bandleader who needs to say something. And by three other musicians and a co-producer (and a faithful manager, Elliot Roberts, somewhere off in the wings) who want only to support and empower him in getting that something said, who let it become their something, as he also lets it become their something, so that finally it's this fabulous creation with endless twists and turns and musical subtleties to please us indefinitely that they have built together.

And perhaps to emphasize the point, which is that "Change Your Mind" is not a jam (it's more like a jazz composition), "Blue Eden," which I regard as the dark side of relationship heaven, a little blues in the night, *is* credited as a joint composition among the four musicians, while every other song here is words and music by Neil Young. What is particularly unsettling about "Blue Eden," which I like a heck of a lot better than I would ever expect to like a Young & Crazy blues jam stuck in the middle of an album, is the way the lyrics snatch bits of other songs—"Change Your Mind" in particular, but also vital chunks of "Train of Love" and "Driveby." What does it all mean? I don't know, but it's very successful at making us *feel* it means something, and that really is all we need to make it so.

"Change Your Mind"'s music is so compelling and pleasurable I don't even flinch at the phrase "magic touch." When you're truly cool, uncoolness just rolls right off you. I laughed when I saw an ad for the album "featuring the single 'Change Your Mind'" (a fifteen-minute single!), but then I realized they must have put out an edited version. It wouldn't be the same. Some tunes just need space to spread out in.

"Safeway Cart" next, and then "Train of Love" and "Trans Am." Vehicles. "I've got to get somewhere." ("My Heart," again.) This is an album about motion.

Motion and stillness. "Trans Am" is a great visionary shaggy-dog story, in one sense a spoof on every dramatic Neil Young narrative that's gone before (including "Driveby," though this in no way detracts from the earlier song's power), but also a sincere and thoroughly charming salute to the modern cowboy's best friend, his car. It's modeled on mock-heroic sixties pop songs like "Ringo" and "Big Bad John," except this time the hero is an automobile, a distinctively American mass-market sports car beloved by young males in the 1970s. The car gets to be the hero of this disjointed narrative mostly through messages contained in the structure of the song (not the lyrics). Song starts with this great guitar figure, a readymade that transports us instantly (how does he get that gloriously low, resonant guitar tone?) into an emotionally very familiar setting, something from the movies, very mythical in a modern sort of way, reinforced perfectly by a ghostly chorus (might be only one voice, but it still sounds like a chorus) superimposing words on the musical picture: "Trans Am." Whew. Narrative starts up immediately, resolving this temporarily into a wagon-train western, but then it takes some funny bounces. Meanwhile each of the four verses ends with that trademark chorus, "Trans Am," and after the fourth verse and chorus the guitar figure returns (a simplified version has been playing throughout the entire performance) and we get a very expressive instrumental last verse, wordless until the final exquisite pronunciation of the title phrase. The Trans Am's role in the lyrics themselves is more suggestive than specific: In the first verse it's an old Trans Am (always old) that the narrator heard the massacre story from (yes, the TA is not just the subject of a yarn, but a spinner of yarns). Second verse is the car's big scene: "It crawled along the boulevard with two wheels on the grass / That old Trans Am was dying hard but still had lots of gas." Western hero. Third verse it shows up in the last line, as though we now realize we've been seeing the scene from the car's point of view: "The old Trans Am just bounced around and took another road." Cool and wise. The fourth verse swerves, de-anthropomorphizing the car, but you can be sure we still perceive it as having a personality, maybe dreaming about its past adventures, even though here it's just an actual car that broke down and "needs a headlight fixed."

"Trans Am." What is achieved here is primarily, as in almost all of these songs, a sound, a mood, a musical experience. The words are part of the assemblage—even though they are the container for the surface narrative (the deeper narrative, I'd say, is communicated by the guitar figure and the chorus) and the source of all specific visual images, they are still in fact just well-chosen elements of the overall (musical) effect. Neil's great, great gift is this ability to ride a feeling. He is phenomenally good at finding the right guitar sound(s) and chord sequences to bring home the mood. He is also very very good at working with other musicians, especially if they happen to be Crazy Horse. With his guitar, and the other instruments, and his voice, and the sound of the band at this moment (that groove, that looseness), he creates a sonic experience in which the role of the words is to point in the direction the feelings are going, without overly getting in the way. A sonic master is a master of space (space *in* time, if you will), and the role of words in a rock-and-roll song is to deepen and focus the space without crowding it or violating its essence. Goofy words (check out the great songs of the Beatles or the Rolling Stones) will often do fine as long as the chorus phrase is right and the other lyrics don't break the mood or cross over some line of insipidness or absurdity.

Anyway, even if they're not the primary reason I love the song, I think the words to "Trans Am" are delightful. In the first verse there's a strange (neilyoungian) transition which can be explained if we accept the suddenly arrived cowboy as the narrator of the first four lines, and which anyway leads into an image that perfectly suits the fantasy (talking cars) mood of the whole piece: "He used to ride the Santa Fe before the tracks were laid." Oh. Astral cowboy. Okay. Second verse doesn't totally gel for me but the imagery works well with the music. Third verse takes us into a timely, political/economic satire (I'll get into the politics of *Sleeps with Angels* in a moment): "Global manufacturing, hands across the sea . . ." The earthquake that upsets the trade convention reminds me of Vonnegut's *Cat's Cradle* and Dylan's "Black Diamond Bay." The last verse is magnificent, very visual (we keep switching movies but it doesn't matter, because we are so immediately and successfully projected into each new scene), with two great moments. In the opening lines, "An old friend showed up at the door / The mileposts flying by." This is inexplicable, I think. But it feels right. Like we saw them fly by as we drove up with him, before he got to the door. Or as Cindy suggests, the mileposts are a cinematic image of the time that's passed since you saw him last. Whatever. Very funny. And then the climax of the big buildup, off to rescue the girl . . . from a broken headlight? Hmm. I like it a lot. Twists and turns. Makes me smile every time.

And "Piece of Crap" is funny in a less subtle but extremely likable way; yes, I know this particular temper tantrum all too well. The spoken parts, the drum sound, the guitar sounds are just more evidence of a guy who knows exactly what he wants when he hears it, each song a different vignette with its own brilliantly intuitive sonic specifications. Sometimes maybe the singer-songwriter bandleader arranger isn't motivated to reinvent his art form for every little song that asks to be recorded—but when motivation and intention and inspiration (and intuition) do get into alignment, and apply themselves not just to a song but to that collective entity called an album (this year's model), look out. "The guy told me at the door . . ." Yahoo! We needed a little catharsis right about now. The transition from "Trans Am" is excellent.

"A Dream That Can Last" turns around the familiar "and then I woke up" in startling fashion—in effect: ". . . and then I didn't wake up . . . thank God!" Why must the album end? Why must the dream always be interrupted by the so-called "real" world? The other side of this fascinating last-song-on-the-album is that it is not an evasion of reality but a demand (as on "Crime in the City" and "Rockin' in the Free World") that we stop ignoring and denying the reality all around us. "I feel like I died and went to heaven" (this on an album whose title song has the chorus, "He sleeps with angels tonight"). "The cupboards are bare but the streets are paved with gold." Here in my neighborhood of San Diego some of the richest and poorest people in the United States live side by side, and the rich and comfortable are working themselves up into a rage of hatred at the poor for raining on their parade. Oh Lord. But Neil's song is about optimism. I think. I wouldn't swear to it. He talks about seeing a glimmer in a young person's eye, and hears the angels say there's a better life for him someday. You can interpret this in all kinds of different ways, or not at all (except that how you feel about the album or the song is itself a kind of interpretation, maybe the only important one). Do I wake or dream? I think he's saying the compassionate and necessary response to what we see is to go on dreaming; meaning, I think, with eyes open. Not TV eyes, either. "Somewhere someone has a dream come true." Why do I feel so strongly that this album is not about the dream of a better life for one slowly aging rock auteur? Or rather, why do I feel so certain that his vision of a better life is one in which the poor people of the earth share more equally, more bounteously, in its gifts? He never says that. Not in words, anyway. Maybe it's in his feelings as he's singing and playing and recording, and those feelings speak to me directly from the music. Or maybe when you really do remember the assignment and make topical music, an album for all of us, its listeners at this moment, autumn 1994, right now, maybe you thereby contribute to our effort to construct a language and a history (read: dream) by the sheer force and joyousness and freshness and honesty of your communication.

The politics of *Sleeps with Angels*? You'll have to determine that for yourself. But I hear a lot of compassion of everyman. And a demand that you, I, all of us change our minds. "It's not too late," says the first song. "(Too late)," says the title track. The message seems to be, It's up to us to choose whether it's too late or not. Are you feeling all right, my friend?

Another paper boat floated out onto the waters of the collective conscious (and unconscious; I love the way music reaches both at once). I, the creature listening, playing the CD, watching the trajectory of the boat, am a part of the beast that needs reprogramming. And I (not the guy who made the CD) am also the reprogrammer. "Change your mind." "It's not too late, it's not too late, I've got to keep my heart." Yeah, well, you've done it again. Thanks, friend, for the encouragement, the music, and yes, the excellent role model.

Don't. That's one way to describe the message I hear. Don't sleep with angels tonight.

Between November 3 and November 9, 1994, I had the good fortune to see **Freedy Johnson** and his band (Mark Spencer on lead guitar, Jared Nickerson on bass, Ron Pangborn on drums) play five shows in San Diego (the Backdoor), Los Angeles (the Whisky twice), and San Francisco (Great American Music Hall and Slim's). The first show he was sleepwalking, and I thought, Well, maybe live performance isn't really his thing. Wrong. The next four club nights were four different flavors of purest musical pleasure. Freedy is a very committed and talented live performer, his current band is terrific, and then, of course, there's the material—something like twenty songs, the same choices and sequence each night for the shows I saw; three-quarters of each of his last two albums (*Can You Fly* and *This Perfect World*), plus one song from his first album and one lovely and improbable cover (Jimmy Webb's "Wichita Lineman"). The material. And the sound of these musicians singing and playing this material. As somebody commented at the shows, you find yourself recognizing and liking virtually every song. How can this be? How can this guy have written and put together and recorded two such extraordinary and enduring albums in a row? I don't know, but I know I'd be derelict in my duties as music-writer person if I didn't urge you (much more strongly that I have already) to go and get yourself a copy of *This Perfect World* and just, um, drown yourself in it. Well, I mean that's what's great about really worthwhile music; you can (and must) get totally immersed in it, and instead of interfering with your breathing, it enhances it, deeper, richer, clearer, more nourishment in and more toxins out. And *This Perfect World*, in spite of whatever expectations you had about what you thought you wanted to be listening to, is almost guaranteed to strike you, after a few listens, as the sort of record you originally bought a phonograph for, you know—makes you feel good when it shares your space, tickles your mind while it massages your spirit, or as Cindy says, "All my judgments disappeared 'cause it was making me *feel* so much stuff."

It would probably be fun to try to analyze Freedy's songs; indeed, many of them invite the listener to unscramble their narratives, figure out what's really happening here, but where I obviously believe that a certain kind of rigorously attentive listening (and, uh, contemplation) can illuminate what Neil Young is already doing to my soul, that approach would not be true to the way Freedy's stuff reaches me. Johnston's songs are all surface and all depth, with nothing in between. Analysis doesn't help. The words are good, the sonics are simple but very good, but the content is located in the melodic hooks and the timing of their arrival, the way they catch us up and wash over us and the way there's always another one coming. Peter Blackstock wrote in a review of the album last summer in the Seattle *Rocket*: "Johnston employs haunting images and carefully selected details to spin intriguing tales of desperate characters. Nevertheless, I'd argue that he could just as well be singing the telephone book and these songs would be nearly as powerful purely on the strength of the music. On his last album's 'The Lucky One,' I remember singing along with the chorus—'On the wheels, on the tabletops, on the handles with my shirt off'—countless times before I realized the song was about a compulsive gambler losing everything he had."

Precisely. I can presume to tell you what *Sleeps with Angels* is about (again and again, contradicting myself as I go along), because the way the album hits me (and I think the way Neil Young generally reaches most of us, when he connects) is that it's *about* something. Neil gives me that good old feeling (hardly ever get it anymore, though Nirvana and Arrested Development have pulled it off) that he's reporting on the state of our collective endeavor. That's what the Stones in particular, and often enough the Doors and Byrds and Kinks and Who and of course Dylan, did for me in my adolescence, and so to a certain extent it's what I'm programmed to most desire from rock music or any music. "Tell us the news of our tribe." Nice to feel one has a tribe, and, of course, one of the downsides of the massiveness of our mass media is one increasingly suspects or fears that one doesn't—do I really know these people? But I'm digressing slightly from the question of how to articulate the quite different musical role of a Freedy Johnston. If he ain't reporting, what's he doing? Well, what these melodic hooks, and the clever phrases they interweave themselves with, full of subtle but challenging feelings, what this kind of musical magic is good for, is *release*. Gets deep into the subconscious. Deals directly with the wound without requiring us to consciously identify it. Let go. It's all right. You are forgiven. Let go. This sort of healing work is not easy to do consistently or responsibly. Freedy's (already) a master. "Why'd you call me? / Must be bad / Disappointed man, where you been?" tells a story of a particular character if and when we listen in that fashion, but mostly and reliably it just hits us as that great-sounding chorus, those dimly understood syllables, full of wonderful emphasis—Yes! Yes!—imaginary hand punching the air with the bass line, feelings, feelings, hearing just the two words "disappointed man" and not trying to put meaning to them but instead jumping straight to our own disappointments and our joy at letting go (that's what a chorus is for) of them. "Hide yourself so well / In this city." That's me, all right. Who among us could fail (with *that* music happening) to identify?

The fact that when you finally hear the lyrics they may be telling a completely different story doesn't matter. Nor does it matter when a song seems to resolve too easily, too clearly, like "Dolores Was Her Middle Name," or "Two Lovers Stop Their Hearts." My experience was that these songs lost some punch for a while, say third through sixth listenings, and then suddenly came right back, having found an ambiguity beyond their surface clarity—not necessarily through a new reading of the words, but because greater familiarity with the music has made reliance on the words and their specific images less necessary, less important. In other words, my dissatisfaction with the surface message of the songs dissolved when I began to connect, through repeated listenings, with the meanings that shimmer ("lovers cry!") in their depths.

Freedy is an improbable success (not huge, nor likely to be, but a success nonetheless, by my measure of things) in this season of circus and spectacle and mass media feeding us quadruple helpings of whatever we seemed to want to eat last week. The song that is carrying him to his new audience (great reviews help get the attention within the business and may help direct the all-important flow of money, but it's still a song on the radio that sells records) is called "Bad Reputation," and it leads off the album. My musician pal's first impression of it was that it was simplistic, acoustic guitar going chunka chunk, but I don't listen with a musician's ears and it always sounded complex and elusive to me. The whole tone of the song changes when the band comes in after the first quatrain, changes again when the ringing guitar starts on "Suddenly I'm in the street," and each time it sounds like now the story is really beginning, so that the sudden chorus catches me completely unready, all these changes in the sound and the words and the melodies setting up a tension and a feeling of motion that are sustained throughout the performance (the chorus hooks—"Do you want me now?"—and the instrumental break partially release but also further build that tension). It seems to me that whether I listen casually or carefully, the narrator is always one step ahead of me, both in what he's saying and in the tone or implication of it: Is he insane? sympathetic? Am I being threatened? Am I a stranger, eavesdropper, friend, ex-lover? innocent victim of obsession? And so forth.

It sounds like I'm talking about the words, and I am, but it's also the subtle intelligence (and beauty) of the musical structure that supports the complexity here, that allows these lyrical phrases to take on so many shifting meanings. What's great about the power of association is that it's open-ended, so that the listener/recipient naturally directs the associative material in a direction that suits his or her unconscious needs. I assume this happens in dreams. It also happens when listening to music, and the better composers and performers encourage it and empower it. I don't want to say more about this song, or the other obvious standout, "This Perfect World," except that the unpleasant narrator may not be a new trick but it's one that Freedy uses uncommonly well. And as I get to a deeper level of my relationship with this record, thanks to the number of listens I've finally given it and also to the greatly enriching experience of the live shows, which are like a third album constructed out of the other two, and just as good as or better than either one . . . as I get to this deeper level I start to think that maybe what's happening or part of what's happening is that, uh, unpleasant narrators need love, too, and we've all got one or several inside us. Or something. And it isn't just talk talk talk. It's harmonies and good guitar sounds and the comfort of the rhythmic structure and the eerie familiarity of the voice.

This Perfect World is music—twelve songs, some kind of intricate suite—to lose and find yourself in. And lose and find and find and lose some more. Words brilliantly crafted, much of the time, to promote specificity and ambiguity (of story, of feeling) both at once. Turning us back, ever back, to the pure bath of feelings in the music.

It's not for everyone. There's nothing alternative about it except the creepiness of some of the stories and the up-from-indie history of the artist and the power of the producer's name (Butch Vig—whatever it was he did as producer here, it worked out splendidly). But there's nothing mainstream about it, either, except the sweetness of those melodic changes, and they come attached in almost every case to powerful and, I suspect, unpalatable emotional baggage. It will be interesting to see if "Bad Reputation" actually becomes a Top 40 hit. Stranger things have certainly happened. Is there a video? Whatever. If Freedy Johnston and band come to your town, I urge you to treat yourself to an experience (four nights out of five) of real artistry; real commitment to the simple unvarnished power of voice (very definitely including instrumental voice; Mark Spencer's guitar tone and presence is a modest beacon in the night) and song. And get the albums. Start with *Perfect World*, if you're not already a convert, and then go on to the very different but equally self-possessed and rewarding *Can You Fly*. You might discover something.

Monster is the title of the new **R.E.M.** album, and it's giving me a headache. Not the title, nor even the sound of the album, but the problem of coming to terms with how I feel about it. I don't like it, and I'm not sure why. I've listened to it a lot over the last few months, and there have been times, even very recently, when I felt I was just on the edge of really getting into it—yeah!—singing along enthusiastically and expectantly and—nothing. Close my hands to capture it and there's nothing there.

My philosophy of listening to music is a fairly simple one: I'm looking for records that I'll really love. It follows logically, since I write about my experience of listening to music, that those are the records I write about. The others—what difference does it make? Maybe I never heard them, maybe I heard them and decided I didn't like them, maybe I heard them and didn't decide, except in the sense that not getting around to listening some more is itself a decision. Anyway, I've always felt I'm fairly ignorant about the things I don't like, and happily so, whereas I do have a certain real knowledge (however subjective) of the things I do like, because we have interacted, I've been nourished by them, we've spent some intense time together. Those records have been *experienced* by me, and I am in fact the only person who has any chance (however slim) of describing that experience. Which I try to do, because, you know, they're such powerful experiences, damn it, they make a difference in my life.

And they have a commonality and a specificity which make them easier to write about than sex (too general) or than my most recent sexual experience (no common specific reference point). You know what I'm saying. *Sleeps with Angels* is for sale at your local store, the exact same album that's on my CD player. So when I write about listening to it, my experience is inevitably different from yours but possibly of interest because we have the common reference point that we're listening to the same record. This does not apply to our sexual experiences (though I suppose tabloid journalism about movie stars, combined with the films themselves, allows us to imagine it does).

Anyway, two months of steady listening and the strongest feeling I've gotten from *Monster* (almost the only one) is *annoyance*. And I feel stupid trying to put down in print my guesses as to why this is so (I'm not one of those music writers who can confidently pronounce damnations—generally all I really know is that something doesn't hold my interest). But I do recognize that my intense enthusiasm for Neil Young's sonic inventions and the stories he tells in *Angels*, and for Freedy Johnston's wonderful melodic hooks and the stories *he* tells on his album, leaves room for curiosity about sonic inventions, say, and melodic hooks, and rock-and-roll rhythms and song structures that *don't* work for me. What distinguishes great from not-so-great? Monstrous question. But at the risk of considerable awkwardness, let me try to guess out loud why it is I don't enjoy or feel friendly towards R.E.M.'s 1994 dispatch.

Borrowing a phrase from my Freedy review, there are some great melodic hooks on *Monster*, but serious problems with the timing of their arrival. What makes a song or an album work for us is a kind of consciousness that is expressed via all the aspects of the music (rhythm, melody, harmony, counterpoint, attack, timing, phrasing, the language, the story, the themes, key verbal and melodic phrases, emotion expressed through the performance, the recurrence of words and melodies and rhythms, the transitions, et cetera, et cetera). Songwriter, singer, musicians, working together, have something to say, and we feel it, feel it in the rhythm, feel it in the melody, feel it in the vocals and the images we get from those vocalized words. Feel it in the way the musicians interact with each other. We are relating not to a hundred distinct qualities but to a single consciousness, often projected onto the singer(s) but belonging in fact to the performers collectively, and more precisely, to the performance. "Driveby" speaks to me. Speaks to me in one voice, words and music and performance acting together as a single entity. It has a flavor, a message, a content in the largest sense. When we listen to good music the world is animate, alive. It speaks to us. We feel and understand.

When it speaks to us and we don't understand, don't feel, we stop listening. Or we listen more closely, if we're given reason to. These latter cases sometimes lead to the biggest payoffs. But when we listen more closely, and stay with it, and still come up empty, we get the flipside of the coin—the big letdown. "Cold again," as Freedy says so evocatively. I really did try to get close to you. Of course, we protect ourselves with a macho dismissiveness: "I went back to the store" (says Neil). "They gave me four more / The guy told me at the door, it's a piece of crap."

The songs I come closest to almost liking (God, I sound bitchy, but there really is a thin line between love and hate, you know) on *Monster* are "Let Me In," "Crush with Eyeliner," and "I Don't Sleep, I Dream." On "Let Me In" I really like the guitar sound and the sound of the voice, and the part of the melody where the voice goes high. And I like the words, including the feeling of the ones I can't quite hear; this is probably the only song on the album where the words don't get in my way at some point. I don't get a feeling for what the song's about, though, and I think that's mostly because it's incomplete. They stopped halfway through the songwriting process. Like one of those Beatles songs where they compress two or three songs together, and you think, Any one of these would have been a great song by itself—and then Paul McCartney's solo career comes along to tell you that's not so. There's some kind of marvelous change or bridge or lyric waiting to happen in "Let Me In," and it never arrives. Whatever it was that wanted to be said here, wasn't wanted bad enough. Next to the slightest song on *Sleeps with Angels* or *This Perfect World*, the strongest songs on *Monster* sound lackluster.

"Crush with Eyeliner" has hooks I like, the obvious ones, going into and coming out of the chorus, but it's sabotaged by unusually dumb lyrics ("We all invent ourselves, and you know me") and by the fact that neither musically nor lyrically do I get any hint of a feeling for the subject of the song; I mean, when Prince does a song about a new lust-object, he makes her exist (as a lust-object). But there's no person here at all. Which could be the point, I suppose, but if it's not really about a person then what is it about? The subtlety escapes me, even though I've genuinely wanted to like the song on a number of occasions. My tendency is to blame the words, but just as words don't deserve all the credit on good rock songs, it's necessarily a lack of vision in the music as well as the words that leaves even eager listeners like myself unable to invent something topical or personally meaningful out of what I'm hearing here. Peter Buck's and R.E.M.'s idea for this album—make it all electric guitar, go for spontaneity, simplicity, noise—was an excellent thought which, in my opinion, just didn't happen to work at this particular moment. So we ended up with a concept instead of communication. "Crush with Eyeliner"—I get it; it's code for, "Let's do a glam-rock remake of *Green*."

"I Don't Sleep, I Dream" is my favorite backing track on the album, but it reminds me of radio hits like "Lonely Boy" by Andrew Gold (1977), in which a very catchy, likable sound is ruined by embarrassingly uncool words, so you resent the way it sticks in your brain (not dumb/cool like Exile's "Kiss You All Over," just embarrassing). I've got "I'll settle for a cup of coffee / But you know what I really need" stuck in my head this month, and while it's not as bad as "Do I give good head?"—also from "I Don't Sleep"—it doesn't please me. In *Musician* magazine, Michael Stipe reveals that "For me, that song ["I Don't Sleep"] is almost an anthem of complete late-twentieth-century overdrive—cyclone-mind-fuck." Too many interviews this time, Mr. Stipe. Far too many cover stories. Too much R.E.M. in my face, like you've finally become U2. The new look (Michael bald with goatee) communicates a desire to say "Fuck you!" combined with a desire to get attention cheaply. I think (and hope, and there's plenty of reason to be hopeful; this is a very resilient band) that all the members of R.E.M. will someday look back on '94 as some kind of low point that had to happen eventually and happened to happen this year.

The strange thing for me is that I didn't have high expectations for this record, and I hadn't planned to review it in any case unless it just knocked me out, so that it should have been easy for me to walk sideways from it early on like I seem to have done with Liz Phair's second album—I don't dislike it, just haven't listened to it enough to know how I feel, and don't feel required to have an opinion. But *Monster*, like two-thirds of Lou Reed's solo albums, somehow turned into this ridiculous tease instead, where I kept thinking I was just on the edge of discovering its fine points, its slow-building genius.

And so I had to write about it, and now that I've done so, I'm still not satisfied. This has a lot to do with the strange relationships we develop with our heroes as they go on releasing product even after they've outlasted our attention span. Lou Reed. The Stones. U2. Pete Townshend. Bruce Springsteen. I'm not trying to be a smart-ass critic here. These people have every right to go on making records (except for the Stones, because they do it only as part of preparation for a tour, like giving interviews and going to the gym) (maybe I am trying to be a smart-ass critic). And I'm aware that many people would put Bob Dylan on this list, and it's true for them, whereas Dylan continues to delight me with his new work more than any other contemporary artist. But rightly or wrongly, these relationships are a big part of how we hear music, both the early part, where we fall in love with them, and the later part, where we hate what they've become but more people love them than ever before . . .

Neil Young (again) told Michael Stipe everything he needed to know before he wrote all these too-clever lyrics about identity and celebrity and the frustration of being not-quite-able-to-love, before he did all these damn interviews. "Is it hard to make arrangements with yourself / When you're old enough to repay, but young enough to sell?" ("Tell Me Why," 1971). Dear R.E.M., you, all four of you or six of you, *are* a commodity at this point. I don't wish to try to tell you how you should respond to that fact. All I'm trying to do is give an honest report of how it feels to hear your new album and see you in the mags at this particular moment in our relationship.

You say you love me madly (last song) and that with love comes strange currencies. And I'm saying, In that case, you owe me something more heartfelt.

Okay. First of all, and let's go right to it, there's a track on **Allen Ginsberg's** new four-CD box set (**Holy Soul Jelly Roll—Poems and Songs 1949–1993**) that arguably deserves to be added to my list of the one hundred best rock-and-roll singles of all time. It's called "Birdbrain"; it was written in a Yugoslav hotel room in 1980 and recorded with a Denver garage band in 1981 and released as a single the same year ("aired a lot on college radios from Berkeley to Harvard and sold three thousand copies before the master wore out"). I never heard it before, but the idea that it came out in the timespan between "Radio Free Europe" and "The Message" is too wonderful for words. It's quite worthy to stand alongside either of those landmarks. It also—and this is one of my requirements for any song that wishes to be considered for the list—sounds as fresh as if it were born yesterday, as urgent as if it were coming over the Internet this evening, being created before your very eyes and ears. "Birdbrain runs the world!!" Amen. This is a truly great live rock-and-roll poem performance, in the holy tradition of the Sex Pistols, Bob Dylan, Chuck Berry and, yes, Allen Ginsberg.

Stop. Start again. How to listen? What is the correct way, if any, that we will have failed if we go to our grave not having performed the act thus at least once? How shall we read and listen? What is the correct way to be present while making love? What is the correct way to be present while sitting in meditation? How are we to properly receive God's blessing? Will we be punished if we screw this up? These thoughts naturally arise listening to Allen Ginsberg's voice, which is, quite self-consciously, the voice of intelligent compassionate American (male, politicized, homosexual) consciousness in the late twentieth century. The outsider. (A rock-and-roll stance, which Ginsberg with his life has shown himself more committed to than most rock-and-rollers, who generally cash in and check out, one way or another, once they've grabbed the world's attention.) And what have we here? Four CDs in a handsome box, five hours of recordings, well-catalogued and in good sound quality and in a format allowing for easy access, quick travel between decades, more than four decades of work represented here, including most of the major poet's major poems (the first public reading of "Howl" in its entirety, Berkeley 1956, with Kenneth Rexroth, Gary Snyder, Neal Cassady, Jack Kerouac, Lawrence Ferlinghetti, Philip Whalen, and Michael McClure among the audience members; also "America" and "Sunflower Sutra" from the same reading; "Kaddish" in its entirety, read to a Brandeis University audience in 1964; "Wichita Vortex Sutra"; "Wales Visitation"; "Please Master"), and something else, apparently equally important to the artist during the past twenty-five years: his songs. Five extraordinary hours, almost a lifetime, of performed art.

This box, I suggest, not any printed book, is Ginsberg's most complete and conscious representation of his work as a whole, his (and perhaps our) *Leaves of Grass*.

I wrote the sentence above, and then, because writing is not as final as live performance, I found myself spending two days engaged in fierce research, reading small and not-so-small chunks of two biographies of the poet and examining his *Collected Poems 1947–1980*, listening to these four CDs some more and studying the excellent and informative booklet that comes with them, just trying to find out whether, if I had just a little more information, I would still dare to make (and, necessarily, attempt to defend) such a claim.

The issue, of course, is this drum I've been beating (not quite to death, I hope) in my writings on Bob Dylan, that "performer" is as legitimate an identity for an artist as "composer" or "painter" or "writer." Or poet. The Harper and Row book called *Collected Poems* is certainly the most complete and useful representation of Ginsberg's work as a page poet (a poet whose work is encountered on paper, in a book). But that work is necessarily a subset of the artist's work-as-a-whole, which in Ginsberg's case includes a huge quantity of journals and preserved notes and drafts and "unfinished" poems plus interviews and letters, *and* a lifetime of live performances. The artist has not only touched people with his published work. He has also touched them, a very great many of them, with his direct communication out loud in their physical presence, in the same room. Allen Ginsberg is a poet, and he is also (I'm sure in some languages the word "poet" must still include this explicitly, like the word "troubadour") a performer. *Collected Poems*, the book, is not only not a complete representation of Allen the performer, it actually doesn't represent that part of his work at all.

Nor does the Ginsberg archive, all those diaries in prose & verse & recording & photograph & press clipping, represent his work. It's too vast. Most of the artist's intent is lost in it (except that part that simply intends vastness, not necessarily to be disdained). (Like a Buddhist master, he happily offers to give you an honest and accurate answer to the question you just asked, if you'll give him forty or fifty years of your time and attention.) Which is not to say it isn't wonderful or valuable—it is indeed one of his greatest achievements, a library of his era that truly stands as an alternate history and that will undoubtedly help shape future historians' perspectives on a great many matters that they may regard as important. Thus indeed one drops one's deliberate pebble into the evolutionary/historical/human flow. One of Ginsberg's great roles, underappreciated but magnificently appropriate for a poet of his times, has been Information Gatherer. He has gathered. He has contemplated. He has published (made public) his findings, his summations. And he has more or less walked from town to town to share the news. What a story.

An archive is too big to be a representation. Even a CD-ROM is too big, most of the time, I suspect. But these four old-fashioned (hah!) audio-only CDs, plus their booklet, tell the story and supply the content, the direct experience, of Allen Ginsberg's art extremely well. Perhaps they also fail my definition of a "complete representation" of the poet's work because they don't include the experience of the poems when read silently, taken in by eyes rather than ears, a very important experience in regard to a writer like Ginsberg. But they don't leave out the poems; whereas the book does leave out the performances. So I end up saying that I'm not certain of the accuracy of my sentence . . . but I do think this box set is likely to be the most thorough possible introduction or reintroduction to Allen Ginsberg's genius. His poetness. His art. The power of his presence (and of his perseverance).

I guess the question I've been pursuing in my reading the last few days is, To what extent does Ginsberg regard himself as a performing (as distinct from a writing) artist? How important is that aspect of his work? The answer is not as clear as I think it is with Dylan. Dylan has frequently made comments to interviewers (throughout his career), directly or indirectly emphasizing his sense of himself as a performer, someone who plays guitar and sings to people, as opposed to a primary identity as a songwriter or a maker of records. Ginsberg's sense of himself is somewhat different. I would say he thinks of himself as a speaking voice, that speaks more or less equally well through printed page or recording or live performance. The great vision of his life, in fact, was an auditory vision at age twenty-two in which he heard "a deep rich voice" reciting William Blake's "Ah Sunflower." Michael Schumacher writes, in his biography of Ginsberg (*Dharma Lion*; highly recommended), "In one shudder of illumination, Allen reached the understanding that poetry was eternal: A poet's consciousness could travel timelessly, alter perception, and speak of universal vision to anyone attaining the same level of consciousness. Poetry, Allen understood, as did Blake, was a vehicle for visionary statement." So the content is vision, but the form is speaking. One of Ginsberg's primary spiritual practices, for many years, has been chanting meditation. The power of voice.

Not words. Voice.

But not necessarily performance. Voice comes through on a page. Ginsberg heard Blake's voice on a page before it took life in the air around him. And on the other hand, performance has played a very significant role in Ginsberg's career. His initial success, with "Howl," came as a result of the impact of the poem's first public performance, in San Francisco, on October 13, 1955. He has spent a great deal of his energy ever since touring and giving readings. Indeed, there is a strong argument that the Beat poets, and Ginsberg in particular, brought the oral tradition back to American poetry. Schumacher cites Gary Snyder's observation that the collective reading on October 13 was "a curious kind of turning point in American poetry," and says it was "the beginning of a surge of poetry readings that brought poets into contact with their audiences and reestablished poetry as an oral form."

It can't be a coincidence that "Howl" 's reinvention of audible poetry occurred at exactly the same time that Bill Haley, Little Richard, Chuck Berry, and Elvis Presley were discovering/reinventing rock and roll. (The night of October 13, 1955, Elvis was on tour somewhere in the midwest, opening for Bill Haley and Hank Snow. "Rock Around the Clock" and "Maybellene" had recently been huge hits, "Mystery Train" was climbing the charts, and "Tutti Frutti" was newly released.) Rock and roll and Beat poetry didn't converge until Bob Dylan's arrival on the charts ten years later, but from that moment forward they were inseparable—"God Save the Queen" and "The Message" and "Smells Like Teen Spirit" form a historical continuity with "Howl" and "America" at least as much as they do with "Rock Around the Clock." The idea of getting up onstage and telling the country what you think of it—while simultaneously screaming out the secrets of your own private soul—was a brilliant invention (as always, obvious enough in hindsight), a breakthrough.

The October 13 "Howl," alas, was not taped; the recording on disc one is from the repeated-by-popular-demand six-poet reading in Berkeley five months later, by which time Allen had written the rest of the poem (fascinating that it caused such excitement even before he completed and read the Moloch section, part two, which is the core of the poem's incandescent power). By this time Elvis was on RCA and everything was different, but anyway the historical vibe attached to this thirty-minute recording is intense—Kenneth Rexroth's introduction and silly banter at the start from the crowd of alcoholic poets are included and really help to place us there, present at the moment. Unfortunately, the performance itself is not a good one, better in the latter parts but still not doing the poem—which was *written* to be performed—justice. Hugely more effective, indeed quite marvelous, is the performance from that same evening of "America," a stand-up comedy routine with an edge on it sharp enough to slice open the sky of our shared false reality. It's striking, too, to hear Ginsberg say (first public reading of this), "America, I'm putting my queer shoulder to the wheel," and to realize that in this case the brash young man did do exactly what he promised. It's hard to think of another poet during the past forty years who has worked as steadily or as earnestly at the task of national (and planetary) transformation.

The best thing on the box set, and it is astonishingly good, is the sixty-three-minute reading of "Kaddish" on disc two. From start to finish, voice and poem are gripping, lucid, keenly emotional (it's hard to think of a piece of music that's made me feel so vulnerable and open so quickly, so enduringly), and radiantly beautiful. The poem is about the poet's childhood (and adulthood) with his mother and her insanity and incarceration, written on the occasion of her death. This reading, simple, straightforward, heartfelt, and worthy of Ginsberg's masterpiece, was originally released by Atlantic Records in 1966.

I notice that I refer to the poem as a masterpiece, not the performance, even though I am reviewing a collection of performances. This is certainly different from the way I write about a Dylan song, and I think indeed that Ginsberg is a different sort of artist than Dylan is—two-thirds writer, one-third performer, as opposed to the other way around. But what complicates this is that Ginsberg is a writer who, as much as possible, writes as if he were performing. Under the strong influence of Neal Cassady and Jack Kerouac, he adopted spontaneity as a primary writing tool, and in many cases identifies his poems as having been written on a car ride or in an airplane or sitting up in bed, at one sitting, as they came out, with light revision after the fact (Kerouac, of course, tried to avoid revision altogether). So with Ginsberg, more than with Dylan, the original writing is a performance, now-I-start-talking-and-let's-see-what-comes-out. The stage performance then becomes a re-creation of this original performance. For Ginsberg—very different from Dylan's approach—there does seem to be a Platonic ideal form of each poem, which is reached for in live performance and attained or not in varying degrees. The idea of each new performance as a new statement, which I get from listening to live Dylan tapes, is not so present in Ginsberg. His writings are not as plastic. They are soliloquies to be delivered, with different emotions and implications in different contexts, but not springboards for an entirely new act of creation.

Much of the material included on *Holy Soul Jelly Roll* is musical. There are readings by Ginsberg to which music has been added, readings with live musical accompaniment, and many songs. Ginsberg's singing voice takes getting used to. It's coarse and not very tuneful—really, not very musical by any ordinary standards. And yet the man's determination to make music, his patient cheerful stubbornness, is finally irresistible. He has been actively working on getting his songs out to the world (in his fantasies, to a mass audience, like Dylan or the Beatles) for twenty-five years now. This box set surely will mark his greatest success so far in this endeavor. (In 1989 I read a rave review of his album *The Lion in Winter* and went looking for it eagerly. It was nowhere to be found, and although I was not as persevering as I should have been, I have never run into a copy of it in all of my hours of browsing in record stores. His considerable fame notwithstanding, Allen Ginsberg records are not hot items. But one suspects this Rhino box will have a certain cachet . . .)

Songs I like: Lotsa stuff, most of it on disc four, which is titled *Ashes & Blues*. In addition to "Birdbrain," which takes the mantralike aspects of "Wild Thing" and pushes them to their even-more-stripped-down logical conclusion, there's punk rock in the form of "Capitol Air" (recorded live with the Clash in 1981), which is charming but forgettable, and "The Little Fish Devours the Big Fish," a chilling, angry song about Nicaragua in early 1982 and its relationship with the United States, driven by Allen's spirited vocal and some great Elvin Jones drum-whacks (catches the German-marching-song side of punk very nicely). "CIA Dope Calypso" is conceptually brilliant (if the *New York Times* won't publish the facts I've dug up about CIA-sponsored opium-smuggling, I'll broadcast them via a pop song) but it gets irritating. "September on Jessore Road" is challenging and moving—Ginsberg is reporting on his experience of visiting, as poet/journalist/witness, the refugee camps on the road between Bangladesh and Calcutta, at the time of the floods that left up to seven million people homeless and starving. This one I strongly recommend; its combination of repellence and beauty, compassion and self-importance, are powerful, disturbing medicine. The vocal performance is superb, full of feeling without sentimentality or melodrama—except in the finger-pointing section; in effect the place where an American has a right to feel angry, asking why his own government is not responding, and answering that they're too busy killing babies in Indochina. Bob Dylan's weird piano accompaniment is appropriately hypnotic and eerie; Hal Wilner seems to have done a great job of salvaging and creating a workable musical track out of two unsuccessful sessions eleven years apart. For twenty years this song went unreleased—it was published as a poem in AG's *The Fall of America* in 1972, but I'm not at all sure it works as a poem on paper. Ginsberg's paradox is that a poem/song like this, clearly intended to get the world's or America's attention, goes largely unheard, perhaps specifically because the author chose to write it in a form that he imagined would bring it to the largest number of people. So that the motivation for working in the song-form is to go public in a bigger way (he has certainly said as much at times), yet the result is the opposite. Allen toys with this riddle in the notes on this song in the booklet, in which he has the chutzpah to say he wrote this song about starving humans in order to impress Bob Dylan (Dylan the same month wrote "George Jackson," a good song on an important subject which also sounds as though it was mostly intended to impress someone) (it was a strange moment). Allen then acknowledges that he had high expectations for the poem/song, and was disappointed that "my magnum opus . . . hadn't resulted in fame, fortune, beauty, sublimity, and public proclamation. But I was over-ambitious, actually, and vain." I don't think Allen Ginsberg ever really intended to achieve fame and fortune by capitalizing on a famine in Asia. We all have egos whispering fantasies in our ears, of course, but—and this may be the explanation for Ginsberg's paradox—ultimately we are judged (and may judge ourselves) not by our thoughts but by the results of our actions. Allen's track record is very good in this respect.

I like a song that isn't on disc four, the prehistoric "Green Valentine" (from 1954) on disc one. It's haunting and reveals the singer that Ginsberg always was, frustrated perhaps when he turned his conscious attention to it but pure beauty and soul communication at unself-conscious moments like this one. I'm excited by quite a few different spoken poems in different parts of this box, but one of my particular favorites is a 1992 performance of an excerpt from "Wichita Vortex Sutra" (1966), in which AG is accompanied by a pianist playing music written for the purpose by Philip Glass. This is a gorgeous duet which, if this box turns out to be the vehicle by which a new generation discovers Allen Ginsberg, could become one of his best-loved creations. I also need to mention two other excellent poems and performances, the elegant "To Aunt Rose" (written '58; performed '86) and the raw ecstatic "Kral Majales," captured almost at the same time it was written, May 1965, immediately following Ginsberg's election as the King of May and his subsequent expulsion from Czechoslovakia. His walk-on in Dylan's "Subterranean Homesick Blues" video dates from this same week in planetary history.

Alongside the quick spontaneity of most of Ginsberg's great work is a slow deliberate willful concentration on a handful of conscious endeavors—even the great loves of his life, Cassady, Kerouac, Orlovsky, often seem (in his writing) like conscious decisions as much or more than passions, mind as well as flesh deciding this is love, and will determining to go the distance. One finds this in the causes that he champions in his writing—decadeslong obsession with details of CIA dope smuggling; why? (because it's Allen we know why, he tells us, archiving and baring his own obsessiveness as well as the results of the search)—and also in his spiritual and aesthetic endeavors. The conscious obsession that stands out on *Holy Soul* and in the history of Ginsberg-as-musician is his effort to reset William Blake's songs to music (their original tunes being long lost). Allen's sincere (and stubborn) primitive as a musician is a tonic, a truly unusual perspective—though he doesn't always seem to realize that if you are this deliberate about each step it may be centuries before you're ready to fly.

For myself, I respect Ginsberg's Blake recordings and the tremendous importance he has attached to this "project" for more than twenty-five years now, but after repeated listenings to the thirteen songs included here, I am only just beginning to find pleasure and personal meaning in them for myself. At first it was all a blank, and even now I apprehend but dimly. The one piece that appealed to me early on was the atypical "A Dream," which creates a fascinating, mysterious mood, particularly centered around the rhythmic shift that takes place in the middle of the song. It's the only Blake piece with drums, and the one least anchored in voice and lyric. Ginsberg makes much of the fact that Blake performed these songs for friends on a pump organ, the same instrument Allen used to compose his Blake tunes and similar to the harmonium he performs these songs on (at most of his readings and live appearances). But I wonder if there was a rhythmic quality to Blake's own performances that Ginsberg, despite his reverence for Blake, is not in touch with? My personal favorite of his Blake performances is the version of "Nurse's Song (Innocence)" that he performs with Denise Mercedes somewhere in Bob Dylan's movie *Renaldo and Clara*. The chorus haunts me; after a number of listenings it suddenly becomes ecstatic, transporting, open door to an unexpected universe. I'm not as fond of the version included on *Holy Soul*, though I appreciate its value as a document of live Blakean roadshow; but Allen adores it, and quite possibly I'll see the light one day.

Two songs here, both recorded with modest help from Bob Dylan, "Vomit Express" (1971) and "Airplane Blues" (1982), manage to achieve a musical groove that ennobles the simple lyrics by opening up a space of deep feeling—they contrast with most of the other songs by being music-driven rather than lyric-driven, so that, like rock songs, much Dylan and most Neil Young, for instance, they open the heart through musical connection first and then direct its attention towards the themes stirred up by the lyrics (friendship and camaraderie in the former song; awareness of one's place in the universe in the latter). But Ginsberg achieves his greatest nobility and success as a singer on four of the simplest performances included here: "Prayer Blues" (1973), "Gospel Noble Truths" (1976), "Father Death Blues" (1981), and "Do the Meditation Rock" (1989; the dates are dates of performance, not composition). These are beautiful songs, great poems of extraordinary depth that cannot be separated from their music or from the impact of the singer's voice. They are also, I think, the sort of songs that have the potential to become new and different luminous entities every time they're performed—I would be most interested to hear tapes of alternate versions from other years. Here the voice of the poet and the voice of the performer become one, in the simplicity of speaking from one's melodic, feeling heart about the basic issues of life and death and how to cope with daily challenges. "Prayer Blues" is about submitting to the will of God (here named "Jesus Christ," just to shake up listener and singer, and also to acknowledge the mythic role of the divine in human form, the He with whom we may identify), in the context of the poet having recently broken his leg. Allen's voice and harmonium lean on each other so eloquently we can feel the universe vibrate. "Gospel Noble Truths" may be "a short-form summary review of the nut of Buddhism," as the author explains, but what enlivens it is the in-your-face quality of the performance, which seems to progress from formal received truth to direct (and familiar) confrontation between the singer and his resistant Self, abstract meditation struggle somehow become real, flesh, loving, angry, personal, authentic. And sweetly musical. "Father Death Blues," written in an airplane on the way to his father's funeral, is as fine and gentle a love poem as I've heard the poet speak or sing. And "Do the Meditation Rock" is joyful, instructional, exhortative (speaking to himself as much as to us, so it feels just fine), and somehow transcendent. It's in the voice. Generosity, indeed.

Finally more poems, a flood of poetry, nicely narrowed down in this collection (as in a public reading) so we can focus in and give attention to what's before us. I like the final poem/performance especially, and admire the sequencing that leads up to it: "On Neal's Ashes," "September on Jessore Road," "Father Death Blues," "Do the Meditation Rock," "After Lalon." "After Lalon" (written 1992; performed 1993) is a vivid funny wise sympathetic benediction to such a public act as this poet's life work, as encapsulated and spewed out in this five-hour package—a good match for the opening bookend, "Walking at Night in Key West." Listen to the two voices. The closeness and distance between them, 1954 before the flood and 1993 long after, tells the whole story. "Oh when the saints, shall go insane . . ." "Allen Ginsberg warns you, 'Don't follow my path to extinction.' "

It's a good story. Kudos to Hal Wilner, who selected and organized and remixed and brought to fruition this box of wonders. I heard and saw Allen read this past September, at McCabe's Guitar Shop in Santa Monica, California—the other time I went to a reading of his was in 1969 in New York City, and he gave outstanding, deeply moving performances on both occasions. At McCabe's, as on the box set, he read the courageous, difficult "Please Master." It is above all, I think, a request for permission to be oneself. It is also a graphic description of a sexual act between a bisexual man and a gay man, with sadomasochistic elements. And tender elements. It's difficult to read before an audience. It's difficult (for me, anyway) to listen to. Ginsberg challenges his listeners. He challenges himself. He's a kind of rock star, certainly, but no more than Bob Dylan has he retired to the Old Rock Stars Home. A working poet, working performer. Walking on a wire with no net live in your town this afternoon. Or on your CD boom box.

Go see him if you dare. And yes, I recommend the album.

What's a poet? (What's a rock star?) As Allen Ginsberg has strived through the past three decades, unsuccessfully (but with his usual dazzling pratfall dignity and hard-earned grace), to be Bob Dylan, **Leonard Cohen** in 1966 or so tentatively put his poet/novelist's toe in the pop/rock water and has been swimming along grimly and charmingly being Leonard Cohen, songwriter and singer, ever since. His exceptional new album, *Cohen Live*, shows what can happen if you try hard enough, long enough, to put across your poetry in the form and language of music. You might succeed. You might find yourself, at age sixty, not even on the map of contemporary poets or novelists, but surprisingly and securely ensconced among the better musical performers (and songwriters, but the truth is no one can begin to sing your little masterworks as well as you can) of your place and time, "speaking to you sweetly from my window in the tower of song." With a hefty book of lyrics disguised as poetry (*Stranger Music: Selected Poems and Songs*) well distributed in the bookstores, just like any rock star, and a new compact disc of live performances, a career retrospective that just might be (tough call, because *I'm Your Man* is certainly a classic) the finest album you've ever released.

What is good about *Cohen Live* is very simply this: It's a pleasure to listen to. An album, like Freedy's, that asks to be put back on the phonograph, and then makes me glad I played it, every time. A surprising record that isn't too long at seventy-two minutes, that allows my mind to wander but also pulls me back in, at the same spots and at different spots, over and over again. It has a funny quality to me whereby in a sense it's one long song. This although, unlike *Sleeps with Angels* or *This Perfect World*, it doesn't have songs that are paired with each other or characters that recur. It doesn't even (I'm giving you a completely subjective impression now; I realize someone else could and would hear it quite differently) strike me as having themes that recur, although I would have sworn recurrent themes was what Leonard Cohen was all about. But this performance, actually an amalgam of performances in Toronto and Vancouver in the summer of 1993 and in Amsterdam, San Sebastian, and Austin in the spring and fall of 1988, is like a single delicious grandiose multicolored but consistently textured narrative, a picaresque story that starts at the end ("Dance Me to the End of Love") and ends near the beginning ("Suzanne takes you down . . .") and speaks eloquently and heartbreakingly and meaningfully and wittily at each station of the heart along the way. It's a live album that works. There aren't many of them (as opposed to live tapes of whole concerts, which very often work if you're into the artist), but those that do click can have a magic, a spontaneity, a fullness (unself-consciousness) of feeling not found on any studio recording. Something special and different.

Let it seep into you. This album's one long wandering narrative (diary of a lifetime of emotional adventures) full of feeling.

Which is what I'm looking for. I'm a needful listener. I'm looking for language and history, mine, ours, for right now (new history is myth revised to describe right now), and I recognize it first and foremost by the way it feels. That's what gets and holds my attention. That's what allows me to hear and endlessly appreciate the nuance of what the storyteller has to say.

A voice. The storyteller's voice. On most of his studio recordings, Cohen is too caught up with his own cleverness; he can be a masterful seducer but that mood of despair that hangs over everything (romantic despair, oh spare us, what a pose) has to do with some ultimate inability to seduce himself. Onstage, however, everything changes. Band and audience, music and communication, transport the singer into a free, ecstatic place where cleverness is harnessed and put at the service of a great joyful unflinching generosity of spirit. The narrative that results, the storyteller's voice we hear, is the voice of the performance, the music, the song. Song *is* words, of course, and now we can really listen to them and take in all the subtleties of the story, now that we are already swept up in the power and heartfelt honesty of the melody, the ensemble, the sound.

We're having a great musical experience. It starts for me, like an overture, with the first wordless bars of "Dance Me to the End of Love," keyboards, guitars, vocal chorus, violin, I respond immediately, opening myself to the melody and its drama (just like the audience that applauds when the "la la" chorus comes in), I'm in love with this tune, this prelude. What does it say to me? It's like the start of a movie, a child hearing the first words of an often-told bedtime story, something familiar and orchestral conjured up from my past and brought forward to the present, romance, theater, an invitation. I wasn't into ballroom or any sort of elegant dancing when I was an adolescent, but it doesn't matter, a universal chord is struck, and I respond. Enchanting melody. Wonderful arrangement. I dance.

"Take This Waltz" (title of a Cohen song, not on this album). He knows how to woo me. I dance.

My favorite words in "Dance Me to the End of Love" are "La la, la la, la la, la la," but those other sounds he's making also touch deep parts of me. Cohen is a stonecutter, quite the opposite of Ginsberg. He labors over every phrase, every word, polishing and reconsidering and improving. Where Dylan and Young say that most of their best songs come very quickly, Cohen reports that the good ones tend to take months of stalking, maybe years. The result (Cohen's technique works as well for him as Ginsberg's or Dylan's for them) is an extraordinary compression, lyrics like a tiny Chinese box whose contents turn out to be huge.

"Dance me to your beauty with a burning violin." We see biblical and historical images, Solomon, Nero (very funny), we know and feel that the dance is one of seduction, and that the singer (we can hear it in the tone of his voice) is celebrating this talent, a willing supplicant, delighted that she (the other, the lover) has this ability to inspire desire, to believe in and dramatize her beauty. "Dance me through the panic till I'm gathered safely in." Swoop, female (Cohen's a famous heterosexual) as mother/protector, again in a totally positive context, and what courage and skill it takes to put these two lines next to each other and make them belong together. They do belong together, but most men (and women) compartmentalize these aspects of the female, especially in their love poetry. But Cohen is one of the great contemporary male appreciators of women. And of love in all its complexity and beauty and pain. "Lift me like an olive branch and be my homeward dove." Let us become symbols of peace to each other, and in the active tense, with other actions of love simultaneously evoked: "lift me," "be my homeward dove" (come here). Cohen's symbolism is never simplistic (I love simplicity, but I hate simplistic symbolism) but always multilayered and evocative, with the ambiguous and the specific all interwoven with each other, generating not one but dozens of carefully interrelated images and meanings.

In poetry like this, images can also evoke their opposites (as an absence evokes a presence): the "olive branch" / "dove" line might also remind us that lovers fight—and maybe he's singing these words as an olive branch, a peace offering, after an argument. This in turn makes this a line (and a song) about healing.

The second verse is the most intimate (or anyway, the most sexual). One of the elements of these performances, particularly relevant and suggestive in this song about a man and a woman, is the use of two additional vocalists, both women, whose voices come and go in a careful choreography throughout the songs. This second verse has a female harmony voice singing alongside Leonard's (slightly lower volume). She wasn't there in the first verse, and will be gone again in the next (she returns for the fourth and the reprise). So when he says, "Let me see your beauty," she's saying it, too. The second part of this sentence, "when the witnesses are gone," is quite wonderful. It evokes the essential privacy of sexuality and sexual interaction, that special world that belongs only to us two, with just a taste of lustful impatience to be in that world. It perhaps acknowledges the almost universal truth that we show more of our beauty to (are more beautiful when we're alone with) our lovers. It reminds us that we the listeners are voyeurs (unless you hear him as singing to you, a different and probably more powerful role than the one I choose when I'm hearing this song). And I just like the sound of that word, "witnesses," and the way it serves as the blossom in the flower of this sentence. And these perfectly metrical phrases (precisely suited to the great fox-trot rhythm, regular, regular, with surges), and the sweetness and sauciness of the rhyme ("Babylon"). And more. Most of this reaches us unconsciously, or semiconsciously. But it reaches us. And although it's great poetic writing, it couldn't begin (I think) to reach us as powerfully if it were words on paper (unless we were reading it after having already taken the performance into our bodies and minds).

There's a dance in the male/femaleness of the "la la" chorus, too. In the prelude it's purely female (the two voices blend marvelously). Then there's a violin break between second and third verses, but the "la la"s don't return until after the fourth verse, and this time Leonard's voice joins his accompanists' (Julie Christensen and Perla Batalla). It's male-and-female for the final chorus also, the recessional after the reprise. (That reprise is the first verse again for the first half, but in the second half, "Lift me like an olive branch . . ." becomes "Touch me with your naked hand, touch me with your glove." His language delights. It just truly delights.)

Language and structure. I like the way he tells the story.

"Dance me to the wedding now" starts the third verse (he knows what comes after lovemaking in his partner's mind). "We're both of us beneath our love, both of us above" bears a lot of thinking about. "Dance me to the children who are asking to be born" (fourth verse) is gorgeous, and again both bold and rare. Part of what sex is about is the desire (whether yielded to or not, always a desire) to have children. Not often acknowledged (especially in such an upbeat context) in a pop song. (Especially in a rock-and-roll song, although I guess one has to ask whether Cohen is in any sense a rock artist. My answer would be yes, actually, in the one specific and important sense that he wouldn't have been able to carve out a niche for himself, with his voice, in any genre other than rock or folk, and the kind of orchestration he's matured into has little connection to most people's concept of "folk." Rock is—still—where the creative go when no one else will have them.)

"Dance me through the curtains that our kisses have outworn." Poverty and grace. Duration. What a magnificent song.

And there are a dozen more. Three are from Cohen's first album, *Songs of Leonard Cohen* (1967), four are from 1984's *Various Positions*, two each from *New Skin for the Old Ceremony* (1974) and *I'm Your Man* (1988), and one apiece from albums released in 1968 and 1971. Nothing from *The Future* (1993), reportedly at the request of the record company (don't dilute the new product). The selecting was presumably done by the album's producers, Leanne Ungar ("broadcast engineer" on Cohen's tours in '88 and '93) and Bob Metzger (guitarist on those tours), though Cohen probably had some input. In any case, the selection and sequence are very good, very successful, giving us, as I suggested before, quite a different picture of Leonard Cohen and his work and even his worldview than we get on his studio albums, a picture much closer to the one he paints when you come to hear him in concert.

It's the portrait of a man who loves women and spends his life sparring with them, portrait of a deeply spiritual agnostic, portrait of a (sharp-eyed) pessimist and cynic who loses his cynicism and becomes an unself-conscious romantic the moment he opens his mouth to sing, onstage, with his fellow musicians. Above all, it's the portrait of a person who loves the sound of music and the act of performing.

There's an actor in Cohen—none in Dylan, I think, and Young and Ginsberg are the sort of actors who are magnificent but can only play themselves. But Leonard walks through this imaginary evening with us, picking up the roles of a repentant lover ("Bird on a Wire," in which Leonard also plays a crooner on the boards belting out his "greatest hit"), a wild-eyed and hilariously accurate prophet ("Everybody Knows"), fire as a conscious entity ("Joan of Arc"), unrepentant and newly politicized lover ("There Is a War"), white knight and perfect suitor ("I'm Your Man"), disembodied questioning voice ("Who by Fire?"), and so forth. Cohen's approach to performing with a band is as different from Dylan's as their approaches to songwriting (although the results are similar—concerts so rich and varied they inspire fans to collect and listen to and compare live tapes, and to attend a series of live performances, not just one, whenever they have the opportunity). Both delight in and insist on playing with a band. Dylan apparently tells no one what he wants but is happiest in a white heat of musical interaction, when the music really puts feeling and spontaneity into his singing, and vice versa. Cohen on the other hand seems to tell every musician and singer exactly what he wants, and is happiest when each player knows their part and is inspired to sing or play their hearts out within it. Cohen's performance aesthetic is Apollonian, Dylan's Dionysian. But both paths lead to the same goal: ecstatic expression, a work of art that reaches a sublime intensity bordering on catharsis and then is over, gone. To be attempted again, perhaps, tomorrow evening. And that's what one lives for.

I like all of these songs and performances, and am capable of stopping to focus in, in fascination, on any one of them. Stories, scenarios, that unfold and unfold. If I were more of a Cohen fan—I mean a more active and educated listener, as I am of Dylan's work—I'd probably be frustrated by this record, because it mixes together different shows and different years, and because any fan can come up with performances of individual songs from any given tour that he or she believes to be far better than whatever made it onto the official album. But ignorance is bliss, and sometimes a doorway to unself-conscious appreciation. If Leonard can be even better than this some nights, and I don't doubt it, then still this album is the perfect vehicle of introduction to such possibilities. And a great pleasure, at least for those of us who are only partially initiated, in its own right.

Besides "Dance," my favorite tracks here are the other three songs from *Various Positions*, "Hallelujah," "If It Be Your Will," and "Heart with No Companion" (it does seem as if he deliberately set out to remake an overlooked or inadequately recorded album), plus "Joan of Arc" (first recorded on *Songs of Love and Hate*, 1971).

"Hallelujah" can be considered the only new song on *Cohen Live*, because this live version contains entirely new lyrics for the first three verses (the last verse stays the same), which seem to tell a completely different story (except that the retention of the climatic verse makes it more like a parallel story, different era, situation, and theme, but arriving at the same unique and compelling emotional state, like the fact is here I am and the speculative part is how I got here). The early lyrics, which are as good or better as isolated verses, but maybe less satisfactory in overall effect (one is left dazzled by the cleverness and scope of the yarn but uncertain whether this was really a story or just a display of beautiful feathers) are biblical and touch on basic Cohen themes: the dark power (and glory) of sexual attraction (Samson's in there, and Delilah as seductress/rapist, combined with the song of Solomon); music as universal metaphor (in which we see muse-guided King David composing "Hallelujah"); and man as spiritual being standing up to the tyrannical God of the Old Testament: "You say I took the Name in vain / I don't even know the Name / But if I did, well really, what's it to ya?" Marvelous. The new lyrics seem much plainer on the page, but they tell the sort of story that songs exist to articulate: waning days of a love relationship, pain, loneliness, dissatisfaction with self, but—the payoff—each verse and the song itself climaxing with a refusal to renounce the power and glory of the experience. This is "better to have loved and lost" writ large, with riveting imagery and unmistakable conviction. What a performance! "Yeah but it's not a complaint that you hear tonight / It's not the laughter of someone who claims to have seen the light . . ." The "secret" title of both songs is "The Broken Hallelujah," and its theme is always the lover, the individual, as a passionate Job, praising Him unconditionally even while standing amidst the sorrow wrought by His, or Love's, hand. Declaration of indomitable faith (as in Neil Young's "Will to Love"). And also some kind of strange proud vulnerable expression of willingness to apologize (to human lover) and to reconnect. A magnificent performance.

If I were Leonard Cohen and were asked to name a song or a poem that I might hope to be remembered by, I can imagine nominating this version, this performance, of "If It Be Your Will." The song is a prayer, simple and profound and full of quiet beauty. Its impact is twofold: the depiction/expression of the speaker's relationship with the "you" he's praying to; and the love and empathy and visionary fire of what he is (so cautiously and recklessly) praying for. Nowhere else in the Cohen oeuvre that I'm familiar with (not even "I have seen the future, baby, it is murder") does he so convincingly and successfully take on the ancient Hebrew role of prophet. In the first verse he offers his voice to God, not by offering to speak for Him but by the more meaningful ego-sacrifice of pledging not to speak at all "if it be your will." This is the genuflection; Cohen's execution of it is moving, filled with an understanding that comes only from long and difficult contemplation.

(You may wonder now why I described these performances as a portrait of an agnostic; I answer that this song's language can be applied as meaningfully to "fate" or "the universe" or "the way things are" as to a divine power. I use the word "God" here because once you take away the projection of "humanness" or "beingness" onto Him, then that word *means* "fate" or "the universe" or "that to which I pray." Listen in your own heart to the chords that are plucked in it by this song; you may find clarification of what it is that you believe in and defer to, if anything.)

In the second verse, the prophet, raising his head from his knee, turns to an alternate possibility: that God wishes truth to be spoken, and him to speak it. His voice starts to take on enthusiasm as he promises, "From this broken hill, I will sing to you . . . all your praises they shall ring." The broken hill is his imperfect human self, surely (not claiming to be without sin). My idea that he's a prophet is challenged a little by this language that suggests that his truth and praises will be sung, not to the people, but directly to "you." But that can be another role of the prophet, as we see in the next verse: to speak for the people, to God. Another possibility is that the "you" he is addressing is in fact us. He is speaking to the people. We will his silence or allow his singing. And we ultimately have mercy on our poor selves, or not. He is humbly entreating us to be merciful, to allow and embrace our own healing.

In the third verse the limits of the divine are hinted at ("If it be your will, if there is a choice"—an admission that we don't know what rules there might be that govern the higher powers, or to what extent our fate is already written and not subject to entreaty). But the singer, emboldened by this feeling of being listened to, gathers passion as he reads his wish list: "Let the rivers fill, let the hills rejoice / Let your mercy spill on all these burning hearts in hell . . . If it be your will to make us well." With real grace he portrays the poverty of our emotional/spiritual/physical existence—speaking, I believe, on behalf of the vast majority of humans, as well as himself—and asks God, like a supplicant in the plague years, to have mercy on us here and now. This is very beautifully expressed and sung. (The performance is Leonard on guitar, his voice joined subtly and touchingly by Julie Christensen's and Perla Batalla's voices. A faint keyboard comes and goes in the background. There are three songs on the album from Cohen's performance on the *Austin City Limits* telestage in 1988; this is the only one that was included in the broadcast.)

The last verse builds to an emotional crescendo by continuing the same thought (he doesn't repeat the "If it be your will" phrase at the beginning this time), which is now transformed somehow from entreaty to vision: "And draw us near and bind us tight / All your children here in their rags of light." We have been trained, in the last few verses, to expect an outpouring of emotion at this moment, start of the third line, and indeed this is the payoff: "In our rags of light, all dressed to kill." What's going to happen? Why, we'll arrive at the meat, the essence, the verb and object of this entire supplication: "And end this night." Deliver us. Lift us like an olive branch. Put an end to all this darkness.

I find the singing and the words, "In our rags of light" ("their" has become "our"), to be utterly beautiful and heart-wrenching. A thousand appropriate interpretations could be made of Cohen's vision; the one that sticks with me is similar to my impression of Teilhard de Chardin's vision, of the impending unification and evolution of the human species (and all life on earth). It's typical of Cohen to twist the knife, confront us with the darkness that is part and parcel of the beauty, "all dressed to kill." It's a turn of phrase, of course, indicating that we're all dressed up (in our "rags of light," extraordinarily apt image) and ready for the big moment. And as the rags point to our physical poverty, "dressed to kill" reminds me of how we are at each other's throats, in Bosnia and the American inner city and all over the world, emblem of our desperation and the hell (the "night") we see around us.

Music, a few notes, can be so transformative. The performers make their voices soul-naked as they wrap themselves in melody-clothes. We listeners let down barriers that we hold constantly in place when listening to those prophets who speak without musical accompaniment.

The next song, "Heart with No Companion," is joyous despite its title, offering suitable relief after "If It Be . . ." 's climactic acknowledgment of our human condition. "Now I greet you from the other side of sorrow and despair / With a love so vast and so shattered it will reach you everywhere." Cohen may be one of the modern masters of the couplet form. The music and performance are sparkling; it's here that the joy can be found. The words themselves don't seem that cheerful ("Through the days of shame that are coming . . . though your promise count for nothing, you must keep it nonetheless") but they are certainly prophetic, and since perhaps those days are already upon us, they contain some very good advice. Stand by your values, though they seem to be doing you no good at all. Stay true to yourself, and to our children's children. And (the music seems to be saying) do it with enthusiasm, with love, with open heart.

"Joan of Arc," more "la la la"s. Inspired (highly original) myth-making. Great use of language: "I saw her wince, I saw her cry; I saw the glory in her eye." The visual image is so well sketched, so powerful—and I love the dance of the two voices, here and throughout the song—and then we are sucker-punched by the moral or commentary in the last two lines, unexpectedly applying her story as told here to our own individual longings for love and enlightenment. Brings tears to my eyes sometimes. Of rage. And empathy.

Consciousness is being expressed in all aspects of this music. A story is being told. The rhythms and melodies and the sounds of the instruments and voices appeal to me. That's all I ever asked for. The task of making it topical is something I as listener will accomplish, anytime you'll meet me more than halfway. Speak your truth, with gusto and sincerity and a good beat and keening melody that speak to all my cellular memories, and I'll find a way to hear my truth in it, I promise. Your story meets my story. And their union has children, who go forth and multiply.

Consciousness meets consciousness. In our rags of light. That's the never-ending story.

8

August 9, 1995. When I picked up the phone in the morning and got the news from a friend in Germany, I naturally thought of the day Daisann called me from New York to tell me John Lennon just died.

So today was the day, all over the world and in our memories from now on, when Jerry Garcia died. And yes, I miss Jerry, and I miss the **Grateful Dead**, whom we all presume also died today. The day the Dead died. But not the day the music died. Jerry was not stolen from us like Buddy Holly. He had lived an extraordinarily full and creative and productive, enjoyable, satisfying life. And so had his group, and so have his community had a great long run as a public united-by-music community.

A phone call from Germany in the morning. And a party, a gathering, at Moonlight Beach here in Encinitas at night. And what a party! "I will survive." Yes, Jerry, you will, that became ever more clear to me at the gathering. You son of a bitch, you made it, you're immortal now. Your music, and something else, what music carries: your spirit.

This is not meant as a eulogy. Not just a farewell. It's an on-the-run essay on rock history. This is a truly memorable and significant moment in rock music and "counterculture" history. Let me tell you why. Not everyone understands the power and beauty and significance of the Grateful Dead. But rock-and-roll history and contemporary cultural history are meaningless or blind if they think the Beatles are more epochal in rock history than the Grateful Dead. Both are equally at the very heart of the story. And until we understand this, I think, we misunderstand the story.

And what happened today is, more than anything else, an occasion for reassessment. No one had as long or great a run in the rock-and-roll playground as the Grateful Dead. I'll tell you why I think so. But first let me say a few words about the Jerry Garcia I first met back when he was still called Captain Trips, and also a word or two about the Monday-night gathering of 150 joyously grieving Deadheads under the full moon at Moonlight Beach, August 9, 1995.

"A long strange trip"? Yeah. It's not just a cliché. It's a particularly fitting metaphor for the artist's (or poet's or even the would-be revolutionary's) life in our era. One big acid trip, and/or one long journey, that goes on and on. And even though Jerry Garcia did live only fifty-three years, he lived them at least as fast and fiercely as Jack London lived his thirty-nine. It's a fabulous story, but never mind. Jerry was a fabulous character and a brilliant and influential musician. But the story of the Grateful Dead is the one that must inevitably endure as a legend (myth) through which we all attempt to understand our times, our own history. What is rock and roll? A kind of popular music. And the Grateful Dead, if you think about it, have redefined the meaning of the word "popular." Fuck record sales. Don't let history be written by the bean-counters. *What about the connection made with people?*

Recollections of Jerry? No big deal. Just his openness and friendliness and natural generosity. I was an eighteen-year-old kid from the East Coast in a San Francisco bar called the Matrix, keen to see Jefferson Airplane play; the manager said I could only stay if I got hold of an ID to show, just in case. And another early-arriving patron, J. Garcia, offered to loan me his driver's license for the evening. Why not? A few nights later I heard his band, New Year's Eve '66/'67 at the Fillmore Ballroom. Two and a half years later, reversing the direction of my cross-country exploring, I arrived at the Liberty New York Holiday Inn after a long flight from California on the red-eye. I needed a place to sleep for the ten hours before the Woodstock Festival was scheduled to begin. And there was Jerry; he still hardly knew me but was always ready to help a stranger. He gave me the key to his room—he didn't need it for those hours. Next day, under the backstage performers' tent, he sat and rapped expansively about the progress of our Movement. Always interested, always insightful, always full of ideas and visions. He liked to share them. Talking backstage, or playing the guitar and goading the band along, onstage. No shortage of strangeness. Read Michael Lydon's account (in his book *Rock Folk*) of a road trip with the band in 1969 ("They see themselves as keepers of the flame").

On the night of Jerry's death, I saw that flame burn on Moonlight Beach. (And when I got back from that bonfire celebration, I turned on the computer and 1,600 postings had been made, mostly in the last few hours, on the Internet newsgroup rec.music.gdead. People reaching out to each other in response to this enormous (and yet, for many, strangely light) sense of loss.

What most impressed me at the beach gathering was how its spontaneity and character and mood exactly mirrored the best tribal moments I can remember from rock festivals, Dead shows, Rainbow Gatherings, political demonstrations, et cetera, et cetera, that I've experienced over the past thirty years. Where do these extraordinarily joyful and free and (in the best sense) high young Grateful Dead fans keep coming from, year after year after year? And as full of grace and inspiration now, even now, as at the first San Francisco or New York Be-Ins. The innocence of the moment. Here we are. Let's drum, sing, dance, hold hands, form a circle on the beach, be joyous and some-how unself-consciously holy together. The perfect wake for Jerry Garcia and for the era of the Grateful Dead (no shows this fall). And somehow one couldn't doubt that the vacuum left behind will find a way to be filled. A new way, not the same way, not under the same name. How myths and great moments touch our hearts and leave us with a hunger for what comes next, which we then proceed to create, collectively. Now I'm talking about culture rather than music. But the significance of both the Beatles and the Grateful Dead is how closely the two can be joined. The music both expresses and defines the political culture, on a popular level. And yes, "the people" do have a role in history, despite our fascination with kings and football stars. Sure, there were people at the gathering with Jerry's face on their T-shirts. But this is no ordinary cult of personality. Rather, it's personality as a talisman for a strangely indigenous and natural cul-ture, albeit genuinely distant from European/middle-class values. Oh well. The Grateful Dead are the pied pipers of this country and this era. And not just the guys in the group. Their songbook. Their songs.

Far more than any nineties indie-rock band, more than Nirvana or the Offspring or even Fugazi, the Grateful Dead have, throughout their astonishing thirty-year hegemony, tilted at the windmill of cor-porate/mass-media–defined pop culture. No one has come remotely as close to holding out for a genuine alternative. They had a different vision. And history will record (depending, of course, on who tells the story, the children of the revolutionaries or the Tories) that they made it stick.

Why do the children respond to the pied piper? Books could be written trying to answer this question. But the incontrovertible fact about the Grateful Dead story is that, in spite of the media-fed eternal obsession of youthful consumers with fashion—what's new? what's cool? what's hot?—the ridiculously unfashionable Grateful Dead have maintained a popularity among a constantly renewed and very young audience—new crops of seventeen-year-olds and twenty-two-year-olds seemingly every two years, every concert season—that is demonstrable to the bean-counters by the fact that no rock band has sold as many tickets in the United States year for year over the last few decades. But never mind the numbers. If you've been to the shows, or even if you just go to the gatherings like the one at Moonlight and the many that I suspect are still to come, you've seen the pied piper in action. "Come, hear, Uncle John's band . . ." Not Jerry. Not even Pigpen. *John.* Who is that guy? Some kind of spirit. Some kind of evangelist.

"Come, hear, Uncle John's band" (oh, those durable Robert Hunter lyrics; in an effective gestalt, everyone plays his/her part) "playing to the tide / Come on along and go alone; he's come to take his children home." Native American legends no doubt predicted such things.

There is a mystery that surrounds the accomplishments of supremely popular—which is to say, beloved—musicians. For enduring and far-reaching popularity in the rock pantheon, I find it easy and appropriate to speak in the same breath of the Beatles, the Grateful Dead, and Elvis Presley. The mystery is and continues to be the way people in large numbers respond to this music, and the symbology or mythic weight the providers (creators) of the music assume.

People still love the Beatles, and what they love are their recordings. And the myth of their success is so large and so much a part of its time, its historic and cultural moment, that no one could truly dare fantasize of being the "next" or "new" Beatles. No explosion of popularity, one song or work of art after another after another, is likely to equal that in our era. Superficially, briefly, perhaps, especially if all you care about is "how much money is it earning?" but mere marketability is not enough to allow some upstart to displace the Beatles from their centrality in the rock-music myth. The mystery has to do with more than units sold. It concerns the way the music touches and awakens people. And the way the music becomes interwoven with the hopes and dreams and visions and sense of identity of a generation or a cultural/political/social moment.

So that forever after, when we think of that moment in our lives or our awakening, our growing and learning, we hear that music—and vice versa. And I don't just mean because we were there. Myths have a way of refreshing themselves, surviving into succeeding generations.

When John Lennon died, the possibility of a Beatles reunion ended, though indeed the Beatles were already "history," because it had been a decade since they last made a record together, and no one really expected that to change.

The death of Jerry Garcia is different because what people love about the Grateful Dead are not primarily the recordings (the officially marketed ones), but the shows and the songs and the context that shows and songs exist within and create. And even as Jerry's body finally gave up on him, people were standing in line (competing, working) to get tickets for the Fall '95 Grateful Dead shows. And until that sad morning there was a band, a working band, despite the loss of Pigpen and Keith and Brent, and no one could have felt certain there would be no new songs added to the G. Dead songbook. But now it's different. The band is done. And so, therefore, is the era. No journalistic hype this time. It's the simple truth. And some of us can already feel the change in the winds.

Why is this musician's, and this band's, death, a historic and significant moment? Not just because there will be no more Dead shows or new Dead music. But rather because, when the document is signed at the bottom (completed), it becomes law. When we know the band (and its most charismatic figurehead, embodiment) is dead, then we by our nature suddenly get the message in a new way (look at what happened to Elvis's mythic role in American culture when he died).

I suggest that Jerry's death changes the way rock-and-roll history will henceforth be read and written, because suddenly the Dead will cease to be the humongous, huge, invisible man of the story. We will all of us, not just the Deadheads, begin to acknowledge and treasure them and feel and be aware of the impact of what they've done, what they allowed us to give to ourselves through them.

As a, ahem, rock critic, I know the shortcomings of the critics' and commentators' attention spans. We always think we know the forest and so sometimes overlook the trees, even when they are very broad trees indeed. In 1978 I was at a Neil Young concert in San Francisco (the one that was filmed and recorded as *Rust Never Sleeps*), and promoter Bill Graham came over to me (we knew each other from days on the road a decade earlier with Jefferson Airplane and the Dead; on one bus trip from Expo '67 to Toronto, I was tripping like all the band members, and Bill, the only "unstoned" soul on the bus, was rapping out to me his life story) and shouted, "What are you doing *here?!*" I protested that I loved Neil's music and wanted to hear it, but it turned out what he meant was, How could you be here at this relatively ordinary event when the *Grateful Dead* are playing at Winterland? He insisted and carried on, and when I said I wanted to hear Neil through, he gave me the name of a person to ask for at Winterland and how to go in the side door once Neil's concert was finished. So my wife and I went and heard the last fifteen minutes of the show, and I was stunned. I realized, *I'd forgotten about the Grateful Dead!* In 1968 I'd thought they were the best band in the world. And then somehow they'd drifted from my attention. But Bill was a huge fan of the Grateful Dead to his last days. He loved their performances. If you are skeptical about my argument for the centrality of the Grateful Dead to the mythology and history of rock and roll and indeed our collective culture (and, in a sociopsychological sense, our sense of community), I wish Bill Graham were here to grab you by the collar and get in your face and set you straight. As only Bill could. Jerry wouldn't need to make the case. He'd just shrug and grin and let his eyes twinkle, and then get involved in the telling of a story. The recounting of this afternoon's vision.

If you've never been to a Grateful Dead concert, I'm sorry about that, but the fact is they had a different way of making music. As with Miles Davis, you had to learn the language. And young people in particular seemed to find it quite easy and rewarding to learn. I won't go into the details here, my main purpose in writing is just to note that we've passed into a moment when, from now forward, we will be more aware of the role the Grateful Dead have played in making the world in which we are or perhaps someday will be living. Visionaries in action. Keepers of the psychedelic flame. A rock-and-roll group, a gestalt, a victorious experiment in collective and communal creativity. There haven't been many groups that truly functioned as a group—the Beatles are one fine example—and most that did for a glorious while then broke up. But the Dead didn't break up or lose their vision or their talent or their collective sense of purpose. Thirty years on the road. No one has come close, not even the Rolling Stones, because though the latter kept working sporadically, that to me is different than actually continuing on as artists and visionary Prometheans genuinely striving to bring us light or some other form of revolution. A matter of opinion, I guess.

A gathering of Stones fans mourning Keith's passing would be a sentimental event for me; I truly worshiped their music once. But I can't imagine such a gathering offering any of the exhilaration that the Moonlight wake for Jerry provided instantly to almost all of us who took part. Of course there was also a gathering in Ocean Beach twenty miles south of here, and ones in San Francisco and elsewhere—friends have called and told me of gatherings they took part in New York City and Bowling Green—and on the Internet that afternoon there were desperate requests for information on get-togethers in Kansas City, Monterey, anywhere! What made the gathering I was at so special, I think, was the deep sense of community among the participants, even if some were strangers to each other, and beyond that, the instrument of our connectedness: the songbook. People sang, to guitars, to conga drums, or chanted lyrics while the drumming continued. Such an opportunity for sharing. A song might have been written by the Incredible String Band, but it had been performed by the Dead, and that put it into the community's collective songbook, through which we connected and spoke to ourselves and each other. The Dead spoke to their audiences (and found their own hearts at a given concert moment) through song selection and sequence. And then we and they shared in what happened as a result, as they played and sang and we listened. A collective, ephemeral, and also eternally affecting, creation.

The songbook has been closed, and—wait and see—has achieved immortality. Its continued power and presence may be felt musically, socially . . . We'll see. I don't think I've begun to say all I could about the Grateful Dead's and guitarist/singer/mascot Jerry Garcia's extraordinary accomplishments in taking the psychedelic visions and values of a particular tribe and moment and living them through their music and performances and life-choices, in such a public way that new models and new possibilities have been made available to the collective unconscious, in ways that have already and may continue to make a tremendous difference on our art, our culture, our music, our sense of our selves.

Jerry worked hard; and loved to work: When the Dead had a night off from their extraordinary demanding schedule, there was usually a Jerry Garcia Band concert somewhere or some other musical performance by some version of Jerry Garcia and Friends. He loved to play. He also played hard, and perhaps lived a little less long as a result, but his religion was staying true to himself. And so he did.

And what survives? The tapes, of course, and the songbook, and the story. And, I think, a myth that will go on growing, as we notice and remember and appreciate, more and more. I haven't been an active Deadhead for many years, but I've always understood and respected and appreciated them, even if my choice was to focus my obsession on getting to Dylan concerts. And the night of Jerry's death, I felt completely accepted and recognized as one of the tribe. Good. This feeling may grow. "I am a Berliner," JFK proclaimed in Berlin. "I am a Deadhead." I can imagine other sorts of rock-and-roll fans or cultural revolutionaries making such a claim in the future, as a new way of saying, "Rock and roll will never die." Roll over Beethoven. And tell John and Jimi and Hank and Billie the news.

INDEX

INDEX